POPE JOHN PAUL II

A Man & His People

This edition published in Canada 1985 by Collins Publishers,
    100 Lesmill Road, Don Mills, Ontario.
© 1985 Illustrations: Gamma, Paris, France and
    Colour Library Books Ltd., Guildford, Surrey, England.
© 1985 Text: Colour Library Books Ltd.
CLB 1324
Display and text filmsetting by Acesetters Ltd.,
    Richmond, Surrey, England.
Produced by AGSA, Barcelona, Spain.
Colour separations by Llovet, S.A., Barcelona, Spain.
Printed and bound in Barcelona, Spain by Jisa-Rieusset and Eurobinder.
ISBN 0 00 217452 9
Dep. Legal. B-41.483-84

POPE JOHN PAUL II
A Man & His People

Text by
Trevor Hall & Kathryn Spink

Designed by
Philip Clucas MSIAD & Sara Cooper

Produced by
Ted Smart & David Gibbon

COLLINS
ROYAL

With St. Paul we repeat: "For the love of Christ restraineth us". Right from the beginning we wish to see our ministry as a service of love; this will permeate all our actions.

Address *Urbi et Orbi* given at the end of the conclave. 17th October, 1978.

Christ, allow me to be and remain a servant of your unique power, a servant of your power who is filled with gentleness, a servant of your endless power, or rather, a servant of your servants.

Homily on the official inauguration in St. Peter's Square. 22nd October, 1978.

IN the silent hours of the night of the 28th September 1978 the thirty-three day pontificate of John Paul I, the "smiling pope", came abruptly if peacefully to its conclusion. High above St. Peter's Square the light in the papal apartment was shining, but unbeknown to the world, the See of Peter was vacant, Rome was without its bishop and the Roman Catholic Church was without a. Head. It was not until 5.30 am when Father John Magee, private secretary to the pope, concerned at the failure of John Paul I to appear promptly for Mass, went to the pope's bedroom, that the tragedy was discovered. The man who had appeared so strikingly alive during the previous day's public audience and address to the bishops of the Philippines was found dead in bed, a copy of à Kempis' "Imitation of Christ" open by the bedside. A doctor was called and it was concluded that death of acute coronary thrombosis must have occurred at approximately 11 pm the previous night and so, sadly, the man who had loved people had died alone without the sacraments of the Church. At 10 pm, whilst preparing for bed, he had been given the news of the murder of a left-wing youth in Rome and had sighed, wistfully "Even young people are killing each other now." These were his last recorded words.

As the news of John Paul I's death spread, the world received it with uncomprehending shock. The death of Pope Paul VI on 6th August of the same year had been a sad blow but it had not been altogether unexpected. He himself had remarked to pilgrims at Castelgandolfo as early as 1970 "The clock of time moves inexorably forwards and it points to a forthcoming end" and when the end finally came he had had fifteen years to make an indelible mark upon the papacy. Pope John Paul I's reign on the other hand, had appeared like a promise of hope cut cruelly short before it had time to come to fruition. His homilies had promised a pontificate in continuity with his predecessors – extending back as far as Pius XI. In particular he had claimed "the pastoral plan of Pope Paul VI, our immediate predecessor, has most of all left a strong impression on our heart and in our memory". Yet in the short time that he was granted as pope the man who had once confided "I am only a poor man, accustomed to small things and silence" had brought a new look to the papacy. His refusal to be crowned with the triple-tiered papal tiara as a symbol of regal power, which he saw as wholly unsuited to the "servant of the servants of God", indeed his rejection of any concept of 'coronation' or 'enthronement' was not simply a demonstration of humility, but a definite statement about the Petrine office itself. The ceremony by which he became pope was not a coronation but "the inauguration of his ministry as supreme pastor", a ministry which promised to be one of transparent compassion and honesty of a kind likely to erode some of the barriers of conservatism surrounding the Vatican. While, therefore, his body lay in state in the Sala Clementina and subsequently in St. Peter's, there were few among the endless stream of mourners who came to pay their last respects who did not note with sadness that his red shoes showed so little sign of wear.

Within the Vatican the death of a pope is the starting point for a complex sequence of traditions for which grief, however great, must be temporarily set aside. On the death of John Paul I, the French-born Vatican Secretary of State, Cardinal Jean Villot, became *Camerlengo*, or administrator of the Holy See, a position he would hold until a new successor to Peter had been elected. For the second time in so brief a period the rituals must be observed. The dead pope's forehead must be tapped three times with a silver hammer, his name called and the question posed; "Are you dead?". Once more the seal in the Ring of the Fisherman, engraved with an image of St. Peter in a boat, fishing, a symbol of papal power, must be shattered with a hammer. Every coin new-minted in the Vatican City and every stamp issued must bear the words *sede vacante* and the Vatican newspaper must carry the same imprint indicating that the throne of Peter is un-occupied. Even the uniform of the Swiss Guards must be changed to the dark blue color of mourning.

The same grief was no doubt aggravated by anxiety at the strain on Vatican coffers. Each time a pope dies, and again when a new Pope is elected, a bonus is paid to all Vatican dependants from cardinals to street cleaners (one of John Paul I's less popular acts was to cut the instalment paid on his election by half). Then there are the arrangements and expenses directly involved in the holding of a conclave; the cost of fares and organization of accommodation for many of the 111 conclavists who cannot afford to pay themselves, as well as the expense of preparing the Sistine Chapel, the papal apartments and the robes. Considerations of this kind inevitably create anxieties on a purely practical level but even more serious on this occasion were the implications to the Church as a whole, of the necessity to search once more for a man capable of bearing the onerous office of pope. As one cardinal later remarked: "A mourning on top of another mourning – it is a very grave trial for the Church and we must truly pray. Who knows what awaits us now?" The role of pope, by virtue of its very basis, can be no easy one. The three-fold scriptural foundation of the office as successor of St. Peter: the pope is the rock-apostle upon which the Church of Christ is built (Matthew 16:18-19); he is commanded to "confirm the brethren" (Luke 22:32); and to feed the sheep and the lambs of his flock as a witness of love (John 21:15-17), imposes upon one man an almost intolerable burden of responsibility and authority. Despite the fact that John Paul I abandoned all the titles that theologians had condemned as unscriptural in favor of "pope, bishop of Rome, supreme pastor", the full range of titles traditionally associated with the office:

Bishop of Rome
Vicar of Jesus Christ
Successor of the Prince of the Apostles
Supreme Pontiff of the Universal Church
Patriarch of the West
Primate of Italy
Archbishop and Metropolitan of the Province of Rome
Sovereign of the Vatican State

gives some indication of what is involved. The ruling of Vatican City, an independent and sovereign state with its own yellow and white flag, is in itself no small task. Something in the region of three thousand people are employed within the Vatican walls, although not all of these are citizens. Citizens are not born to the status, but are created because of the work in which they are currently or were once engaged. Cardinals resident in Rome, whether employed or not, automatically join the ranks of citizens which also include the Swiss Guards and all active members of the papal diplomatic corps. The actual administration of this small but vital state, which despite the fact that its nearest water is the rather dubious Tiber, is actually entitled to its own fleet, is undertaken by the Cardinal Secretary of State assisted by a cardinal pro-president and a commission of cardinals. Nevertheless the ultimate responsibility for the Vatican City and its contents rests with the pope, and popes have in general taken this responsibility seriously. This can be but a small task, however, by comparison with that of being leader of the estimated 700 million Roman Catholics in the world. As leader of the Roman Catholic Church, the pope must not only establish and maintain relationships with Church hierarchy throughout the world but must also walk the tightrope of international diplomacy, and be capable of arguing convincingly, but patiently, the position of the Church in an often antagonistic world of science and politics. Furthermore he must maintain harmony between radicals and conservatives within the Roman Catholic Church itself – all this too must be undertaken in the knowledge that when speaking *ex cathedra* on matters of faith and morals he will be regarded within the Roman Catholic Church as speaking with the voice of God Himself and therefore, with infallibility. It is a task which has created in many a supreme sense of isolation. The Lateran Treaty of 1939, between the Italian government and the Church, may have allowed the pope to move outside the confines of the Vatican City but he was still restricted by the necessity for prearrangement. John XXIII's chauffeur, Guido Gusso, recounted how the Holy Father delighted in failing to give the requisite two hours' notice of his intention to go out to the *carabinieri* so that he, like everyone else, could stop at the red traffic lights and wave and bless his people. John XXIII did much to break down the barriers of formality which existed between the pope and even his closest aides. He abolished the custom of always eating alone on the grounds that there was no scriptural foundation for it and rejected the kind of exaggerated ceremony which had meant that in the time of Pius XII officials knelt even when speaking to the pope on the telephone. As Lawrence Elliott writes in his book "I will be called John", ". . . it ran counter to his Bergamesque sense of brotherhood and he was continually ordering people to their feet. When an aged reporter from *L'Osservatore Romano* assured him that he was perfectly comfortable conducting an interview from his knees, John threatened to leave the room unless the man sat in a chair." Despite such progressive steps, however, when John Paul I became pope there still remained enough ritual to make him lonely, so much so that he resorted to telephoning the mother superiors of religious orders for a chat.

The cardinals who assembled in Rome in October for the second conclave of that year were all too aware of what strength, both spiritual and physical, was required of a future pope. Significantly, the man who was to become John Paul II, then Cardinal Wojtyla, had welcomed the election of John Paul I with the words: "Certainly he who has taken on his shoulders the mission of Peter – pastoral responsibility for the entire church – has also taken on his shoulders a heavy cross. We wish to be with him from the beginning of his road, for we know that this cross – the pope's cross – is part of the mystery of the world's salvation which has been accomplished in Jesus Christ." Had this cross proved too heavy for one man to bear? Certainly John Paul I's early death was a warning against choosing someone whose health was fragile. The 111 conclavists looked closely at his abbreviated pontificate to see what could be learned from it. John Paul I had been elected for his pastoral qualities, for his ability, to communicate with people, and in this respect their choice would appear to have been emphatically vindicated. During the *Novemdiales* sermons which preceded the conclave, Cardinal Confalinieri also pointed out that John Paul I had stressed "the integrity of faith, the perfection of Christian life, and the discipline of the Church." It was a deep hunger for the nourishment of solid spirituality which, according to Confalinieri, had drawn the crowds to the pope. There were those also, however, who had seen the image of the genial figure who loved children, the poor and the third world as dangerous because it had not been tested. His death according to some had been timely because it had spared him the problems on Puebla, on women priests or inter-communion. The way seemed to be pointing towards a people's pope but towards a pope who was also strong-minded and firm in his doctrinal teaching. Furthermore it was suggested that Pope John Paul I's ignorance of world affairs had placed him at a disadvantage. He had, for example, warmly received General Videla, President of Argentina, unaware that this might offend Latin American Catholics who were at that very time preparing a Puebla meeting intended as an unpleasant surprise to the military dictatorships with their "doctrine of national security". The need for someone who was politically aware and competent was made all the more poignantly obvious by the fact that shortly before the conclave, rockets were dropping upon the Maronite Christians of the Lebanon, and in Italy itself the Red Brigades were active again. In this election experience of world affairs must count as an important consideration.

Pope John Paul II at his meeting with General Wojciech Jaruzelski in Wawel Castle, June 22, 1983.

Most of the important work in a papal election occurs before the actual conclave, as the cardinals meet, discuss and get to know each other. In an atmosphere of tension, for each one knew that he, like everyone else, was subject to close scrutiny, the lessons to be learned from what had gone before were thrown open for discussion, and with them the names of the most likely *papabile* (those candidates having the necessary qualities for pope), among them Cardinal Lorscheider, the man for whom John Paul I had consistently voted in the August conclave; Cardinal Siri of Genoa, an archconservative ardently supported by the Italian Catholic Press; Cardinal Benelli, the favorite of less reactionary Italians, and Cardinal Hume, strongly supported in London by both the *Times* and the *Guardian*.

As, however, the cardinals, wearing red cassocks, white surplices and red birettas gathered on the 14th October in the Pauline Chapel, beneath Michelangelo's frescoes of the crucifixion of St. Peter and the conversion of St. Paul, nothing was certain. Most, if asked as they processed in reverse order of seniority through the Sala Ducale, beneath Bernini's cherubs into the Sistine Chapel itself, would have considered another Italian pope most likely, but a non-Italian was by no means excluded. Indeed, during the mass "for electing the pope" Cardinal Villot, expounding on the Gospel of St. John, had placed all such considerations in their proper perspective by applying the verse "You have not chosen me, I have chosen you" directly to the conclave. Human abilities must be taken into consideration, but ultimately the mandate of the college of cardinals came from God's choice and not "from the human qualities that we may or may not possess."

The system of the conclave was first established in 1271 with the election of Gregory X. Since then the rules have been repeatedly modified but one factor has remained all-important – that of secrecy. The very name derives from the Latin *cum clave* meaning "with key" and refers to the fact that the cardinals are not allowed contact with the outside world. When, on Saturday 14th October, the cardinals began entering the crucible of the conclave, 88 other persons such as kitchen and medical staff were already in there, having taken a vow of secrecy which bound them on pain of excommunication from revealing what occurred during the course of the conclave. The cardinals too, must first listen to a solemn reading of parts of the apostolic constitution, *Romano Pontifici Eligendo*, and in particular Nos. 55-61 on secrecy. Anyone discovered using or planting "technical instruments, of whatever kind, for the recording, reproduction or transmission of voices and images" (No. 61) would have been instantly ejected at this stage. Then each cardinal took the oath of secrecy on the Gospels: "Above all, we promise and swear to observe with the greatest fidelity and with all persons, including the conclavists, the secret concerning what takes place in the conclave or place of the election, directly or indirectly concerning the scrutinies; not to break this secret in any way, either during the conclave or after the election of the new Pontiff, unless we are given special faculty or explicit authorization from the same future Pontiff (No. 49)."

Only then could the conclavists repair to their rooms or "cells" – some to dark little offices tucked away in obscure corners, their telephones carefully disconnected, others to huge Renaissance reception rooms hung with

Canada, September 1984.

ornate chandeliers. The doors of the Sistine Chapel were sealed. The conclave had begun.

In view of the vow of secrecy, it is impossible to tell exactly what occurred in the course of the voting which began soon after nine o'clock next morning when the cardinals processed into the Sistine Chapel, took their places at the twelve wooden tables set out in rows, and cast their votes on cards headed with the words *"eligo in summum pontificem"* (I choose as the supreme pontiff). There has been some suggestion that Cardinal Karol Wojtyla had some intimation of what was to come. Certainly it is true that in the August conclave which elected John Paul I, seven votes had been cast for him and, while this was not a significant number, it did indicate that his name was one which had been given some consideration. Cardinal Stefan Wyszinski, the Primate of Poland, had told a group of friends in Poland that he could not envisage his fellow cardinal as Primate but rather that he was destined for "greater things" and with disturbing insight the woman whom Karol regarded "almost as my grandmother", Mrs. Irena Szkocka, had predicted his

'It is cold up there on the mountain.'

election many years previously. On her personal copy of the prophetic poem by the poet and playwright, Juliusz Slowacki, beside the words:

> "He has made ready the throne for a Slav Pope,
> He will sweep out the churches and make them clean within,
> God shall be revealed, clear as day, in the creative world,"

she had written unwaveringly "This Pope will be Karol." It is perhaps true to suggest, however, that it is one thing to recognize in a person the qualities which will one day qualify him for "greater things" and another to attribute to him the private certainty of a specific happening. Friends and journalists who were with Wojtyla at the time of and shortly after his receiving the news of John Paul I's death, have noted that he was greatly disturbed by it and that he became absent-minded and remote, and have interpreted his reaction in the light of his knowledge that he might be the next to take upon himself the mission of Peter. The question of Cardinal Wojtyla's personal conviction must remain open. What is certain, however, is that when a news photographer was taking photographs of the cardinals before the conclave, Wojtyla laughingly remarked "Why are you taking so many photographs of me? You certainly don't believe I might be the next pope." His last act before disappearing into cell No. 91, assigned to him during the conclave, characteristically equipped with a quarterly review of Marxist theory, was to ask his Polish hosts in Rome to book him on the first plane to Krakow, without waiting for the installation ceremony of the new pope.

Apparently endorsing the view that Cardinal Wojtyla's election was not, at least initially, a strong likelihood, when the conclavists cast their votes and approached the altar in the Sistine Chapel, for the first time giving their oath: "I call to witness Christ the Lord who will be my judge that my vote is given to the one whom before God I consider to be elected", they seemed to be looking in accordance with tradition for an Italian pope. Dedicated observers of Vatican activity have produced what may be considered a fairly reliable account of the progress of the voting and in the first ballot the main contenders' were Cardinal Guiseppe Siri of Genoa. Giovanni Benelli of Florence and Cardinal Pericle Felici. In the second ballot many of the votes previously cast for Felici went to Benelli, but still he failed to achieve the necessary two thirds plus one majority, and so during the first day the abortive struggle to find an Italian pope went on. As the day progressed, however, an increasing number of votes for non-Italians, among them Karol Wojtyla, began to emerge and by the end of the day, as black smoke rose once more from the stove in the corner of the chapel and appeared via a somewhat undistinguished flue above St. Peter's Square, the Cardinals must have realized that they were now looking for a non-Italian pope.

On Monday morning, on the sixth ballot, the number of votes for Wojtyla increased noticeably and it is said that he was so visibly shaken at the prospect that Cardinal Wyszinski, fearing that his friend might refuse the Papacy, took him to one side and reminded him that it was his duty as a cardinal to accept. The last ballot (it is not certain whether it was the seventh or the eighth) was conclusive. Then, with apprehensive solemnity, Cardinal Wojtyla was asked whether he would accept the election. With tears in his eyes, he paused so long before replying that many feared he would refuse, and when he finally did speak it was to refer to the words of Pope Paul VI's "Constitution on the Election of a Pope":

"We ask him who is elected not to refuse the office to which he has been elected for fear of its weight, but to submit himself humbly to the Divine Will; for God who imposes the burden sustains him with his hand lest he be unequal to bearing it; in conferring the heavy task upon him, God also helps him to accomplish it and, in giving him the dignity he grants him also the strength, lest in his weakness he should fall beneath the weight of his office."

In carefully compiled Latin came the reply: "Knowing the seriousness of these times, realizing the responsibility of this selection, placing my faith in God, for Christ, for the Virgin Mary, the Mother of God, respecting fully the Apostolic constitution of Paul VI . . . I accept."

There was another long pause and then: "Because of my reverence, love and devotion to John Paul and to Paul VI, who has been my inspiration and my strength, I shall take the name of John Paul."

The conclave applauded and the master of ceremonies, acting as notary with two assistant masters as witnesses, drew up a document, a legacy to history, concerning the acceptance of the 264th Pontiff and the name taken by him.

Outside in St. Peter's Square an excited crowd of Romans and tourists had been waiting expectantly since the first morning of the conclave. For two days a large and motley assembly of churchmen, television crews, nuns, reporters, children carrying helium-filled balloons, and pick-pockets had been curiously united by an all-absorbing preoccupation with smoke-signals issuing from an otherwise nondescript stove-pipe in a cornice of St. Peter's. The most dedicated smoke-watchers had even brought their camp-stoves in order to avoid leaving the celebrated chimney to satisfy the demands of their less dedicated palates. Seven times the huge crowd had bubbled with excitement as smoke began to appear from the chapel, some had even begun to shout triumphantly *"Viva il Papa"*, but seven times the chemical pellet, now used instead of the traditional wet straw, gradually turned the smoke black, and the crowd resigned itself to waiting once again. Reassuringly, a voice on Vatican Radio reminded its listeners that the average length of twentieth century conclaves was three days and that the conclave of 1922 had lasted seven days. By the evening of the second day there were those who could not help recalling that one nineteenth century conclave had lasted more than 50 days – and so the tension mounted. Then, at 6.18 pm, the smoke began to rise again, this time unquestionably white. *"E bianca!"* the crowd whispered, then shouted, cheered and clapped. The world had a pope – but who on earth was he?

The Pope returns to Rome after a visit to his homeland in June 1979, and is greeted by Guilio Andreotti.

As more and more Romans rushed from all parts of the city to the already packed square, the lights came on in the Hall of Benediction, the tapestry was unrolled from the balcony and while Pope John Paul II changed into his new vestments, of which Gammarelli's, the Vatican tailors, had provided a number of different sizes, Cardinal Felici appeared, smiling, on the balcony. In Latin he proclaimed "I announce to you a great joy. We have a pope." Then

came the name: "Carolum Cardinalem Wojtyla . . . who has taken the name of John Paul." The crowd was at once astonished and delighted; astonished because their newly elected pope was a stranger, delighted because the man whom they gradually identified as a Pole had taken the name of his much loved predecessor. The air resounded with cheers and expressions of amazement as the realization slowly dawned that in electing the first non-Italian pope for 450 years the conclave had moved as far away as possible from the conventional certainty of old Rome and turned its back on centuries of tradition.

When, within the hour, Pope John Paul II appeared on the balcony to bless the crowd, he was greeted with all the warmth that the Italians, as a nation, feel for Poland as a land which has known so much suffering, the more so because their very first encounter with the new pope was in itself a breach of tradition. Tradition demanded that he merely gave his blessing – *urbi et orbi* – in Latin but this stranger chose to speak to them first in almost flawless Italian:

"Dear brothers and sisters, we are all still saddened at the death of our beloved Pope John Paul I and so the cardinals have called for a new bishop of Rome. They called him from a far-distant country – far and yet always close because of our communion in faith and Christian traditions. I was afraid to accept that responsibility, yet I do so in a spirit of obedience to the Lord and total faithfulness to Mary, our most Holy Mother. I am speaking to you in your – no, our Italian language. If I make a mistake, please correct me. I would like to invite you to join me in professing our faith, our hope and our fidelity to Mary, the Mother of Christ and of the Church, and also to begin again on the road of history and of the Church. I begin with the help of God and the help of men."

If there had been doubters among the Roman crowd, these few words delivered with obvious emotion and in a voice which suggested both humility and strength, went straight to their hearts. He had used "I" instead of the ceremonial "we", he had identified himself as their bishop and he had corrected the words "your language" to "our language". Again the cheers soared into the night sky. When, finally, Pope John Paul II gave the Latin benediction, waved and disappeared, those who lingered in the square below were preoccupied by all the possible effects of a Polish pope upon the world at large, but the atmosphere was one of jubilation and above all one of excitement. To the people of Rome the man from Poland had appeared as a vision of dedication, faith and strength. In Poland, to the people who had known and loved him for many years, the pathos of the papacy was perhaps more readily apparent. In the Catholic weekly newspaper *Tygodnik Powszechny.* Tadeusz Zychiewicz drew attention to the private tragedy of those moments when the clapping and cheering stops: "It is a heavy and terrifying burden they have placed on his shoulders. It is cold up there on the mountain. With all our hearts we wish him the strength to bear the cold, knowing as we do that he will not only be cold but alone. May God be always near him". Those who were with Cardinal Wojtyla shortly after his election will recall a picture of him seated beneath Michelangelo's "Last Judgement", his head in his hands, his body slumped – already alone.

When, on the 16th October, news of a new era in the history of the papacy was broadcast to the world, congratulations were plentiful and so, too, were speculations as to the thinking behind the cardinals' choice. President Jimmy Carter's message of congratulations pinpointed some of the reasons why many believed the Polish cardinal had been selected: "I add my congratulations and my sense of joy to that felt around the world at your selection as Pope. Twice in eight weeks, the College of Cardinals has had to choose a new leader for your church and a spiritual guide for the world – and twice they have given us choices which have filled the Church and the world with new hope. Like your predecessor, Your Holiness has shared the experience of working people, and understands the daily victories and defeats of human life. As a theologian, a pastor, and a worker, you also understand the most extreme tests that life presents. You know what it is to struggle for faith, for freedom, for life itself, and your insight into these modern dilemmas will enrich, and be enriched by the enduring traditions of your Church."

Beyond this kind of reasoning, it was claimed that John Paul II had been elected because he was well-connected and well traveled. His active part in the Second Vatican Council and his membership of the Synod of Bishops had brought him into contact with the "International Church" and he had traveled extensively in Europe, Canada, the U.S.A. and Australia. He was known to be a man of intellect, a linguist who spoke Italian, English, Spanish, French and Russian, and doctrinally a supporter of Vatican II. Like his predecessor he had the ability to draw people to himself; unlike his predecessor he was physically strong and at 58 was the youngest pope to be elected since Pius IX. His life had been a continued witness to pastoral experience, and as a Pole, he was, of course, the ideal person to cope with the threatening problem of euro-communism. Doubtless all these considerations were valid, but doubtless too, there were others equally well qualified in each of these different respects. Could it be that those attempting to reason in this way were falling into the very trap against which, on 21st October, John Paul II himself warned journalists; that of plunging "boldly into a far-reaching analysis of the problems and motives of Church personalities at the risk of passing over the most important aspect, which, as you know, is not political but spiritual"? Could it be that beyond the intellectual theorizing and the political speculation, the true reason for his election lay in the simple and perhaps unfashionably unsophisticated fact that the cardinals recognized in him a man of God, a man of love? Significantly it was only those who did not know the man who were truly surprised at his election.

At the time of his election there were many who knew little or nothing about the new pope apart from the fact that he was a Pole. Before the conclave, "The Inner Elite: Dossiers of Papal Candidates" had asserted with great authority: "A study of the processes that bring a man to the cardinalate show the extent to which each has been given a certain mind-set and imbued with a given system of values. A key element is isolation from the normal influences of human experiences at an early age and immersion in a homogenized ecclesiastical culture." Now, either with a view to verifying this kind of theory or with a view to predicting more accurately what was to come, the world received with absorbed interest whatever snippets of information could be gleaned about the life of this man "from a far-distant country" and the small town of Wadowice, where the boy Karol had grown up, assumed overnight an overwhelming importance.

Facing page: John Paul II at Mentarella, October 1978. Above: Karol with his mother, Emilia Wojtyla.

In looking at the early lives of those who have risen to positions of prominence, there is always a danger of viewing otherwise insignificant details in the light of what was to follow, and of seeking to show that the outcome, now known, was inevitable from the very beginning. Bearing this in mind the life story of a pope is, nevertheless, of interest and it is worth seeking beyond the hand-written entries which record Wojtyla's life in the Parish Register at Wadowice: Born 18th May 1920; baptized 20th June 1920; ordained priest 1st November 1946; consecrated bishop 28th September 1958; made archbishop 30th December 1963; became a cardinal 9th May 1967 and finally – 16.x.78. *in Summum Pontificem electus, Joannes Paulus II.*

Karol Wojtyla was born in Wadowice, near Kraków, into a poor family. His father, after whom Karol was named, was a retired lieutenant of the Corps of Supplies, first in the Imperial Austro-Hungarian Army, then in the Polish Army, and his small pension permitted only a modest apartment on the first floor of number 7 Koscielna (Church) Street. Little is known of his very early years. His own writings are conspicuously lacking in autobiographical detail and it is possible that his parents were at this stage largely concerned with their elder son, Edward, who after proving himself to be of exceptional intelligence at his high school, had qualified as a doctor and was now hoping to become a consultant. It is known, however, that in 1927 Karol entered the "Universal" or primary school in Wadowice and that he remained there until he was eleven. A school photograph taken at this time shows him as a serious-faced boy with the close-cropped, almost scalped look of many of his Polish contemporaries.

Wojtyla was to have his first close encounter with tragedy early in life. In 1929, at the age of forty-five, his mother Emilia died and shortly afterwards the elder son, Edward, on whom so much hope had been focused, died tragically of an attack of scarlet fever contracted in the hospital where he was working. Inevitably these two deaths, occurring in rapid succession, left their mark on the boy. Monsignor Kazimierz Figliewicz, at Wawel Cathedral in Kraków, who has known Karol from his earliest days, recounts how "looking closely at him, one could find traces of the experience". As a result Karol drew closer to his father, who was a loving but stern parent, and a believer in military discipline. Karol, or rather Lolek, as he was known to his friends, (Lolek is a frequently used diminutive of Karol) was subjected to a rigorous daily routine of mass, school, a meal, one hour's play, then homework followed by early bed. Discipline and hard work at an early age was to bring its rewards, however. In 1931 Karol and his friends moved to the boys' Gymnasium and there he earned the reputation of being something of a genius. He is remembered by teachers and schoolmates alike as being good at everything and yet, possibly even more remarkably, as being not a priggish but rather, a friendly and stimulating companion. Although while he was still very young he developed a life-long love of Polish literature, he was not totally absorbed in bookwork. His strong, stocky body was ideally built for any number of sporting activities: football, swimming, hiking, canoeing, and above all skiing in the Tatra mountains, which then as now formed a fundamental part of the psychic make-up of Wojtyla. Throughout his life the Tatras have been a place for meditation and a place of refuge in times of stress, but from his very earliest years they epitomized his love of freedom. It was at school too, that Wojtyla first showed his talent for dancing (he excelled at the complicated Polish folk dances) and for acting. He was an active member of the school drama group, so much so that he was entrusted with the time-consuming and challenging task of producing many of the plays himself.

Section 71 of the Parish Register in Wadowice.

The house in Wadowice where Karol Wojtyla was born.

From the accounts of those who knew Wojtyla as a child, he emerges as the almost too perfect all-round pupil, and working on the principle that there is no virtue in excellence if it comes too effortlessly, it is perhaps reassuring to note that piety is not the foremost quality for which he is remembered. Doubtless, however, Karol's father's deep religious convictions left an impression on the boy and it must be noted that he served as an altar-boy each morning at mass. The parish priest whom he assisted harbored a secret hope, for some years, that Karol would one day choose the priesthood. It was a hope too, which was reiterated by the erstwhile Archbishop Metropolitan of Kraków, Prince Sapieha, who visited the school in Wadowice shortly before Karol was to take his school-leaving examinations. The boy with the sonorous voice and careful speech was chosen to welcome their distinguished visitor and he did so with such fluency and obvious ability that the Archbishop is said to have inquired whether Karol had shown any inclination towards the priesthood. A schoolfriend of Wojtyla's, looking back on their shared schooldays, remembers him as "somehow different". "He was remarkable for his versatility. He was in many ways an extrovert but what really set him apart from the rest of us was the other side of him, which could be reflective, contemplative, even mysterious." This delicate balance between extrovert and introvert and his wide range of talents led many to believe that Karol Wojtyla was destined for something special. When, however, at the age of eighteen he left school, having graduated top of his class, it was not with the intention of following the example of most Poles who excelled intellectually, and entering the priesthood, but with a view to joining the world of the theater.

In the same year, 1938, Karol and his father moved to Kraków, a city of magnificent art and architecture, dominated by the fortified castle on Wawel Hill, the home of a succession of Polish Kings and a proud historical seat, and by the adjacent Cathedral, one of Poland's greatest religious centers. An inscription on an effigy in the city describes Kraków in glowing terms: *Cracovia totius Poloniae urbs celeberrima* – "Kraków, most celebrated of all Polish cities" – but the eulogy was well founded, and remains so today, for not only did the golden age, when the city was the capital of the Jagiellonian dynasty linking Poland to Lithuania, leave a rich heritage of artistic masterpieces, it also gave to the world a great seat of learning, in the form of the Jagiellonian University.

It was here that, after spending the greater part of his summer vacation working on the roads, Karol enrolled at the start of the new academic year. He joined the Department of Philosophy, one which already boasted an impressive number of scholars of international repute, to read for a degree in Polish language, literature and philosophy. Once again, his contemporaries at University remember him as a student of great academic ability but also as a young man who was good-humored, friendly and understandably popular. The subject he had chosen to study gave him an excellent excuse for joining the students' experimental drama group 'Studio Dramatyczne 1939', a theater workshop which experimented in developing new dramatic ideals. Here his hopes of becoming an actor seemed nearer fulfillment when he took part in the "Knight of the Moon", a drama based on an old Kraków legend. With his large, muscular frame and his beautiful, haunting voice, he played the part of Taurus, the bull, so convincingly that his fellow-players were determined he was destined for theatrical stardom. Wojtyla enrolled in optional elocution classes; in his spare time he began to study for a diploma in drama; he became one of the few privileged undergraduates permitted to join the élitist Polish Language Society and, in addition to all this, he still found time to write poetry and folkloristic ballads, after the style of the then popular Zegladowicz, which he recited during poetry-reading evenings organized by the students. By the end of his first year at University Wojtyla was deeply immersed in the academic life and almost oblivious to the distant rumblings of Nazi boots on the march across Europe, but this was all to change suddenly.

On 22nd August 1939, to the astonishment of the world, Germany and Russia signed a peace treaty. Allied to Russia, Germany's visions of walking over Europe seemed relatively unimpeded and when, on 1st September, Karol Wojtyla made his way to mass at Wawel Cathedral (for despite all his other activities, he had by no means abandoned the church), it was to the sound of bombs falling over Kraków. The Blitzkrieg offensive against Poland had begun. Within a few days the 14th Army had reached Kraków and the policy of exterminating Jewish and Polish *Untermenschen* began. A select few were to be preserved as servants and laborers for the Reich but intelligence and education levels were for obvious reasons to be kept to a minimum. The closing of the Jagiellonian University marked the beginning of an attempt to eliminate systematically the intelligentsia, the nobility and the clergy. Many of Kraków's academic staff were sent to Sachsenhausen concentration camp; some were subsequently released but most were never seen again.

Those academics who were not arrested did not, however, remain idle. Instead, they went underground, organizing themselves into groups, so that tutorials, seminars and examinations could be held secretly in private houses. Students were also in grave danger – to be identified as such meant death or removal to a concentration camp – but with grim determination that learning should not be denied by military oppression, many continued to study at the "underground university". Among these was Wojtyla, who enrolled without hesitation as a second year student of philology. The way to avoid deportation was to show oneself to be useful as a laborer for the Reich. The possession of an *Arbeitskarte* (work card) meant some security at a time when those without one were instantly deported to the camps, and so Karol mingled with the working people and went to break stones with a sledgehammer in a quarry belonging to the Solway Chemical Works outside Kraków. Karol was later to be "promoted" to assisting the shot-firer by packing explosives into holes in the rockface and stringing up fuses and eventually he was transferred to the water purification department of the Solway factory, where he carried lime in buckets suspended from a wooden yoke. It was all hard labor, however, alleviated only by the company of friends. Among these were Juliusz Kydrinski,

who had been in the same seminar group as Wojtyla at the Jagiellonian University and who was later to become a well-known writer, Krauze the quarry foreman, and the daughter of one of the factory directors who used to bring Wojtyla welcome snacks to restore his strength. Karol, despite the bitter cold and what amounted almost to convict labor, managed to find time for the humblest of the workers, trying to improve working conditions and helping to provide for their recreational, cultural and spiritual needs. The discipline of his childhood stood him in good stead. Karol studied at night, was one of the first to join the new underground Rhapsodic Theater as an actor and co-producer and still found time to write. Under the pseudonym of Andrzej Jawien he wrote articles later published in the Catholic newspaper *Tygodnik Powszechny*, plays on Biblical themes and poetry – poems

Karol with his father in Wadowice in 1928.

which, like "The Quarry", speak with imagery that is both beautiful and powerful of work, of the workers, and of human emotions and which, despite the censors, point beyond the suffering to a God, who means salvation.

"How splendid these men, no airs, no graces;
I know you, look into your hearts,
no pretence stands between us.
Some hands are for toil, some for the cross . . .

...Whoever enters Him keeps his own self
He who does not
has no full part in the business of this world
despite all appearances."

> from "The Quarry" translated
> by Jerzy Peterkiewicz.

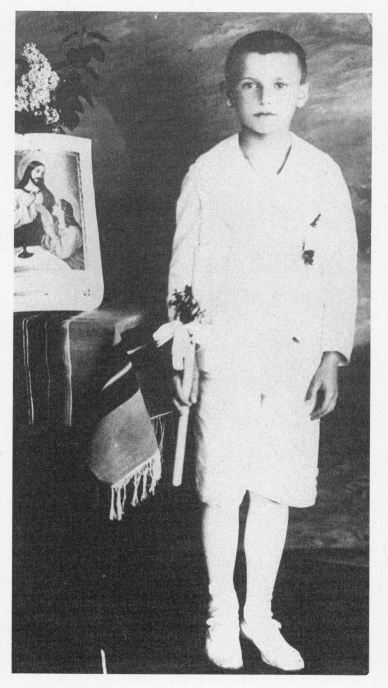

First Communion.

At this time Wojtyla was also profoundly influenced by a simple, uneducated ascetic with the very highest spiritual standards. Jan Tyranowski was a tailor by profession and also a dedicated Christian, with enormous spiritual strength, much of which was drawn from the writings of St. John of the Cross. It was he who introduced Wojtyla to the teachings of this sixteenth century mystic concerning the *via negativa*, and the concept of finding God in a darkness devoid of sensual pleasure may well have held a particular appeal at a time when such pleasures were few and far between. It was he who also organized the "Living Rosary" prayer circle, of which Karol became a diligent member and he who formed the Catholic Youth Association of which the young student was at one time chairman. Despite the rigors of Nazi-occupied Poland then, Karol still managed to pursue his intellectual – and now, increasingly – his spiritual interests. The rigors, however, were not to be underestimated. Returning from work one night, Wojtyla collapsed with exhaustion in the street, only to be hit as he fell by a passing German truck. Karol lay in the road, unconscious, with a fractured skull, until he was found next morning by a stranger who took him to hospital.

The precise point at which Karol Wojtyla abandoned his hopes of fame under theater spotlights and committed himself to a study of theology with a view to becoming a priest remains something of an enigma – so too do the exact reasons for this apparently sudden change of course. The ever-imminent possibility of arrest and interrogation prevented the ready exchange of such confidences – even between the closest of friends – and even Karol's fellow-students at the illicit university remain uncertain at what stage the change in studies took place, although many have attempted to hazard guesses. Some have suggested that it was Karol's road accident which called him to revise his intentions and others claimed that a second, similar, accident only a short time later endorsed the call which he then decided to answer. Kydrinski recalls that in the early spring of 1941 Karol's father died while staying at the young writer's house. Wojtyla spent the entire night kneeling beside the body of the man who had been his pillar of strength and his point of reference on so many issues. At twenty Karol Wojtyla was left virtually alone in an exceptionally arduous world and this moment of extreme personal tragedy has been seen as the turning point in his life. No doubt these incidents had their role to play, but to see Wojtyla's decision as a "turning point" suggests perhaps too dramatic a change, for under the influence of his father, and later of Tyranowski, Karol had always been a committed Catholic. It is significant also that Karol himself did not recognize the gap between his dramatic and literary interests and his priestly vocation as so yawning a gulf. Later, as a well established priest, he was to write of the relationship between talent and vocation, "Priesthood is a sacrament and vocation, while writing poetry is the function of talent, but it is talent also which determines vocation." Also significant is the fact that beyond the romanticized image of a young man determinedly holding his own and helping others in defiance of enemy occupying forces, lay the brutal reality of suffering and deprivation – his own and that of everyone around him. During the Nazi occupation Karol Wojtyla helped Jews to evade arrest by supplying them with Aryan identification papers, but for every one that escaped, countless others died from starvation, cold, punishingly hard work, bullets and ultimately from Cyclon B gas. Suffering either dispels or strengthens faith and the savagery of these years seems to have called Wojtyla to the service of others, for some time in 1942 Karol enrolled at the illegal theological department of the Jagiellonian University in the certain knowledge that discovery meant death.

Above: Karol Wojtyla senior (the man with moustache and shaved head) in a school photograph. His son sits one place removed from him. Facing page: John Paul II at Assisi, November 5, 1978.

While continuing his work at the Solway plant during the day, Karol studied at the underground seminary for two years. Then, in August 1944, shortly after the Warsaw uprising, Gestapo and SS Units purged the streets of Kraków in an attempt to discourage its citizens from attempting a similar insurrection. All males between fifteen and fifty found in the streets were rounded up, and shots were heard throughout the city, but Wojtyla, who remained quietly at prayer in the house which he shared with the Kotlarczyk family in Tyniecka Street, was not discovered. Nevertheless, Adam Sapieha, the same Archbishop Metropolitan of Kraków who some years previously had recognized the potential of the schoolboy welcoming him in Wodowice, took "Black Sunday" as a signal to gather his small, scattered group of seminarists into the archbishop's palace. Here, the imposing drawing room was equipped with twenty or so camp beds and converted into a dormitory for the seminarists, who were at last able to abandon their working clothes for black cassocks. They were to remain in the palace and study in the relative safety of the archbishop's protection. Archbishop Sapieha, although he stood for two of the things most ardently condemned by the Germans (he was both a prince of the church and a prince by birth), had remained conspicuously unafraid of them. When, occasionally, the German Governor General, Hans Frank, chose to afford him the dubious privilege of a visit, the old man took a defiant delight in serving him the coarse black bread and the beetroot conserve which formed the staple diet of the half-starved Polish people. For reasons best known to them, the occupiers had chosen to delay the elimination of this churchman, so beloved by the people of Kraków, and few dared to enter his precincts. Yet the dangers for Wojtyla were not altogether over. He continued to help distribute anti-Nazi newspapers and to assist Jewish families, and so found himself on a list of "unwanted persons". He was forced to abandon his work at the Solway Plant and the fact was of necessity reported to the German "Arbeitsamt". On the intervention of Adam Sapieha, however, Wojtyla's name was miraculously "lost" from the absentee returns submitted to the Germans, and for the remainder of the war the clandestine seminarist "disappeared" altogether from German eyes.

The war ended in Poland early in 1945, but the Russian "liberators" brought a very dubious "peace". In January a Government of National Unity was set up, with Wladyslaw Gomulka – one of the leaders in the A.L. Russian-backed Resistance Group – as Vice-Premier and Secretary-General of the Workers' Party, and the Moscovian Boleslaw Bierut as President of the Republic. Understandably, the exiled former Polish Government, now based in London, refused to acknowledge the new administration and so the bitter struggle, this time frequently of Pole against Pole, began again. It was in an atmosphere of tension and chaos that Wojtyla completed his studies to be a priest. He enrolled as a third year student at the reopened Jagiellonian University only narrowly to escape arrest once again, this time by the Russians, and it would merely have been for singing patriotic songs with a group of other young people in a church square, in a defiant and traditional cry for freedom. Fortunately, the group succeeded in dispersing in time and Wojtyla completed his studies. His overall performance was described by his professor, F. Rozycki as *emminente* i.e. more than excellent, and on 1st November, 1946, Karol Jozef Wojtyla was ordained priest by Archbishop Adam Sapieha, in the archbishop's private chapel. He celebrated his first Mass on the following day, All Soul's Day, in the crypt of St. Leonard in Wawel Cathedral.

With his godmother, Maria Wiadrowska, during the late thirties.

卐 卐 卐 卐 卐

Despite his unquestionably unconventional preparation for ordination, the talents of the new Father Wojtyla had not gone unnoticed. Once again Archbishop Sapieha intervened and Wojtyla was sent from a Poland struggling to recover from the westward shift of its frontiers (the Poles had regained, after 600 years, some of the half-obliterated cities of Germany and at the same time lost huge areas of land to the Russians), to the majesty and splendor of Rome. On a hill overlooking the city, the young priest spent two years studying at the Pontifical University Angelicum under the guidance of the Dominican Fathers. Here he wrote his dissertation on "The Concept of Faith in the Writings of St. John of the Cross". Significantly, the mystical poet, for whom faith appears as a series of paradoxes, had not lost his appeal with the end of the Occupation and, indeed, many years later, when Pope Paul VI called upon Cardinal Wojtyla to lead a Vatican retreat, he was still to draw on St. John's beautiful testimony to the paradoxes of a transcendant God:

> *"To attain to this which you know not*
> *you must pass through that which you know not.*
> *To attain to this which you possess not*
> *you must pass through that which you possess not*
> *To attain to this which you are not*
> *you must pass through that which you are not."*

The University dissertation, completed under the direction of a French Dominican who saw in St. John of the Cross a confirmation of the theses of Thomas Aquinas, was awarded nine points out of ten by the examining professors. The defence of the thesis was awarded fifty marks out of a possible fifty. Wojtyla's first venture outside Poland had won him academic acclaim and had placed him for the first time on the broad stage of the Universal Church. It had also given him a good command of Italian and his summer vacations spent among Polish exiles in the Pas de Calais and in Belgium had improved his working knowledge of French.

When, therefore, Father Wojtyla, D.D., left the cultural and intellectual sophistication of Rome to return to the Poland of 1948, it must have come as a surprise to many that he was sent as priest to a small parish apparently at the very end of the world. At that time Stalinist terror was at its highest pitch. In Poland the Communist Party was condemning even its own more moderate leaders – those who, although confirmed Communists, were looking for a Polish rather than a Soviet orientated communism. Secret police weeded out innocent people whose opinions were considered in any way "hostile", and prisons overflowed with the victims of unlawful and illicit arrests. While, however, in many parts of the country, people trembled at the sound of an early morning knock at the door, Karol Wojtyla presided over an old church in Niegowić surrounded by huge lime-trees, and a house set in a kitchen-garden and orchard where chickens picked their way, undisturbed, through the vegetables. Perhaps the decision of Sapieha, now a cardinal, had not been so lacking in foresight. Certainly the villagers responded with warm appreciation to the man who arrived in Niegowić with only one small suitcase and placed himself entirely at their disposal. When one of his parishioners fell ill, the young priest would cheerfully take his place among the laborers in the fields, and pastoral visits to distant farms were undertaken on foot or on the back of a passing wooden cart. Tales of the kindness and generosity of Father Wojtyla are still told regularly in Niegowić today. In return, while Wojtyla was their incumbent, the villagers flocked to church and listened, enthralled, to the sermons of a priest whom they recognized to be "a truly good man".

When, after only one year, Wojtyla was transferred from Niegowić, he left behind him a brand new church, which he had helped to build, and a congregation of friends that he would retain for the rest of his life. Much to the amazement and confusion of his new parishioners in the busy parish of St. Florian's, in Kraków, the new priest arrived not in a taxi, but in the very least salubrious of farm carts, his worldly possessions were all mysteriously contained in a single suitcase and his faded cassock was punctuated with dark gray patches. The people of St. Florian's, at first dismayed by Wojtyla's lack of concern for considerations of dress and physical well-being, were soon to discover that theirs was a priest who not only preached asceticism as a means of spiritual growth, but one who practiced it also. It is not known whether the man who is now Pope, like Pope John XXIII, swore a vow of poverty. What is known is that he frequently opted to sleep on the bare floorboards in preference to a comfortable bed; that at times he did not allow himself the luxury of sleep at all, passing the night in silent devotion in the church, and that all attempts to induce him to protect himself from the bitter Polish winter with overcoats, or even a cardigan, proved abortive. The

congregation of St. Florian's grew to accept and admire his "unusual" ways and many recall with affection that at times the demand for him was so great that Wojtyla resorted to "hiding" in the confessional to snatch a few much needed moments for prayer and meditation. In particular he had an affinity with the young. Surrounding himself with students and young workers, he would organize cycle rides and hikes for them, accompany them skiing or simply take them into the mountains to speak to them of a God whom the Marxist educational system had attempted to oust altogether. They, in their turn, regarded him as an uncle, calling him *"Wujek"* (little uncle) and teasing him with friendly familiarity when, for example, he "switched off" i.e. lapsed into thought and ran off the road with his bicycle. He was also, however, the man to whom they turned for advice and whom they respected greatly, joining with him to say a "field" mass by the roadside, in a tent or in some laborer's cottage.

Wojtyla's first parish at Niegowic.

Work of this kind by a Catholic required much courage under Stalinism, but Karol Wojtyla gave himself up to it wholeheartedly. That is not to say, however, that he had altogether abandoned his love of the theater. There are still those in the offices of the Catholic monthly newspaper, *Znak*, in Kraków, who remember a shabbily dressed young priest clutching the notes for a play he was completing, on the subject of the Polish painter Brother Albert. Again the subject matter is interesting, for Brother Albert sacrificed his dedication to art to give his life to the poor. Wojtyla's identification with him is easily understandable. Yet by some strange ironic twist, or through the workings of some Divine Will, Wojtyla was compensated for the sacrifice of his dramatic career. The man who had surrendered the spotlights and the stage found himself addressing huge "audiences" every time he preached a sermon, for people came from miles around to hear his voice proclaiming the Gospel message, with obvious heartfelt sincerity and in a manner that was comprehensible to everyone.

Wojtyla in his diocese of Krakow.

Sadly for the people of St. Florian's, in 1951 Father Wojtyla's sermons were interrupted, for at the insistence of his former professor of theology at the Jagiellonian University, Fr Rozycki, Wojtyla decided to continue his academic studies. A few months previously, to the bitter grief of the people of Kraków, Cardinal Sapieha, their "invincible Cardinal" had died, and his successor, Archbishop Eugeniusz Baziak, granted Wojtyla dispensation from pastoral duties with a sabbatical for further studies. Wojtyla chose to pursue his interest in phenomenology and above all in Max Scheler, attempting to reconcile such contemporary theories with the traditional teachings of St. Thomas Aquinas. Scheler built largely on the "logic of the heart". Feeling is central to his work and love is the way by which goodness and other values are discerned. "Unless we love, we cannot know" is a premise fundamental to Scheler's teaching. It is a premise which has also exerted a lasting influence on Karol Wojtyla, and his thesis, entitled "The Possibilities for Building a System of Christian Ethics on the Basis of Max Scheler", in many ways foreshadowed all his later philosophy and his writings.

Wojtyla's work was accepted by the examining professor as a suitable dissertation for a junior professorship. It was presented in 1953 and approved in 1954, shortly before the Theology Department was closed down by the Communist authorities. However, once his teaching certificate had been obtained, Wojtyla was invited to give several lectures at the University of Lublin; the lectures gradually became a regular feature and after only two years he was offered the chair of Ethics. At thirty-six Wojtyla thus became a fully-fledged professor, the Head of Lublin's Institute of Ethics. Then, on 4th July 1958, the Pope appointed Professor Father Karol Wojtyla as titular bishop of Ombi and bishop auxiliary of the Kraków diocese. Wojtyla, Cardinal Wyszinski remembers, was out canoeing at the time. It was only after many hours of trying that Poland's Primate managed to contact him, tell him of the Holy Father's wishes and ask him whether he accepted the appointment. "Yes", came the characteristic reply "but now can I go back to canoeing?" Within a matter of hours he was back on the lakes.

The consecration ceremony took place in Wawel Castle Cathedral on 28th September 1958. The day was damp and overcast and inside the cathedral the darkness was lightened only by spattering candles, but a story which has already become something of a legend tells, with all the poetic symbolism of a master painting how, as Wojtyla in accordance with the order of service raised his miter to the heavens, a shaft of warm sunlight penetrated the stained-glass windows and fell on the solitary figure of the newly-anointed bishop. The congregation of relatives, friends, parishioners from Niegowić and St. Florian's and even fellow workers from the Solway plant were convinced that here was one of the Lord's chosen.

The new bishop himself obstinately refused to alter his life style to that of a man "set apart or above". As he was later to reaffirm in his retreat on the "Sign of Contradiction", he saw the kingly mission of Jesus Christ as handed on to the Church in a very special way in the pastoral authority exercised by the bishops under the direction of the successor to Peter, and by priests and deacons under the direction of their bishops, but this did not absolve them from respecting the "kingliness" in every man, which stems from Christ the good shepherd. "The bishop who visits the communities of his Church is the authentic pilgrim who arrives at one after another of the good shepherd's sanctuaries preserved by the People of God, sharers in the kingly priesthood of Christ". It was no part of a bishop's role to become separated from the other sharers in this kingly priesthood. Bishop Wojtyla still had the capacity to fill a church, but he wanted also to reach beyond the believers to those who doubted or even denied the faith to which he was so totally committed. Each week he opened his apartment for a party of a different kind. Professional people, students and workers, no matter what their creed or status, were invited to share a glass of wine and an *oplatek* wafer – a wafer of unleavened bread – which the Poles traditionally share with each other on Christmas Eve as a symbol of friendship and harmony. This would lead to discussion and, frequently, also to a joyful rendering of Polish folk songs. These evenings were the beginning of other activities. Marxists, Roman Catholics, intellectuals, laborers – all would set off on outings organized by Poland's youngest bishop, who was still dressed in a threadbare cassock, still traveling through the streets on a bicycle, and still living in a tiny, two-room apartment.

It was while he was Bishop of Kraków that Wojtyla fell ill. The recommendation of his doctor was that to prevent any recurrence he should take plenty of exercise. The bishop needed no second bidding and the doctor's orders merely added more justification to what he was already doing, for in between his official commitments and his other pastoral duties, he was still cycling, kayaking and skiing with groups of enthusiastic students. With them he seemed to relive his own student days and sometimes indulged in most "unbishoplike" behaviour. One American lady in particular must have been very surprised to discover that one of the group who serenaded her, as she lay in hospital with a broken leg, was the Bishop of Kraków.

In 1962, on the death of Archbishop Baziak, Wojtyla was elected Vicar Capitular and so to all intents and purposes was placed in charge of the diocese. Then, on 30th December 1963, Paul VI appointed him Archbishop of Kraków, and on 18th January 1964 he took over as Archbishop Metropolitan. Still Wojtyla obstinately ignored the comments of the Metropolitan curia that his cramped lodgings were unsuitable for an Archbishop. The curia scored one of their few victories over him, however, while he was away from Kraków for a few days. In his absence they went to his lodgings, removed his few personal possessions and deposited them in the Archbishop's Palace. Wojtyla, on his return, was furious and when he did finally admit defeat and move to the Palace it was only to baffle the housekeeper by arriving bearing a canoe and paddles. She had never seen such unorthodox ecclesiastical accoutrements.

The Archbishop's Palace in Kraków is an imposing building with spacious rooms proudly displaying priceless paintings and furniture that once belonged to Polish Kings. Even here, however, Archbishop Wojtyla managed to secure himself a small, spartan bedroom more suited to his tastes. His frayed cassock was a constant source of

embarrassment to his chauffeur and he was always penniless. He determinedly refused all payment for his professorship at the University of Lublin and what salary he did receive vanished without trace in the direction of those he considered to have greater need of it. Father Pieronek, who acted as Wojtyla's secretary when he traveled to Rome in 1967 to receive his cardinal's hat, recalls that on that occasion the cardinal had no red socks. The Felicjanki Sisters' Convent had presented him with the robes, but en route to the Sistine Chapel Wojtyla realized that his only socks were black. The Roman shops near the Chapel proved to be sadly lacking in red socks, so too did the cardinals' laundry at Santa Marta and so, even on this auspicuous occasion, Wojtyla's appearance was not what his chauffeur might have wished.

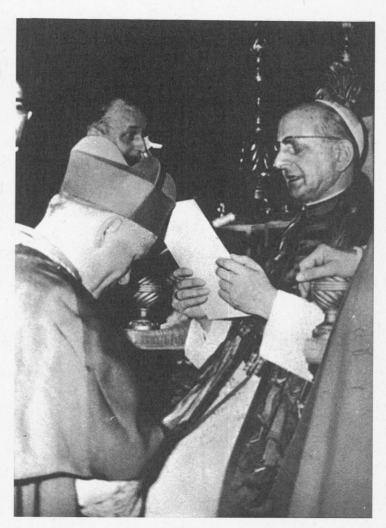

Cardinal Wojtyla receiving his cardinal's hat from Pope Paul VI in 1967.

Karol Wojtyla's energy was apparently endless and every minute of his day was carefully planned. Starting at 5 a.m., the first hours of the day were generally allocated to a Mass, prayer, reading and above all to seeing people. His office was always open from 11 a.m. until 1 p.m. for anyone wishing to see him and he always made a point of visiting the poor and the sick – even in the early hours of the morning. When Kydrinski's mother lay dying in Kraków hospital, the Archbishop left his bed in the middle of the night to be with her during her last hours. Driving round the city, Karol would work in the back of the car on papers and books drawn from what seemed a bottomless briefcase. He also had the disconcerting ability to read or write while conducting a conversation and still recall exactly what was said. Many, too, will vouch for the fact that Wojtyla never forgets his friends, colleagues, parishioners or any of the multitude of people who have helped him in his life. At Christmas he went without fail to visit the workers at Solway whose loyalty he has never forgotten.

Yet, despite his heartfelt commitment to the duties of his office and to the people who surrounded him, Wojtyla managed to remain an avid sportsman throughout the twenty years in which he presided over Kraków. Asked once whether it was quite becoming for a cardinal to ski, Wojtyla replied unhesitatingly "It is not becoming for a cardinal to ski badly". This was not one of the Kraków cardinal's failings for it is not for nothing that he has been called the "Scourge of the Tatras". Dressed in baggy trousers and using old-fashioned skis – for he emphatically refused to spend money on new ski equipment – he would snatch a few hours in the mountains, often to the amazement of others whom he encountered on the snowy slopes. On one occasion in particular he is said to have lost his way, when skiing alone, and crossed the Czech border by accident. Discovered by a Czech patrol, he was arrested and held for some considerable time by security police who refused to believe that the man before them was really, as his official documents suggested, the Cardinal of Kraków.

The young Bishop of Krakow.

In his former diocese of Krakow, 'Wujek' is not forgotten.

before he could swim in it. "Naked he appears but a man" must surely have been the principle underlying the Vatican statement that some people would take offence at seeing the pope in a swimming costume. In view of this, it is understandable that there are those who seek to "humanize" their spiritual father. Less understandable is the fact that attempts to show that the pope is a man like any other have exactly the opposite effect. Strangely, the knowledge that Pope John Paul II has carted piles of frozen excrement from the blocked lavatories left by the SS in the Theological Seminary used as their headquarters during the Occupation, serves only to enhance and not to detract from his mystique.

✶ ✶ ✶ ✶ ✶

Tales of this kind concerning the man who now sits at the head of the gigantic apparatus of the Roman Catholic Church are endless. When a man is elected pope he runs a grave risk of disappearing behind a formal image and a cloud of somewhat informal mythology. In the nineteenth century Alphonse Daudet wrote a poignant story about a small boy who repeatedly stayed out late, playing. When he returned to confront the wrath of his parents, he would announce solemnly "le pape est mort" (the pope is dead). The effect was so devastating that when his family awoke in the morning and found that the pope was not dead, they were so pleased that they forgot to punish the boy. The story illustrates admirably simply, although naturally with some degree of poetic exaggeration, the legendary stature and importance which the life, or indeed the death, of one man assumes overnight, when he becomes the successor to Peter. The formality which traditionally surrounds the papacy, the style of dress and the style of address, are all designed to raise the pope from the level of the individual to the level of the universal and archetypal, from that of the human to that of something much greater than human. John Paul II had to shield the swimming pool at his summer residence at Castelgandolfo

Those who, in the days following the election of John Paul II and preceding his inauguration, scrutinized the life that had gone before, were concerned not so much with the "human element", as with the element that had placed him in a position where the demands were almost superhuman. Bearing in mind the requirements outlined in "The Inner Elite. Dossiers of Papal Candidates" they glanced briefly at his personal life, noted with some surprise that in some ways he had not been "isolated from the normal influences of human experience at an early age" and then turned to the "ecclesiastical culture", to his public life – to his role in the church both in and outside Poland. After all, the fact that a man is a good skier does not make him pope, nor does the fact that he is a poet and nor, the more cynical might argue, does the fact that he is sincerely committed to the service and the love of people. More significant, many suggested, was the fact that he was Polish, for to be Polish meant to come from a land where nationalism and Catholicism were irrevocably linked and where Catholicism had proved itself to be the effective enemy of oppression and the champion of human rights. It meant that Pope John Paul II had survived the paradox of a country in which the Polish Communist Party officially holds the monopoly of power over a population which is overwhelmingly Roman Catholic.

In the year AD 966 the Polish ruler, Miezko, married a Christian princess from Bohemia and in doing so, himself became a Christian, thereby bringing Poland under the jurisdiction of the Church of Rome. The adoption of Roman Catholicism removed the main pretext for the German encroachments which Poland repeatedly suffered, but it also turned "Polania semper fidelis" into an exposed limb of Catholicism on the eastern boundaries of Central Europe. Successfully combated attacks from both East and West increased its sense of national identity and on the strength of this Poland elected to identify itself with Rome. When Boleslaw, Miezko's son, persuaded the pope and the Holy Roman Emperor to make the diocese of Gniezno an archbishopric it not only gave Poland independence from German ecclesiastical hierarchy, but also strengthened the links with Rome. Polonia became a sovereign state in 1024 by virtue of the pope's permission and so began a long tradition in which the equation of Pole and Roman Catholic became the symbol of the separate identity of the nation, a symbol which has endured to the present day.

The Poland into which Wojtyla was born was a young nation which had risen like an independent phoenix from the fire of the First World War. He belonged to the first generation of free Poles for nearly one and a half centuries. Three months after his birth the Red Army was defeated at the gates of Warsaw and the new nation began courageously to rebuild its thousands of demolished buildings with renewed faith in the future and a faith in God and the Virgin Mary, which had been increased and strengthened by the oppression of the nineteenth century. Religion had indeed served as the "mainstay of the people" during the days of the Partitions, for the Russians, Prussians and Austrians had all ruled their respective parts of Poland with an iron hand. During Wojtyla's early youth, however, the prevailing atmosphere was one of triumphant hope. Then came the German Occupation. Once again, it was the Church which led the struggle against the Nazis. One thousand Polish churches were destroyed by enemy action during the Second World War and three thousand priests were killed or lost their lives in concentration camps. There were many among the clergy who showed exceptional bravery, but of these one man in particular must be remembered, not only because he epitomizes the Christian Spirit, but also because of the interpretation Wojtyla placed upon his death.

In his home town of Wadowice, the election of John Paul II is celebrated with a Mass.

In Poland, the inauguration of the Polish Pope was the first Mass ever to be shown on television.

Father Maksymilian Kolbe was well known throughout Poland as the guiding light in one of the world's largest monasteries, Niepokalanów. Together with his friars he built here not only a center for prayer, but also a completely self-supporting community which included among its many facilities a printing press compiled of all the most modern equipment. From here, in 1935, he launched a daily Catholic newspaper which was soon to become one of Poland's best-selling publications. In September 1939, however, the Nazi forces took over this flourishing center and many of the religious community were deported to Germany. Among them was Father Kolbe. This particular imprisonment lasted only a short time. In December, Father Kolbe, wracked with tuberculosis and suffering painful abscesses, was released and instantly began a mission for Polish refugees. He also wrote articles in his magazines designed to prick the consciences of the Nazi persecutors. So it was that in 1941 the priest who had made such a courageous stand for freedom, was arrested for the second time by the Germans and sent to become prisoner 16670 in Block 11 at Auschwitz. Subjected to constant blows, flagellation and starvation because he refused to deny his faith in Christ, Father Kolbe was eventually incarcerated in this, the camp prison known to the inmates of Auschwitz as the Block of Death. It was in Block 11 that the court sessions were held, passing up to a hundred death sentences in the hour, in the name of some satanic justice. Once sentenced, prisoners were made to undress. The lucky ones were then afforded the dignity of dying with their faces turned to the wall outside in the courtyard; the not so lucky were simply executed in the lavatories. Many never even reached the courtroom, but died in one of the block's infamous cellars, where they suffocated in the heat and the stench or simply starved to death. One thing was certain – no-one who entered Block 11 ever came out alive.

Father Kolbe, initially in Block 14, was brought to one of these cellars following the successful escape of a prisoner. The camp authorities demanded the death of ten men as a reprisal. The prisoners of Block 14 were paraded before an SS officer who selected at random ten men to die of starvation in a windowless underground bunker. Father Kolbe was not among the chosen victims, but as one of the prisoners cried out in despair, a figure stepped out of the ranks and offered to take his place. "Who are you?" asked "Butcher" Fritsch, amazed. "I am a Catholic priest" came the reply.

In the wretched, stifling atmosphere of an underground cell in Auschwitz, Father Kolbe led his companions in fervent prayer, and hymns resounded through the concrete corridors. As one by one the starving wretches collapsed and died, Father Kolbe continued to comfort, to reassure and above all to pray. Finally, after a fortnight, only the priest and three other prisoners remained. The authorities, needing the cell, decided that their victims were taking too long to die, and sent a common criminal to accelerate the process. Father Kolbe, his face still calm and radiant, himself gave his arm to the executioner to receive an injection of phenol.

On 17th October 1971, Maksymilian Kolbe was beatified by Pope Paul VI and at Auschwitz in 1972, on the first anniversary of the beatification, Cardinal Wojtyla addressed a multi-national audience: "Auschwitz" he said "is a place in which the command to love was replaced by the imperative of hatred" . . . "But God's Providence manifested itself at last, towards the end of that terrible time of trial of which Auschwitz has remained the ultimate symbol. The life and death of Maksymilian Kolbe show the power of love victorious over hatred, and of the power of the human spirit to survive."

Above: John Paul II with President Giscard d'Estaing of France, October 1978. Facing page: John Paul II celebrates Mass in a suburb of Rome, December 1978.

To Wojtyla also, the most crucial factor in the story of the blessed Maksymilian Kolbe was his reply to the inquiry of the SS man, Fritsch – "I am a Catholic priest." Throughout Wojtyla's life the figure of Father Kolbe was to act as a model of what priesthood represented, for it was in his capacity as a Roman Catholic priest that Kolbe sacrificed his life to be a source of comfort and love in the last terrible hours of his fellow sufferers. Priesthood is an "expression of the meaning given to man and the world by their relationship with God" and the true priest "simply by being who he is, expresses this meaning and at the same time conveys it to the world and to man in the world." Oppression and persecution serve only to make this meaning, as expressed in the priesthood and in the Church, more apparent.

On October 21, 1978, the newly elected pope held a meeting for two thousand journalists.

At the time when Karol Wojtyla was ordained priest, shortly after the conclusion of the Nazi occupation, the Provisional Government was treading carefully in its relations with the Roman Catholic Church. It regarded Catholicism as an irrelevant vestige of a bygone era and fully intended to oust the Church completely in the course of time but, for the moment, its primary interest was in the consolidation of its own power. Indeed, overt confrontation with so influential a force as the Roman Catholic Church in Poland would be, at least, embarrassing. Ironically, both Hitler and Stalin contributed to giving the Church the strong position it now occupies in Poland. Hitler's systematic slaughter of Polish Jews, and Stalin's annexation of the eastern provinces with their large Greek Orthodox and Uniate population, raised the proportion of Roman Catholics among the Polish population to more than ninety percent. This fact, coupled with the Church's greater strength as a spiritual, historical and patriotic force, called for caution on the part of the Communist Government, and Poland became the point of measured confrontation, co-existence and dialogue between Marxism and Catholicism. This does not mean to imply, however, that there were no acts of open hostility between the two bodies. As early as 1945 the government suspended the Concordat with the Vatican, for example. At Yalta the agreement between Churchill, Roosevelt and Stalin had endorsed Russia's claim on Poland's eastern territories, and the Potsdam agreement had attempted to compensate for this loss by restoring to Poland the ancient Slav territories which for 600 years had been under German rule. The shifting of Poland's frontiers naturally made her the target for German resentment and the Vatican refused to appoint diocesan bishops to the new Polish territories, or even to recognize the post-war frontier until a peace treaty was concluded.

No doubt the Soviet-orientated government would have revoked the Concordat in any case, but the attitude adopted by the answering anti-Communist Pope, Pius XII, provided a pretext for the government to "defend Polish National interests". In 1948 a number of Church organizations, among them Catholic Action, were officially declared illegal. Two years later, Cardinal Sapieha and Stefan Wyszinski, the newly appointed Archbishop of Warsaw, complained to President Bierut, who was also First Secretary of the Party, that the Government was acting in bad faith in its dealings with the Church and the government reciprocated by accusing the bishops of adopting an attitude of hostility towards the People's Republic. On 14th April 1950, Communist representatives signed a paper recognizing the Pope as supreme head of the Church in all matters relating to church order and to faith, and in exchange the bishops acknowledged the restored western territories as part of Poland and agreed to appeal to Pius XII to appoint bishops for the new Polish dioceses. Accordingly, Cardinal Sapieha went to Rome and begged the Pope, on bended knee, to accept the compromise. Pius XII remained intractable, however, and in Poland, mistrust of the Vatican's *Ostpolitik* increased.

The relations between Church and government grew progressively worse under Stalin's regime. In the Autumn of 1953, Wyszinski, now a Cardinal, was confined to a monastery, where he was to remain interned for three years, and by the end of the year eight bishops and nearly one thousand priests had been arrested. The number of arrests increased rapidly in the following year and depression prevailed throughout Poland until the death of Stalin, and Kruschev's denunciation of his crimes. Then hope was born again, for when in 1956 Gomulka came to power it was to promise to follow "the Polish road to socialism". In an expansive gesture of good will, he released all those who had been imprisoned for their faith and re-instated Cardinal Wyszinski as Primate. The persecutions were not, however, over; the struggle had merely become more subtle. It was a battle between ideologies for the souls of the nation's young, for their commitment either to Poland, the model home of the "new man", or to Poland, the historical bastion of Christianity. As a young priest, Wojtyla would not, it may be argued, have been involved with the fluctuations of the highly complex relationship between Church and State, yet the most tragic aspect of the struggle lay in the fact that it sought to strike at the heart of Everyman and that it intruded, unwelcome as it was, into everyday lives. Perhaps nowhere is this fact more poignantly expressed than in the first socialist new town of Nowa Huta, where the church of the Mother of God, Queen of Poland, now rises proudly and eloquently from the junction of Karl

ately the new man, much to the embarrassment of the authorities, decided that the one item most essential to his needs was a building in which to worship God. Persistent attempts to dissuade him failed miserably and in 1957 permission to build a church was finally granted, and a site was allocated for the purpose. The people of Nowa Huta immediately had the site blessed, and a cross marked the spot where their new church was to be constructed. Then, in 1960, the government decided that instead of the promised church, they would build a school on the site and sent workmen to remove the wooden cross. The workmen met with hundreds of believers who defended the land, which they had already been using as a place of open-air worship, with a barrage of stones. Police replied with tear gas and severe penalties were meted out on the "rioters" but the cross remained and the faithful continued to assemble for regular Masses, held there despite the rigors of the climate.

Among those who celebrated mass on this unusual site was Karol Wojtyla. As bishop and archbishop, Wojtyla

Shortly after his inauguration, pilgrims and posters await the arrival of the Pope at the Marian Shrine of Mentarella.

Marx and Great Proletariat Avenues. The history of this soaring, concrete tribute to freedom and to faith provides an admirable example of how, in a city built "without God", the determination of its citizens prevailed, in defiance of persistent opposition from the government.

The town of Nowa Huta was built in the early 1950s around the massive Lenin Steelworks, not far from Kraków. It was intended as a showpiece for socialism, the model home for the model socialist man who would not, of course, wish to live in the religious and reactionary atmosphere of historic Kraków. Disregarding all financial considerations, the government generously erected the concrete jungle they believed to be socialist man's heart's desire – wide roads imaginatively named, gray high-rise flats and a huge bronze statue of Lenin. Everything was provided except a church, a facility which, it was anticipated, the new man would not require. Unfortun-

was constantly involved in arguments and discussions regarding Nowa Huta's church. Abhorring any incitement to violence, he nevertheless used every conceivable means of putting pressure on the authorities. Finally, in 1967, permission was given to build. A huge crowd gathered for a celebratory Mass in the open air, dampened by a persistent drizzle. Under their umbrellas the people knelt to pray in the mud beside a foundation stone which came from the tomb of St. Peter in Rome, and which bore a message from Pope Paul VI: "Take this stone to Poland, and may it be a corner-stone on which a church will stand at Nowa Huta dedicated to the Queen of Poland". The delays and obstructions were by no means over, however, and it was not until 1977 that the church stood in its entirety. On 15th May, it was finally consecrated by Cardinal Wojtyla. The apparently simple requirement to build a church had meant seventeen years of determined effort. It had involved argument and suffering, but the completed building, with its Chapel of Reconciliation containing the moving sculptures entitled "Christ in Auschwitz", is a living monument to the fact that in Nowa Huta at least, as Cardinal Wojtyla proclaimed: "the will of God and the people who worked here prevailed". He added: "Let this be a lesson!".

The fight for the church in Nowa Huta was just one of numerous confrontations in which Wojtyla, as he rose in the ecclesiastical hierarchy, became increasingly involved. In 1966 Cardinal Wyszinski decided to celebrate one thousand years of Polish Christianity in a highly distinctive fashion. While exiled in a monastery he had read Sienkiewicz's account of the famous victory of the Poles over the Swedish invaders in 1655. According to Sienkiewicz, on the eve of this all important battle the ruler John Kasimir swore on oath on behalf of the nation to serve God and the Blessed Virgin, to rid Poland of foreign invaders, and to improve the social conditions of the Polish people. Wyszinski's idea was to call upon the people of Poland to make a similar but suitably adapted commitment during the years of preparation which culminated in the millennium celebrations. In 1956 the bishops led the country by taking a vow at Czestochowa, and so began a series of sermons and catechesis designed to make all Polish Catholics aware of their responsibilities.

Wojtyla as bishop, and subsequently archbishop, was deeply involved in these preparations and it is interesting to look more closely at the kind of promises Wyszinski, and with him Wojtyla, called upon the Polish people to make. In the course of the preparations they were asked to commit themselves to:

On November 5, 1978 John Paul II visited Assisi, to pray to St Francis and to bless the Franciscan fathers.

John Paul II arriving in Rome after his visit to Mexico in January 1979.

1) allegiance to God, the cross, the gospels, the church and her shepherds and to the sacred land of their fathers
2) fighting against their national vices
3) doing everything to help the nation's children to live in a desire for justice
4) defending the sanctity of marriage, and guarding the family unit, so that within that unit Poland's people can live peacefully and without fear
5) testifying to their devotion to the Mother of God and following her virtues
6) retaining in every Polish soul the grace which is the source of divine life
7) guarding, with eyes turned to the crib at Bethlehem, all unborn life
8) educating the young generation in loyalty to Christ
9) defending the sanctity of marriage and promoting Christ's rule in family life.

The list is, in its entirety, an act of outright defiance of the government. It is also characteristically Polish and characteristic of Wyszinski in its nationalism, traditionalism, tenacity in faith and its Mariology. More significant to those who wished to place Wojtyla in the context of a specific ecclesiastical culture is the stress on family·life – the product, it may be suggested, of a society in which the family unit is one of the few areas which has remained to a large extent outside the reach of Communist indoctrination – and the determination to protect unborn life. In recent years, the government in Poland, thinking to win the loyalty of the people away from an unsympathetic church, has made abortion legal; the Church, scorning such cheap tactics, has remained unwavering in its attitude both to this and to contraception.

Examples of government harassment are numerous. In 1970 Gomulka was deposed after bloody riots in the Baltic coastal cities, and his replacement by Edward Gierek again brought a thaw in Church-State relations. By 1973, however, the Church and the State were once again at loggerheads, this time over the question of religious education. Official reports emphasized the need for a unified educational system designed to prepare young people for adult life in a "socialist" Poland. The school timetables were to be so arranged that it would be impossible for children to attend church for religious instruction. The bishops' response was vehement. "Such intentions", they argued, "could deny a person his fundamental right to freedom of conscience and religion which are guaranteed by the Polish constitution. State laws cannot be contrary to God's laws otherwise they are not binding." Riots in 1976 over steep rises in the price of food brought further friction. Wojtyla, together with other church leaders, announced publicly that the people had a right to protest. The Polish bishops took up the issue of religious freedom in a pastoral letter which pointed out that the State was using the people's taxes to propagate atheism in a country which was indisputably and overwhelmingly Roman Catholic. In a sermon at Nowa Huta, Cardinal Wojtyla underlined grievances which were very close to the hearts of the steelworkers: "The government does not allow you to be promoted because of your beliefs, nor are you allowed to worship in a building." Then on the Feast of the Epiphany he made one of his most memorable and characteristic addresses: "It is difficult from the point of view of human dignity, from a humanistic point of view, to accept atheism as a political program. For it is understandable that a man may seek but not find; it is understandable that a man may deny; but it is not understandable that a man may find himself forbidden to believe. If you wish to fill a given office, to reach a given position, you are forbidden to believe. Atheism as the foundation of national life is a painful misunderstanding from the point of view of true human progress. For it is necessary to respect what is in man."

He went on to stress the obligation of the faithful to speak out against the enforced imposition of an ideology which was contrary to the conviction of the majority. This was not the impassioned plea of a naive champion of religious faith, but rather the product of a deep rooted and carefully formulated humanism which recognized that freedom must apply to all, not only to Christians. "We do not wish to interfere with the families of atheists – that is a matter for themselves and their own consciences." This was the very essence of Wojtyla's approach to Communism.

Paradoxically, government harassment, intended to restrict the influence of the Church, in practice stimulated it and retarded the process of secularization which was taking place in other parts of Europe. Conflict acted as a stimulus to faith: this was the principle which lay at the roots of Wyszinski's attitude. Wojtyla on the other hand was frequently more conciliatory. When Pope Paul VI made Archbishop Wojtyla a cardinal, the event was seen by many as a political move, as an attempt to "counteract" the intransigent Wyszinski with the younger, suppler Wojtyla. Whatever the reasoning behind the actual appointment, the Polish government no doubt hoped to exploit the differences between the two men. The government failed miserably – the Cardinals remained united in their stand – but the difference in approach remained marked.

His Holiness among the Polish community in Rome.

Wojtyla, like Wyszinski, would never compromise his principles, but he had the ability to place Church-State relations on the level of controlled dialogue. Wyszinski distrusted intellectuals, Wojtyla was able to meet them on their own terms. He has a breadth of culture and a profound understanding of Marxism which challenged the Marxists on their own ground, and frequently exposed their lack of knowledge of their own subject. The subtlety of his approach lay in his ability to score points without actually forcing the government into a position where violence was the only resort. He recognized the need to give Polish nationalism its voice without permitting it to shout too provocatively. Wojtyla, while avoiding, wherever possible, direct interference with temporal power, did not hesitate to speak out where necessary for human rights and human values – for liberty, respect for life, fairness, conscientiousness, the dignity of man and a spirit of reconciliation. It was values such as these which, according to him, formed the basis of a harmonious society. His dialogue with Marxism was more, it seemed, a dialogue with atheism, for he was not so much concerned with political Communism as with the challenge which atheism and agnosticism represented to the Christian way of life, and to those values contained in man which make him worthy of respect. Even here, however, Wojtyla had no illusions but talked on the basis of full reciprocity and exchanged concessions.

So, like Cardinal Wyszinski, Cardinal Wojtyla became within Poland a symbol of the Church's resilience, and indeed a symbol of all those trying to retain human dignity. His voice has frequently resounded as loudly as the Primate's on such issues as education – the re-opening of the Theological Faculty at the Jagiellonian University, access to the media, elimination of censorship, the building of churches, freedom from atheistic propaganda and the right to religious instruction. The list of protests is endless, but all came under the broad heading of "human rights", and all were undertaken with a distinctive combination of strength and flexibility which won him the respect of even the staunchest Communist leaders.

Because of its Communist government Polish society is of necessity restrictive, and there is no reason why a voice crying out for human rights within Poland should automatically make a resounding impact on the eardrums of the rest of the world. If Wojtyla came to the notice of the International Church as bishop, archbishop and cardinal it was possibly not so much because of his work within Poland but because of his attendance at, and contribution to, the Second Vatican Council, which brought him to the forefront of Church affairs and which also exposed him to churchmen whose experiences had been very different from his own.

In Kraków, Wojtyla is known as a man upon whom the Council made an indelible impression, and whose ideas and teachings developed very much in its spirit. An examination of the Council, and of Wojtyla's role within it, might, therefore, be a good indication of what kind of papacy the world was about to witness.

On 2nd January 1959, Pope John XXIII announced to an astonished assembly of cardinals his intention of holding a council. His aim was to "spring-clean" the Church of Rome, for central to his belief had always been the idea that the Church, although it possessed the essence of eternal truth, must always be ready to re-interpret it in the light of the Gospel. Wojtyla, who was from the very first an enthusiastic supporter of this Council "inspired by the Spirit of Wisdom and of Love", saw as its starting point the awareness of a crisis situation; a situation arising from a growing indifference to ideology in a society orientated towards consumption and the worship of technology, and oblivious to altruistic values. Given this starting point, the Second Vatican Council was to concern itself with the entire human race, its values and the position of the Church within it. Significantly, Wojtyla considered that one of the prime objectives behind Pope John's summoning of the Council was that of Christian Unity. Asked while the Council was still in session what he anticipated the principal changes brought about by it would be, he replied that he believed that there would be a development of ecumenism on an unprecedented scale, accompanied by an upgrading of the role of the laity in the Church. There would also be an attempt to work out a new Church-State relationship and a new conception of the right to religious freedom. Catholicism would become more universalized, with a different approach to the ancient cultures of non-European people, i.e. de-westernized, and the Church itself would be decentralized by a revaluation of the bishop's authority and a return to the collegiate principle. Finally, he believed that pastoral methods would be reviewed and new ones introduced. In the light of what has already been seen of his life, the emphasis on religious freedom and tolerance and on pastoral care is almost to be expected. The stress on collegiality, which without impairing the primacy of the pope nevertheless distributes greater authority among the bishops, is of interest in view of what was to follow.

It was touch and go whether Wojtyla would be granted a visa to attend the opening session in 1962, but the authorities relented in time and Wojtyla, speaking to the assembly on liturgy and on the sources of revelation, impressed many of the foreign clerics, not least for his command of languages (the proceedings in the first session were conducted in Latin) and for his youthful enthusiasm. It was during the second session held in 1963, however, that Wojtyla really came to notice. On 23rd September, during early discussions on the Constitution

of the Church (Lumen Gentium) he urged that the Church should be viewed as "People of God" before any discussion of the hierarchy was considered. In other words he was asking for a less clerical and more biblical approach to the Church's vision of itself. The implications of this for the theology of the laity were considerable and those who had dismissed all Polish bishops as arch-conservatives were astounded. Wojtyla's scholarship made him one of the principal architects of Lumen Gentium, a document which re-orientated the whole Church, away from the Church constructed as a monarchical pyramid, towards the form of a body in which everyone is responsible for the mission of the Church but each in his own way. The role of the layman is thus in the world where he actually is; it is there that he must build the Church.

In later discussions Wojtyla's profound awareness of the realities of the contemporary world experienced under an oppressive regime brought a sense of perspective to the Council. He insisted on the need for religious freedom for all religious groups, however embarrassing this might be for the Roman Catholic Church. The Church could only demand religious liberty in the face of hostility if it was prepared to concede it itself. Again, speaking on the subject of atheism, his first hand experience came to bear. Out-and-out condemnation, he said, only served to make further dialogue impossible. Discussion should start instead on the basis of a recognition that we are all involved on a common search in the midst of human experience. "Let us avoid moralizing, or the suggestion that we have a monopoly of the truth. One of the major defects of this draft is that in it the Church appears merely as an authoritarian

On February 25, 1979, in St Peter's, John Paul conducted a marriage service for Vittoria Ianni and Mario Maltese.

institution". Because of his valuable contribution to the discussion on religious liberty, Wojtyla had been invited to join the mixed Commission which dealt with Schema XIII, a draft which was eventually to become *Gaudium et Spes*: the Constitution of the Church in the World of Today. In what may well now seem a petty argument about the wording of the title, it was Wojtyla who found the solution by defining it as a "pastoral" constitution, thereby emphasizing that it was concerned not so much with doctrine as with life – with contemporary problems such as war and peace, economic development and international organization and also, at the instigation of Wojtyla, with marriage and the family.

By December 1965, the Second Vatican Council was officially over and the bishops returned to their respective dioceses. It was a further seven years, however, before the documents were actually completed, and Wojtyla returned at regular intervals to Rome. Meanwhile, at home in Poland, he set about implementing the decisions of the Second Vatican Council. Liturgical changes such as the turning of the altar to face the people and the celebration of the Mass in the vernacular rather than in Latin, he, unlike Cardinal Wyszinski, accepted easily, but commitment to the spirit of the Council must go much deeper. As a Church leader, Wojtyla is demanding both of himself and of others. He has always recognized wholeheartedly the need for fidelity to the mission with which he has been entrusted, placing considerable weight on what he calls "the great discipline of the Church". Fidelity means respect for liturgical norms determined by Church authorities; love is the fountain which sustains and the climate in which we grow. Concepts such as the bond of collegiality which binds together the bishops "with Peter and under Peter" must be looked at in the spirit of love and accepted from the heart. What had been explicitly stated by the Council must be instantly put into practice and what had remained "implicit" would become evident with experiment and changing circumstances. In the light of all this and in order to further a full understanding of the Council's decrees, in 1972 Wojtyla set up a Synod involving a large number of clergy and laity to meet and pray together and discuss the draft texts. He also wrote, for the benefit of the synodal assemblies, a guide to the implementation of Vatican II, entitled "Foundations of Renewal".

〰 〰 〰 〰 〰

It may come as a surprise to some to learn that Karol Wojtyla as bishop, archbishop and cardinal still found time to write. Even more surprising for many is the fact that he was still writing poetry. A talent for poetry and the need to give poetic expression to personal sensitivity in a young man deeply immersed in the study of language and literature is not so startling; the same need found in a Church leader profoundly committed to pastoral ministry, to the vicissitudes of Church-State relations within Poland and to the complexities of the Church's role in the world at large, is possibly more unusual. Yet it would seem that, for Wojtyla, writing poetry was a natural and continuing means of expression for an important aspect of his personality, for his poetry appears to span a period from the mid-1940s to as late as 1975. It has been seen that even in his early years, Wojtyla's poems were not merely the

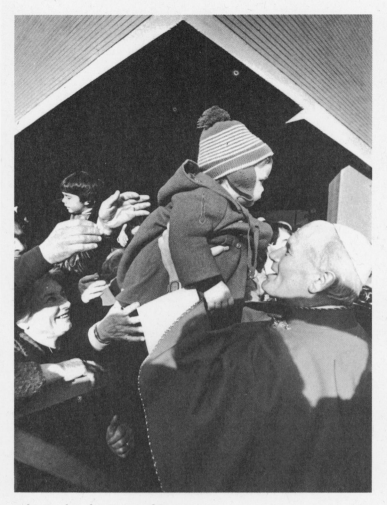

John Paul II, the 'Pastoral Pope'.

sentimental outpourings of an emotional youth, and in the course of time his work developed powerfully until he emerged as what Boleslaw Taborski, another poet, has described as "among the major religious poets of our time". Taborski has referred to him as a "religious" poet. Neither the phraseology nor the imagery of Wojtyla's writings are overtly devotional or superficially "religious". Yet the connection between his poetry and his spiritual works is implicitly apparent. The pseudonym under which his works were published both in *Znak*, the monthly magazine of the movement of Catholic Intellectuals and in *Tygodnik Poswzechny*, their weekly newspaper, is in itself significant. Andrzej Jawien was the name of the hero in a famous pre-war novel, "The Sky in Flames" by Jan Parandowski. The title refers to the young hero's loss of faith, and the choice of pseudonym may well intimate the recognition that faith, in order to be strong, must first be tried and tested. In his poetry Wojtyla frequently takes as his starting point a religious or biblical theme and applies it to the contemporary world in a way which reflects a deeply felt compassion for humanity as a whole. "Profiles of a Cyrenean" for example, recounts how Simon was forced to carry the cross of Christ to Golgotha.

"And then He comes. He lays his yoke
on your back. You feel it, you tremble, you are awake."

Simon is not alone, for we are all of us Cyreneans

*"I know the Cyrenean's profile best,
from every conceivable point of view."*

We must all carry crosses – with which we do not wish to be burdened and against which we try to rebel – so the Cyrenean cycle pinpoints the everyday crosses of individuals in the contemporary world; a car factory worker, a worker from an armaments factory, a woman typing for eight hours a day, a girl whose heart has been broken, the man of emotion and the man of intellect:

"How cramped are your notions, formulas, judgements always condensing yet hungry for content.

Don't break down my defences, accept the human lot; each load must take the direction of thought."

Wojtyla's writings are a powerful witness to his fundamental Christian humanism. They are the poetry of one who has a sympathetic understanding of human emotions, of life, of children:

"Growing unawares through love, of a sudden they've grown up, and hand in hand wander in crowds (their hearts caught like buds, profiles pale in the dusk) The pulse of mankind beats in their hearts."

but above all they are poems of ideas in which intangible truths are given concrete expression. In "Marble Floor", a poem which has recently provoked particular interest, Wojtyla meditates upon the floor of St. Peter's Basilica which becomes the symbolic representation of the role of the Pope.

"Peter, you are the floor, that others may walk over you (not knowing where they go). You guide their steps so that spaces can be one in their eyes, and from them thought is born."

The Pope meets children in the St Basilio area, on the outskirts of Rome, March 1979.

John Paul II pays tribute to the Polish soldiers who died at Monte Cassino in May, 1944.

In addition to poetry Wojtyla has written countless essays, articles and plays. Dealing with a variety of subjects ranging from dramatic theory to detailed insights into human relationships, they all combine to proclaim the message, which he took as one of his main themes of the retreat for the Roman Curia – the words of St. Irenaeus: "The glory of God is that man should be fully alive". His books "The Acting Person", "Foundations of Renewal" and "Love and Responsibility" all emphasize the importance of human experience and of a positive relationship to the humanity and the dignity of others. They also advocate a sense of harmonious community as opposed to isolation. "Love and Responsibility" in particular, deals in detail with the theme of man as an individual, and the difficulties involved in the formation and development of personal relationships. It is a work of Catholic orthodoxy in its attempt to provide a rational justification for the Church's traditional teaching on sexual morality. Taking as its theme the love between man and woman, it advocates, as do the documents of Vatican II, the love that is a mutual self-giving and not a mutual exploitation. The preoccupation with family life which occurs and recurs in Wojtyla's works is, it may be argued, the direct product of life in a society in which this was the only area where a sense of freedom from State directives could be retained, but then would not this same society make the recognition and proclamation of the dignity of man more difficult? The solution lies in the mystery of love that is at the base of all things. In his poem, "Reflection on Fatherhood", Wojtyla foresees the day when God will allow this world to crumble. "And everything else will then become unimportant and unessential, except the father, the child and love. And then also, looking at the simplest things, all of us will say: couldn't we have learned all this long ago? Was not all that always embedded at the bottom of everything that is?" (Excerpt translated by B. Taborski.)

In 1976 Wojtyla was invited by Pope Paul VI to conduct a retreat for the Holy Father and for the Roman Curia. He chose to center his sermons on the prophetic words spoken by Simeon on seeing the child Jesus: "Behold, he is set for the fall and the rising of many in Israel, and as a sign of contradiction" (Luke 2, 34). To Wojtyla the world today is the realization of Simeon's prediction: "If now – on the threshold of the last quarter-century before the second millennium, after the Second Vatican Council, and in the face of the terrible experiences the human family has undergone and is still undergoing – Jesus Christ is once again revealing himself to men as the light of the world, has he not also become at one and the same time that sign which, more than ever, men are resolved to oppose?" Such a world merely emphasizes the need for Christ, who in himself guarantees the essential profile of the "mystery of man". "Given our society today, in which falsity and hypocrisy reign supreme, public opinion is manipulated, consciences bludgeoned, apostasy is sometimes imposed by force and there is organized persecution of the faith – sometimes camouflaged but all the more terrible for that – the Christ who bore witness to the truth is more than ever the Christ for us: *'Christus propheta magnus'.'"*

Skier, canoeist, mountaineer, actor, linguist; a man who was Professor of Ethics at Lublin and committed to a highly complex and carefully defined philosophy and yet was possessed of a faith which found its expression in such simple actions as the heading of his lecture notes with the initials *J* and *M* for Jesus and Mary; the intellectual who was capable of confronting Marxism at its highest level and of impressing the leading theologians of the Roman Catholic Church with the clarity of his thinking; the pastoral priest who regarded the Solway factory workers as some of his most treasured parishioners; the man of action and the man of prayer; a man who risked his life repeatedly during the Occupation and a poet whose works are a moving and glorious hymn to life; a patriot and a citizen of the world profoundly concerned with universal human rights – it is small wonder that in October 1978 a leading editorial article described the cardinals' choice as one displaying a "touch of imaginative rashness". The world, baffled by a series of apparent paradoxes, came to the cautious conclusion that John Paul II was a moderate progressive but not an innovator, but anticipated nevertheless a papacy such as had never before been witnessed. In Poland, people were delighted. Wojtyla's former housekeeper dismissed all question of paradox or complexity with the simple statement "He is a good man" and the Polish government added one more paradox by deciding, after some considerable discussion, to send a telegram of congratulations to the Vatican and at the same time contriving to tell the world that the new pope was the product of a good socialist state.

In the meantime, John Paul himself embarked upon his pontificate with a rhythm of work which was impressive, not least for the fact that he appeared to achieve it without rushing. On the morning of 17th October, he appeared as if untouched by the cold isolation of the "mountain", to deliver in characteristic tones the discourse which was to bring the conclave to its conclusion. It was a speech remarkable for its content, in that it had been prepared in so short a space of time, but to those who knew and understood the man, it was very much a confirmation of what had gone before. In it John Paul II committed himself unhesitatingly to the Second Vatican Council: "Before anything else, we wish to emphasize the continuing importance of the Second Vatican Ecumenic Council. To us this constitutes a formal obligation to see it executed with diligence". He went on to add: "First of all, we must become in tune with the Council, in order to apply in practice what the Council has stated emphatically and to reaffirm that which one usually understands to be implicit, in the light of experiments

undertaken since that time and the demands created by new circumstances". Here, to those radicals who hoped to find it, was some scope for "reinterpretation" of the truth. In the areas in which many were hoping for innovation, such as those of women priests, abortion and contraception, Pope John Paul II did not at this stage commit himself. He did, however, call for close examination of the subject of collegiality, a doctrine to which he intended to adhere: "Most particularly we do encourage an examination of the principle of collegiality, to become more deeply aware of it, and at the same time to enable us to do our duty with greater watchfulness. Collegiality intimately connects the bishops with the successor to Peter and unites them among themselves. It allows them to bring the light of the gospel to the world, to sanctify it through the avenues of grace the Church extends and to assume leadership with a shepherd's care towards all the people of God. Collegiality also means the creation of organizations, partly new ones, partly existing ones, but adapted to today's needs."

The homily delivered on the death of John Paul I had reminded those present that, in a sense, Christ always asks of the successor to St. Peter the same question delivered to Simon Peter: "Do you love me more than others?" The call to papal authority invariably includes a call to greater love, and so in his very first address as pope, John Paul II chose in all humility to respond to that question: "With St. Paul we repeat: 'For the love of Christ

Pope John Paul II in the Vatican in March, 1979.

restraineth us'. Right from the beginning we wish to see our ministry as a service of love, this will permeate all our actions." John Paul's first address was characteristic in many ways: in its profession of loyalty to the Second Vatican Council, in its approach to collegiality, in its expressed intention to continue the steps already taken towards ecumenism, in its reference to the Virgin Mary whose name many years earlier, together with the words *Totus Tuus* (all thine), he had inscribed on his heart and on his coat of arms, and in the special greetings he remembered to include for Poland, *semper fidelis*. Most characteristic of all, however, was his resolve to examine and to undertake the Petrine ministry in the light of its threefold scriptural basis, and in the spirit of that love which is the source that nourishes and the climate in which one grows.

John Paul II's "service of love" began with an energy and a disregard for protocol which was to disconcert some within the Vatican but which was to endear him to many outside it. It is not usual for a newly elected pope to leave the Vatican before he is officially inaugurated but on the first evening after the papal election, John Paul had already "escaped". His compatriot and friend Monsignor Andrea Deskur had suffered a heart attack and been admitted to the Gremelli Hospital four days previously, and so the Pope strode determinedly out of the Vatican to visit the sick man. After a brief, informal audience with assembled hospital staff, John Paul was on the point of leaving without giving his blessing. A whispered reminder was greeted with a smile. "I still have to learn how to behave as pope", he admitted. Yet the addresses delivered in the short space of time preceding the inauguration ceremony displayed no lack of confidence. His dealings with the cardinals, with the press and with the diplomatic corps, revealed instead an air of unpretentious self-assurance and ability.

The "inauguration of John Paul II's ministry as supreme pastor" took place on the mild autumnal morning of Sunday, 22nd October. Attended by a crowd of 300,000 people, among them dignitaries ranging from the Archbishop of Canterbury to the Polish Head of State, the ceremony amounted to what can only be described as a non-triumphalistic triumph. Like his predecessor, John Paul II chose not to be crowned with the papal tiara but rather to be invested with a pallium. This long woollen band has been presented to metropolitan archbishops of both East and West since the fourth century. It is made of lamb's wool given to the pope on the feast of St. Agnes, and is therefore linked with pastoral care. It is placed on the shoulders like a yoke and is in this way a reminder that the service of a Christian is not easy but that, with the help of the Lord, it is light. It is also presented to the metropolitan and to the pope as coming "from the tomb of St. Peter": thus stewardship in the church is linked with the founding apostle. Finally, it is a reminder that the successor to Peter is also bishop of Rome. It was clothed in this garment, steeped in the symbolism of humility, that John Paul II received the homage of the individual cardinals. To the accompaniment of the singing of the text "Thou art Peter, and upon this rock I will build my Church" they came forward one by one to kneel and kiss the Fisherman's ring. Among the first in line was the staunch old Polish patriot, Cardinal Wyszinski, who only a few days previously as Primate of Poland had been Wojtyla's superior. Now the old warrior knelt to make his obeisance, only to be forestalled by his compatriot. Raising the Cardinal carefully to his feet the Pope embraced him three times in truly Polish fashion, then kissed his hand. In Poland, the thousands gathered round television screens to watch the first Mass ever to be shown on Polish television, wept openly. In Rome, John Paul II moved slowly to the altar to celebrate his first pontifical Mass. Before the staring eyes of the omnipresent television cameras he raised the ornate golden chalice, and as he did so, centuries of papal grandeur seemed to many to slip away, leaving only the simplest of acts – that of a man worshipping his creator.

John Paul celebrates Mass in Rome, Easter 1979.

The Pope's homily took as its text: "Thou art the Christ, the Son of the living God" (Matthew 16:15). He saw his role as rock-apostle as that of proclaiming the essential faith of Peter, of placing himself in a position of subordination to the Gospels. His authority must be of the kind that expresses itself not in the exercise of power, but in love and truth and so, watched by countless millions of people all over the world, he uttered an ardent and humble prayer: "Christ, allow me to be and remain a servant of your unique power, a servant of your power who is filled with gentleness, a servant of your endless power, or rather, a servant of your servants". Then came the ringing appeal "Open wide the doors for Christ. To his saving power open the boundaries of states, economic and political systems, the vast fields of culture, civilization

John Paul II chose to spend his 59th birthday at Monte Cassino, where he paid homage to the sacrifice made by hundreds of Polish soldiers who gave their lives there in May 1944.

and development. Do not be afraid. Christ knows what is in man: He alone knows it". Strangely this plea was left untranslated on Polish television. The rest of the world heard it however. They heard also the greetings he added in English, French, German, Spanish, Portuguese, Ukrainian, Russian and Czech, and watched as he insisted on mingling with the crowd after the ceremony was over. They were left with a sense of having encountered, possibly for the first time, a man of a great faith, of great strength and yet of great humility.

The danger of great expectations is always that their actual realisation may prove an anticlimax. As far as the pontificate of John Paul II is concerned, however, it may be said with considerable justification that the reality has proved as interesting as the speculation which accompanied his election. Certainly it has not been a dull pontificate to date and shows no sign of becoming one. John Paul II has shown, perhaps more effectively than any of his predecessors, that popes are not merely stereotyped figures dressed in white, who make occasional appearances on distant balconies and utter ceremonial truisms. If the cardinals were looking for a pastoral pope – a people's pope – their choice has been more than vindicated. From the very first John Paul II made his refusal to be separated from his people by papal etiquette readily apparent. From the moment when, after the inauguration mass, he strode vigorously down to a group of Poles and insisted on greeting personally a number of cripples in wheelchairs, he has been a constant source of nervous

covered the same ground in an estimated three minutes.

John Paul has gone to considerable trouble to quieten any potential discontent among Italians. In Italy, he always speaks Italian and he has let it be generally known that he is only the Pope because he is Bishop of Rome. He has held special audiences for Roman priests, nuns and seminarians, and done everything within his power to fulfil the intention expressed early in his pontificate: 'I intend to do something every Sunday for the diocese.' On Sunday 29th October 1978 for instance, the Pope went by helicopter to visit the shrine of Mentorella, some thirty miles outside Rome, the site of a twelfth century statue presided over by a community of Polish monks. The visit marked the beginning of papal activity, in and around Rome, such as had never before been experienced. Within a few weeks this foreign Pope had visited two shrines; taken possession of St John Lateran, the Bishop of Rome's basilica; visited one of the suburbs of Rome; spent some time at the papal residence at Castelgandolfo; celebrated Mass in Santa Maria Maggiore, the largest basilica dedicated to the Virgin; laid a wreath at the statue of the Virgin Mary near the Spanish Steps, and held a public

anxiety to both his security staff and to papal masters of ceremonies. As the *Tablet's* correspondent in Rome put it, his behaviour is likely 'to give healthy nightmares to protocol slaves until they either fade away or adjust themselves.' Protocol prelates have given up laying protective hands on the Pope's arm and saying *'basta'* to indicate that he has talked for long enough to one individual and it is time to move on. The Holy Father used merely to shrug their hands off with disconcerting ease and continue talking. In vain Vatican officials tried to induce him to walk rapidly through the audiences, or to allow himself to be carried in his gestatorial chair. Prelates hurrying him forward found themselves firmly restrained by a muscular papal arm and the chair was simply ignored. So it is that the journey from the door of St Peter's to the chair at the altar, from which he talks during his overcrowded general audiences, takes John Paul more than half an hour. Paul VI

Facing page: a moment of reflection in New York. Above: the Pope prays at the spot where the body of Aldo Moro was discovered.

meeting with the Communist mayor of Rome, Giulio Carlo Argan. Within days John Paul II was being greeted everywhere with enthusiastic cheers and spontaneous, heartfelt cries of *'Viva il Papa'.* 'At last', was the general feeling, 'we have a Bishop of Rome.'

'Pastoral' has continued to be an important word in the ministry of Wojtyla. It is not for nothing that he referred to the mission of Peter as that of 'pastoral responsibility for the entire Church'. In Rome he has conducted a wedding for a road-sweeper's daughter, baptised a British baby and above all has not been afraid to abandon the ceremonial trappings of the papacy to draw nearer to the people for whom he feels joyously responsible. In August 1979, this most cheerfully unconventional of popes tramped through twelve inches of snow across a mountain top to bless a six-foot bronze Madonna, a tribute to the bravery of Alpine women. With a smile that threatened to melt the snow, and wearing a peaked, white fur cap, a white windjacket and red ski boots, he stood on an icy plateau at 9,792 feet and spread out his arms to welcome a congregation of at least seven hundred people. It is gestures of this kind which have won him the hearts of the Italian people and indeed the hearts of the world at large. In his relatively short time as Pope, John Paul II has already kissed the ground of scores of countries, from the Caribbean to the Philippines and from Scotland to Kenya. In each of these places he has been accompanied throughout his visit by enormous crowds, responding with enthusiasm to the warmth and the concentration which he brings to everything he does, and in each of these places he has made it clear that to him crowds are not merely crowds, but collections of individuals, important in their own right. He has walked among them, laughed with them, sung with them, wept with them, kissed their children – and all this in a way that, even in this cynical world, has not compromised his image as a man of God.

However splendid the trappings of each of the state visits which will take up much of the story which follows, John Paul succeeds in transforming his journeys into pilgrimages – in Mexico, to our Lady of Guadelupe; in Poland to the revered Black Madonna of Jasna Gora. In Ireland he came as a 'pilgrim for Christ', following in the footsteps of Saint Patrick. The highlight of his pastoral visit was his devotion at the shrine of Mary, Queen of Ireland, in Knock. These tributes are not merely lip-service paid to Catholic Mariology, but rather the product of a profound faith and spirituality which somehow commands recognition. When John Paul II kneels to pray, whether it be before the barbed wire fences of Auschwitz, or in the majestic splendour of St Patrick's Cathedral in New York, the most loquacious voices of the materialism he so ardently condemns fall silent.

John Paul has been prepared to bare his soul to the world. On the day before his inauguration he held a meeting for two thousand journalists in the Hall of Benedictions, and without hesitation changed the policy of Vatican dealings with the media, at a single stroke. The Vatican Press Office had previously been described as making 'Kremlin spokesmen seem like chatty salesmen'. The Polish Pope, predictably in the light of his fight for church access to the media in Poland, and of his admiration for freedom of expression experienced during a visit to the United States in 1969, now proclaimed: 'It is my emphatic wish that religious reporters have access to the necessary help from the authorised ecclesiastical departments. The latter must receive them with every respect for their convictions and their position.' After his set piece John Paul II moved through the Hall of Benedictions and, to the horror of those Vatican officials who had anticipated that a non-Italian pope would be nervous and manipulable, proceeded to answer questions from individual groups of journalists. This meeting was to set the tone of his whole approach to the press. It is rare that he completes a flight without spending some considerable time talking to the numerous journalists who accompany him on his journeys. Remarkably, he has survived this 'exposure' to emerge as a spiritual leader, universally acknowledged to be a 'good man', a 'man of love'.

In a world where the motives of a politician embracing a child are immediately suspect, there is a temptation to regard the 'good man' who does the same thing with transparent sincerity, as naive. There are those who have applied the principle that goodness precludes shrewdness

Hands reach eagerly to greet the Holy Father in Gniezno.

The Holy Father responds to the welcome of President Jimmy Carter at the White House in Washington.

to John Paul's 'service of love', but to do so is to ignore his past achievements and to underestimate the intellect which undoubtedly functions as effectively as his heart. The man who impulsively envelops people in his huge and powerful bearhug is, in his business office, anything but impulsive, and it is not for nothing that so many of the world's ecclesiastical and political leaders have admired his insight into world affairs. Those who interpreted his slowness to make new appointments or confirm already existing ones in the Vatican hierarchy as an irresponsible preoccupation with getting to know his diocese have learned from experience to bite their tongues, for now John Paul has the hierarchy completely under control. In March, 1979 the death of Cardinal Villot, the Secretary of State he inherited from his predecessor, gave the Pope, whose preoccupation with human rights, as we shall see, is a deep-rooted conviction stemming not only from personal experience but also from the long-standing traditions of his nation, the opportunity to recast the higher echelons of his government according to his own notions. His new Secretary of State, Cardinal Agostino Casaroli, was involved in the East-West détente policy, and the global human rights campaign. Archbishop Achille Silvestrini, who took over the foreign affairs portfolio, was deeply involved in the Helsinki Declaration on religious liberty and all the resultant moves in the human rights field. The post of *sostituto* (deputy) went to Archbishop Eduardo Martinez Somalo, a Spaniard with a detailed knowledge of the human rights movement in Latin America, and the third foreign affairs post was given to Mgr Andryss Backio, a Lithuanian, with responsibility for Soviet territories. Together they all point towards human rights as the main diplomatic thrust of the Church's activities.

The principle underlying the Pope's global strategy is that ultimately, totalitarian regimes, of any kind or political complexion, are incompatible with human rights. If they deny such basic rights, they can be legitimately challenged, particularly by the Church. If, on the other hand, they concede them, even in part, they are set on a course of self-destruction. To become the effective champion of human rights, the Church must be seen to be even-handed, as between Communist and capitalist regimes, and must be seen to uphold religious freedom and atheist freedom, even where it conflicts with her own interests. Subject to these two qualifications, John Paul, and with him the Roman Catholic Church, is committed absolutely to the cause of human freedom as expressed in the Rights of Man.

Perhaps it was appropriate – certainly natural and understandable – that John Paul should begin what looks like a life-long crusade against the restrictions and injustices of authoritarian regimes with a determined foray into the social and political establishment in his own homeland. Only eight months after his accession, he paid a nine-day visit to Poland to take part in the official episcopal celebrations marking the 900th anniversary of the martyrdom of Poland's patron saint, St Stanislaus. He was quick to make his diplomatic point. On his first day there he met Mr Gierek, the country's effective leader, and told him that the Roman Catholic Church desired not privileges, but 'only and exclusively what is essential for the accomplishment of her mission. In seeking, in this field, an agreement with the State authorities,' he went on, 'the Apostolic See is aware that, over and above reasons connected with creating the conditions for the Church's all-round activity, such an agreement corresponds to historical reasons of the nation, whose sons and daughters, in the vast majority, are the sons and daughters of the Catholic Church. In the light of these undoubted premises, we see such an agreement as one of the elements in the ethical and international order in Europe and the modern world, an order that flows from respect for the rights of the nation and for human rights. I therefore permit myself to express the opinion that one cannot desist from efforts and research in this direction.'

It wasn't a declaration of war – indeed, in the light of the steadily improving relations between Church and State in Poland since 1977, it would have been foolish to appear aggressive – but in the knowledge of what has happened since, it might now seem like one. The Pope saw it as a pronouncement of steadfast intent, a straightforward

And if anyone was under the impression that these were words of hope without expectation, a whistling in the dark for the sake of form, John Paul added more than a touch of realistic warning. 'We are aware that this dialogue cannot be easy,' he said, 'because it takes place between two concepts of the world which are diametrically opposed. But it must be possible and effective if the good of individuals and the nation demands it. The Polish episcopate must not cease to undertake with solicitude initiatives which are important for the present-day Church. In addition, in the future there must be clarity in the principles of procedure which in the present situation have

warning that he was not likely to rest until the ground which Cardinal Wyszinski had so laboriously prepared was properly built upon. Furthermore, he made that intention plain when, a few days later, he addressed a plenary assembly of the Polish Episcopal Conference at Czestochowa, where he spent three days at Poland's most hallowed shrine, that of the Black Madonna at Jasna Gora. Where better to insist, before those whose duty it would be to see his intentions carried out, that the Polish government must 'respect the convictions of believers, ensure all the rights of citizens and also the normal conditions for the activity of the Church as a religious community to which the vast majority of Poles belong'?

Pope John Paul II leaving a meeting with the synod devoted to the family, whose members included Mother Teresa, in Rome, October 1980.

been worked out within the ecclesiastical community, regarding both the attitude of clergy and lay people and the status of individual institutions. Clarity of principles, as also their practical putting into effect, is a source of moral strength and also serves the process of a true normalisation.'

Indeed these were strong words, though no doubt John Paul was fortified in his resolve to pronounce them by the relative geniality of his secular hosts. Nevertheless he was skating – fairly cheerfully, it seemed – on thin ice. He had insisted that his visit was being undertaken for religious purposes only, yet here were several signs of a campaign for social and political rethinking which took timely advantage of the difficulty of defining precisely where religious considerations ended and political ones began. His statement in Warsaw – 'Christ cannot be excluded from the history of any man. His exclusion from the history of man is an act against man' – widened the scope of his justifiable utterances . against possible governmental pressure on students, workers, ordinary citizens and priests. Even national and local newspapers felt

A meeting of two figures who hold each other in high regard – Pope John Paul II and Mother Teresa.

emboldened in the wake of his electrifying pronouncements. One described him, prophetically, as 'a man of rare stature, whose words are more effective than the sword.'

Certainly he lost no opportunity to encapsulate his thoughts for his oppressed countrymen in every appropriate way possible. The formation, in late 1979, of the Polish trades union Solidarity, under its energetic, bold and persistent leader Lech Walesa, seemed to give John Paul a new theme to work upon. He was already preparing a 26,000-word encyclical on the role of work and of the workers in the world today, and its publication in September 1981 showed that he was ill-disposed to conceal or disguise his basic admiration for the new, thrusting organisation that Solidarity had become. 'In order to achieve social justice in the various parts of the world, in the various countries, and in the relationships between them,' he wrote, 'there is a need for ever new movements of solidarity of the workers and *with* the workers. This solidarity must be present whenever it is called for by the social degrading of the subject of work, by exploitation of the workers, and by the growing areas of poverty and even hunger.'

No man, in interpreting these words, could dissociate them from the events of the previous twelve months in Poland. The Pope had, only eight months earlier, received Walesa in audience – an event which had enormously bucked the Polish people and manifestly discomforted the Polish government. As it happened the State need not have worried unduly at that stage; like the Roman Catholic Church in Poland, John Paul was anxious lest Solidarity should make exaggerated demands upon the government,

forcing abrupt and monumental changes in the Polish economy which might threaten both that economy and the political stability which had, after all, accounted for the relaxations in policy from which Solidarity was born. Nevertheless, it did not take long for the Pope to nail his colours prominently to the mast. Only just before the encyclical on work was published, Polish workers, and the officers of Solidarity in particular, had come under threat by the Polish government's abolition of their union, and the introduction of martial law.

The Holy Father had repeatedly expressed concern at the growing polarisation between workers and government back in Poland, and rarely had the issue failed to feature in his most important addresses. After Solidarity was banned, he not only publicly expressed his support for the union, but also demanded its restitution – a demand which, he claimed, did not rest upon its potential for political power as much as upon the fact that its birth in 1979 marked an important and desirable social development. On New Year's Day 1982, he stood before a crowd in St Peter's Square to thank the world at large for its expressions of support for Solidarity – which, he insisted, belonged to the 'actual patrimony' of the Poles – and he reaffirmed their right 'to set up autonomous trade unions, the role of which is to guard their social, family and individual rights.' The problems of Poland, he warned, were 'important not merely for Poland herself, but for all nations and societies, for Europe and the contemporary world.' He was emphatically unimpressed by the Polish government's recent move of doubtful conciliation, in which it had offered workers their jobs back on condition that they abandon their membership of the now disestablished union: 'a violation of conscience,' he condemned it, '... a grave act against man... the most painful blow inflicted upon human dignity.' (He was to go even further the following year when, on his second visit to Poland, he talked of trade unions as 'an indispensable component of social life', and of the right to free association as 'an innate right which is not given to the State to bestow or retract.')

There were many who by then found it convenient to castigate the Pope for having given his support in such full measure to Solidarity as to identify himself with the class from which he himself had sprung, and of which the bulk of the Catholic following in Poland – and indeed in many other countries – was composed. But John Paul had already dealt with that type of criticism. He held that, in his pursuit of human dignity, there was no 'for' and 'against' relating to persons or classes or countries; the struggle involved the attainment of abstract ideals and the physical fulfilment of them. 'Catholic social teaching,' he had written in his encyclical on work, 'does not hold that unions are no more than a reflection of the "class" structure of society, and that they are a mouthpiece for a class struggle which inevitably governs social life. They are indeed a mouthpiece for the struggle for social justice, for the just rights of working people in accordance with their individual professions. However, this struggle should be seen as a normal endeavour "for" the just good; in the present case, the good which corresponds to the needs and merits of working people associated by profession; but it is not a struggle "against" others. It is a characteristic of work that it first and foremost unites people. In this consists its social power; the power to build a community.'

John Paul II meets members of the world's press.

By February 1982, the six-month-old Polish crisis seemed as intractable as ever. Meetings at various levels between Catholic leaders and workers' representatives became regular occurrences, as civil disturbances increased in number and severity in many major industrial areas in Poland. One day that February, John Paul met Jozef Glemp, Cardinal Wyszinski's successor as Archbishop of Warsaw, in the Vatican. The archbishop talked of the 'bitterness and anger' felt by the Polish people, and the Pope later told a meeting of Polish bishops that dialogue between Church and State must be established and maintained. A few days later, the Pope gave an audience in Rome for which trade unionists from all over Europe had gathered. The assembly steeled him into voicing almost unrestricted praise of Solidarity – 'an autonomous, independent union faithful to its initial inspiration, refusing violence even in the difficult situation in which it is living, intent on being a constructive force for the nation. The restitution of effective and total respect for the rights of working men, and especially their right to a union already created and given official authority,' he continued, 'is the only way out of this difficult situation.' John Paul's uncompromising stance gave heart not only to his working countrymen, but also to the many bishops and priests who felt that their own efforts in support of Solidarity were leading them into terminal conflict with the Polish authorities, whose own actions were now clearly guided by the Soviets. But by July 1982, the clergy had another weapon in their armoury.

That month, it was officially announced that, as a result of an invitation from the bishops of Poland, Pope John Paul II would pay a second visit to his homeland in August. The visit had been planned for almost a year – since, indeed, about the time when martial law was imposed – but the bishops had remained confident that matters would have resolved themselves well in time to avoid the cancellation of the trip. Clearly, John Paul's support for Solidarity, expressed in the strongest language, was meant to pre-empt any condition that the Polish government might seek to impose upon him, and that same government's silence on the matter, at least up to the spring of 1982, might well have been construed as a sign of reluctant acquiescence to the unavoidable prospect of the Pope's visit, or indeed as a promise of gradual stabilisation in Poland. Archbishop Glemp was responsible for much of the ground-work *vis-à-vis* the government and when, that April, he reported to the Pontiff that the chances of a Papal visit had diminished, John Paul himself called upon the government to create what he called 'adequate conditions' for a visit to which, he insisted, he was morally committed.

There was a general feeling that, left to its own devices, the government could deliver, but Russian policy soon dominated with unabashed strength and vitriol. The official Soviet media was by now constantly hurling harsh insults at the Pope, on the grounds that he was being encouraged by Western opinion, especially through the influence of President Reagan, deliberately to increase tensions in Poland. The Polish press was noticeably more moderate – though even so he was occasionally taken to task for taking up Solidarity's cause and provoking unrest in the country – but the Pope was clearly content to bide his time. There was something vaguely resembling the calm spirit of compromise and hope for better things in the exchange of messages which accompanied his decision, ultimately, to postpone. He said he did not want the visit to take place in 'a period of nervousness and excitement', while General Jaruzelski, the Polish leader who imposed martial law, promised that the government would do all it could to facilitate a visit in 1983, provided that civil order were restored, anti-State hostility had ceased, and 'an indispensable level of normalisation' had been achieved.

John Paul II greeted by President Monge on his arrival in Costa Rica in March 1983.

By the end of the year, a new date – June 1983 – had been provisionally fixed for the Pope's visit, but despite being conscious of the need not to rock boats, the Church refused to remain silent. Archbishop Glemp delivered a sermon near Kutno in November 1982, encouraging Roman Catholics to increase their involvement in public affairs, to stop accepting supposed restrictions on their political activities, and to seek office in provincial and national assemblies, and in government. Meanwhile, John Paul himself was addressing 11,000 Polish emigrés and pilgrims in Rome, and thundered bitterly on behalf of 'those who are not present today because they are in prison and internment camps. Poland,' he complained, 'does not deserve to be driven to tears and despair but to create a better future for itself.'

Meanwhile, Solidarity interpreted the announcement that the visit would go ahead as a sign that the Polish government, which after fourteen months seemed acutely embarrassed at its inability to terminate martial law, was seeking compromise, and it called off a series of demonstrations planned for the New Year. It proved a well-timed decision; so well-timed, in fact, that it is inconceivable that the moderating, arbitrating hand of the Pope himself did not guide it. By early in the New Year, martial law was partially lifted. Although Solidarity remained, and still remains, a banned organisation, its members and sympathisers were now free to air their grievances and look forward to the Pope's second visit as a focus for their own aspirations. The feeling that a certain oppression had been lifted was compounded when, shortly before John Paul's visit, an article in the official party journal *Trybuna Ludu* quoted the Polish minister for religious affairs as seeking an agreement with the Roman Catholic Church involving recognition by both Church and State of the legitimacy of each other, and a willingness not to interfere in each other's affairs. It was a bland and indistinct aim, failing to give a full definition of its terms of reference, but the message for the forthcoming

visit was clear. 'It is to be hoped,' the minister stated, 'that the Church leadership will manage to keep its pastoral duties separate from any attempt by intransigent adversaries of socialist Poland to take advantage of religion or the Church in their destructive political activities.' One prominent Communist Party leader put the government's stand beyond any doubt. Making a special reference to the Holy Father's prospective meeting with Lech Walesa, he expressed the pious hope that the Pope's visit could help to create the conditions of a complete lifting of martial law, but implied that meetings with members of Solidarity would constitute a political matter because of Walesa's involvement in 'the political game of hostile forces at home and in the West.'

In the event, that meeting, official permission for which was in doubt until the last moment, took place, but in the meantime the Pope was still not inclined to mince his words in an effort to sway the government's mind. Although, in greeting the Pope at Warsaw airport, President Jablonski viewed the visit as 'proof of the considerable advance in the normalisation in the life of the country', and spoke of the 'strong possibilities for cooperation between the State and the Church in resolving Poland's patriotic tasks', the Pope was insistent in his condemnation of the events of the previous eighteen months. Speaking that same day at a Mass in Warsaw Cathedral, he deplored 'the bitter taste of deception, humiliation and sufferings, the deprivation of freedom and the trampling of human dignity' which had been endured by the Polish people since 'the painful events associated with the date of December 1981.'

Much as the authorities might have wished to silence the Pope by reminding him of the essentially religious purpose of his visit – primarily he was in Poland to attend the jubilee of the shrine at Jasna Gora – the Pope justified his socio-political utterances with vigour and consistency. 'The events which occurred in Poland in August 1980,' he said at Katowice on the fifth day of his tour, 'were primarily concerned with the moral order rather than with social issues.' At the Jasna Gora shrine itself, he said that 'men, as sons of God, could not be slaves; their freedom is a measure of their dignity. The sovereignty of a state is closely linked with its ability to promote the freedom of the individual – that is, to create conditions which will enable the people to express their own historical and cultural identity.' And he referred, not too obliquely, to 'all the forms of solicitude which surround those who were imprisoned, interned, dismissed from work, and also their families. You know this better than I. I receive only sporadic but frequent news about it.'

Nor were his pleas confined to the converted. In his talks with General Jaruzelski, John Paul insisted that the Polish government should honour its commitments in order to 'maintain Poland's good reputation in the world, to facilitate her emergence from her national crisis' and, more pointedly, 'to save numerous sons and daughters of the nation – my fellow countrymen – from suffering.' He was even more specific during a public homily in Wroclaw when, without actually referring to the Polish trade union, he included the word 'solidarity' in his text to express his relations with both his Church in Poland and with the people of his homeland. The connotations of his phraseology sparked off a couple of demonstrations (which police could only control by the use of tear gas and water cannon) and a reprimand from the party leadership, who described the Pope as 'the tutor and educator who spreads myths, legends and half-truths amongst the Polish youth.' It did not induce John Paul to modify his tone. On his last day but one, preaching at Krakow, he called for a monumental struggle against 'the wave of demoralisation, indifference and weakening of spirit', and resistance against 'the arrogant use of power.'

For all that, the Polish leadership was keen to paper over the cracks and see the Pope off with at least a veneer of goodwill, and a puff of saccharine official government comment followed his departure. There was talk of the evident 'will to discuss issues which are of significance for Poland and the world', and satisfaction that 'various political expectations connected with this visit had not been realised, since those who had tried to stage political demonstrations had failed to make a significant impression.' Lech Walesa was reasonably optimistic too, though the deputy editor of the *Osservatore Romano* was asked to resign after having inferred otherwise in his report of Walesa's meeting with the Pope. Meanwhile, the USA regarded the outcome of the visit as having provided 'a ray

John Paul II during his brief stay in Nicaragua in March 1983.

of hope', on the strength of which President Reagan would consult anew with his allies regarding his country's future policy towards Poland. This reappraisal was of double significance a month later when, the Pope safely back in the Vatican, the Polish authorities lifted martial law entirely.

In spite of the delicate political and partisan implications of his visit, John Paul revelled in seeing his homeland again for the second time in four years. From the moment when he knelt to kiss the rain-soaked tarmac at Okecie military airport in Warsaw, he felt that his arrival had embraced the whole country. 'I come to the entire homeland and to all Poles,' he affirmed, conscious of the fact that even *his* busy itinerary could not encompass everyone and everywhere. His welcoming by dozens of boys and girls, by young men and women in the full vibrant splendour of their traditional national costumes, proclaimed the pastoral, cultural and homely aspects of his visit. As with his 1979 tour, the programme was thick with the solemnities of his faith – masses in the heart of his old archbishopric, Krakow, at the Black Madonna's shrine at Czestochowa, and in the industrial city – the Solidarity heartland – of Katowice; vespers at Mount St Ann, near Opole; meetings with students and nuns, parochial delegations and episcopal councils at every port of call. He visited Pawiak prison, where thousands of internees had been killed by the Nazis during World War II, and the monastery of Nepokalanow, with its heavily emotional associations with Fr Maximilian Kolbe – the man who died in Auschwitz after having volunteered to take the place of a condemned married man. Kolbe was beatified by Paul VI in 1971, and John Paul himself had canonised him eleven years later in a gesture widely reckoned as not only appreciative but also instructive – for in Kolbe the Pope recognises the ideal of the highly-disciplined priest.

At Blonie, within the archbishopric of Krakow, the Pope led the solemn rite of beatification for two more of Poland's sons, the Discalced Carmelite Raphael Kalinowski, and Albert Chmielowski, the founder of the Albertine Brothers and Sisters. Such a ceremony usually takes place at St Peter's but, as His Holiness pointed out, the tradition had recently been broken when he himself proclaimed beatifications in Manila and in Seville. It had been, he added, 'my ardent desire that my pilgrimage to my homeland should also become an opportune occasion to raise the servants of God to the altars.' At Krakow – 'My Krakow, so dear and loved' because of the memory of 'all the generations that have left a unique expression of their Polish and Christian identity' – John Paul visited his old student stamping-ground, the Jagellonian University, where he was welcomed by the singing of *Gaude, Mater Polonia*, and received an honorary doctorate. He spoke of his days as a clandestine student of theology during the Second World War, and praised the university for having remained at the heart of Polish learning and culture for all of six centuries. He described himself as proud to be 'the son of a nation condemned to death many times, but which has survived and remained itself.'

There were visits to Poznan, Wroclaw and Zakopane – for that controversial meeting with Lech Walesa – but the crowning point of the papal tour was also its prime purpose, namely the final celebrations marking the sixth hundredth jubilee of the shrine at Jasna Gora. The Holy Father celebrated a special jubilee mass there as hundreds of thousands of Poland's young people packed the esplanade

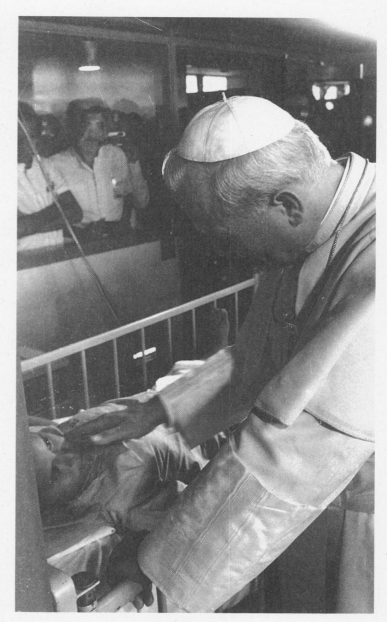

A blessing on a sick Costa Rican child.

below the lofty, elaborately-decorated sanctuary. With them he sang the 'Call to Our Lady of Jasna Gora' and exhorted his audience to 'put up a firm barrier against immorality – those social vices which I will not here call by name, but which you yourselves are perfectly aware of.' And here he slipped in one of his neatly-structured political references: 'Historical experiences tell us how much the immorality of certain periods cost the whole nation. Today, when we are fighting for the future form of our social life, remember that this form depends on what people will be like. Therefore watch!' The following day – a Sunday – he presided at the solemn closure of the sescentenary celebrations, before an august audience consisting of all eighty-eight of Poland's bishops and many visiting cardinals and bishops. His message was one of doing Christ's will – the perfect spiritual freedom. But he could not resist mentioning personal freedom as well, again with a deft turn of phrase. He counselled his audience to make good use of what freedom they had, for, he assured them prophetically, 'people can use freedom well or badly.'

Life has not been easy in Poland since those days. The apparent goodwill of June 1983 was finally dissolved as the authorities began a campaign against the Church less than three months later. Popular association with the Catholic hierarchy was again under threat as, one by one, crosses which had been erected at factories and in schools during Solidarity's heyday were removed. The party press backed that action by lashing out at the clergy. *Trybuna Ludu* railed against 'the fanaticism and intolerance of the bishops', while another news-sheet, *Polityka*, accused the Church of encouraging opposition to the authorities. The clergy attempted to respond in kind, with a point-by-point criticism of Poland's economy, during an ecclesiastical conference at the end of 1983, in which they called for 'proper socio-political reforms' and 'an end to political trials.' But the Politburo would have none of it – 'Militant clericalism and instigatory pronouncements will not be tolerated,' it warned.

Among the priests it accused of fomenting opposition was Fr Jerzy Popieluszko, a Warsaw priest who had been under investigation for two years for allegedly celebrating monthly 'Masses for the Fatherland' at which he was said to have made statements critical of the authorities in front of thousands of believers. He was detained for forty-eight

Above: the Holy Father prays before the tomb of Archbishop Romero in San Salvador Cathedral, March 1983. Facing page: members of the Church listen attentively to the Pope's message during his visit to Poland.

hours in December 1982, before the police claimed to have found explosives and ammunition in his flat. In October 1984 he went missing, and was found drowned in a river. Though four members of the police force were quickly put on trial, Solidarity remains banned, its members tamed. For John Paul – a heartfelt sympathiser from afar – there is much to do before his own people are set free. In the meantime, he can continue the battle of words on appropriate occasions, like the meeting with members of the Polish community in Nigeria during his visit there in 1982. 'These last years,' he said, 'have been a particular trial for the alliance between the nation and the Church. I feel very deeply all that is happening there, and with a loud voice proclaim what the Poles have a right to on the part of their neighbours and of all nations – especially on the part of those nations with which the history of our continent has linked us right from the beginning. I have said this during recent months and recent weeks in regard to the state of emergency, that is to say the state of war, in Poland. These rights are for us a centuries-old heritage.'

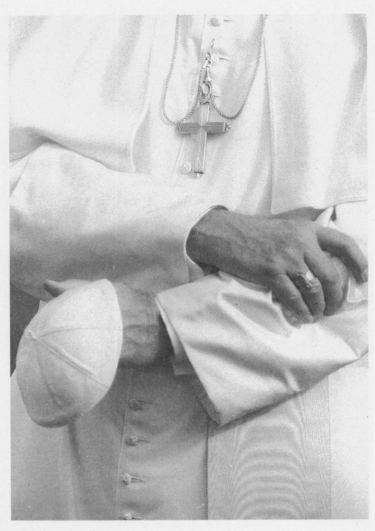

Prayers in Costa Rica.

Czechoslovakia illustrates more vividly the general antipathy between Church and State in many Iron Curtain countries. Czechoslovakia has been in a perpetual state of suspicion with regard to the Catholic Church since Dubcek was deposed in 1969. Poor relations in the 1970s have deteriorated further in the last five years, with State harassment of Catholic clerics and judicial action against clandestine groups which has led to several imprisonments. A reaction typical of the State's fears of militant Catholicism occurred in the wake of the Polish crisis of the early 1980s; the Czech government have allowed virtually no religious meetings since the beginning of the decade and have attacked the Pope personally for 'political clericalism'. The official party journal *Tribuna* denounced him as recently as 1984 as 'one of the most reactionary popes this century. He is calling on the Catholics in Eastern Europe to imitate the reactionaries of the Polish Church in the belief that Communism and the Soviet Union must be destroyed.'

At that point, no fewer than seven bishoprics had fallen vacant in Czechoslovakia, despite the government's willingness to allow the Pope to fill them with his own appointees. John Paul, having by then had his own fill of governmental obstruction of parish priests and interference with Catholic seminaries, decided to abstain in anticipation of a possible political veto on his chosen replacements. Meanwhile, the Czech government followed China, Nicaragua, and other parts of the Soviet bloc in Europe in an attempt to set up a rival, officially-sponsored church organisation called – confusingly, after the title of a papal encyclical – *Pacem in Terris*. By the end of 1983, it claimed that at least half of the country's Catholic priests were members – a figure hotly disputed by the Pope, who denounced the organisation's obvious, indeed blatant, links with official party politics. He had already given his consent to the suggestion of the Archbishop of Prague that priests who had joined *Pacem in Terris* should be called upon to resign, but this only stung the Czech government into putting additional pressure upon loyal, pro-Vatican Catholic clergy. Two priests were imprisoned, for example, in 1982 for practising after having lost their governmental licences to preach; two more followed them into the gaols for alleged illegal activity, including the clandestine taking of vows, the illegal circulation of religious publications, giving private religious instruction, and celebrating mass while unlicensed. Negiotiations between the Pope and the Czech Foreign Ministry at the end of 1983 came to nothing – the Vatican described them as 'difcult and strained' – but this did not prevent the Archbishop of Prague from inviting the Holy Father to visit Czechoslovakia in 1985, an invitation about which the archbishop said he would speak to the government. The signs are not good. Of the seventeen thousand people who signed a petition supporting the idea, several hundred were interrogated by Czech police within days.

That the primary target of the new Vatican policy which John Paul has inspired has been the Soviet Empire was only to be expected. No self-respecting Pole, least of all a passionate libertarian like John Paul II, can admit the permanency of the Soviet occupation of Eastern Europe. An article written by Wojtyla for the Italian magazine *Vita Pensiero* shortly before his election, states vehemently that the EEC concept of 'Europe' is incomplete – the Iron Curtain is a detestable and artificial, and therefore

It is understandable that many regimes operating throughout the world feel that the Roman Catholic Church, a traditionally conservative, establishmentarian and authoritative institution with millions of devoted followers, poses a threat to the national, party or indeed personal loyalty that their political sponsors hope to achieve. Certainly this has been the case close to home, within those European Communist countries which seem almost to revel in their long experience of keeping Western influence, including that of religion, at bay. There has, for instance, been a growing concern in Yugoslavia over renewals of popular interest in religion during the past four years, and the government there – normally comparatively liberal-minded – feared that the situation was not unconnected with a resurgence of Croatian nationalism which would threaten the country's unity. Since 1981, several Roman Catholic clergy have been imprisoned for alleged political offences, and the consequent deterioration in relations with the Vatican culminated in the postponement of a tour of Yugoslavia which John Paul was due to make in March 1984.

But perhaps the story of the Vatican's relationships with

impermanent, division of a culture. The Pope believes that religion, armed with the human rights issue, can eventually undermine the Soviet Empire from within, and so he will maintain the pressure he has already exerted on the regime of Poland – one of the reasons for his return there in 1983 for the 600th anniversary of the shrine of Czestochowa. He also intends to have his prospective trip to Yugoslavia restored to his diary and to persuade the Communist authorities to allow him to visit Hungary and Czechoslovakia and the Catholic communities in Lithuania and the Ukraine.

Much of the Pontiff's intense dislike of Marxism is born not only of fundamental ideological differences, but also of the practical obstacle that Marxism presents to religious freedom – an indispensable prerequisite to the work of the Church in every country, regardless of its political complexion. John Paul put the point crisply in an address he gave in Kenya in 1980. He said then, 'Because she believes that no freedom can exist, that no true fraternal love is possible, without reference to God who created man in the image of Himself, the Catholic Church will never cease to defend, as a fundamental right of every person, freedom of religion and freedom of conscience. And because unbelief, lack of religion and atheism can be understood only in relation to religion and faith, it is difficult to accept a position

John Paul II descends the steps of San Salvador Cathedral, where Archbishop Romero was assassinated on March 30, 1980.

that gives only atheism the right of citizenship in public and social life, while believers are, as though by principle, barely tolerated or are treated as second class citizens.' 'Persecutions today,' he added, during his 1983 visit to Lourdes, 'are often similar to those described in the Martyrology of the Church for past centuries. They include various types of discrimination against believers and against the whole community of the Church. Such forms of discrimination are often practised at the same time as is recognised the right to religious liberty and to freedom of conscience, and this in the laws of individual countries as well as in declarations of an international nature.'

The reasons for the Pope's constant appeals for religious freedom are not merely doctrinal. He has frequently pleaded quite simply and openly in its defence that, without freedom, there can be no proper Church operations. 'The Church does not claim any privileges,' he insisted while in the Philippines in 1981. 'She wants only to be free and unimpaired in pursuing her own mission. The principle of freedom of conscience and of religion is enshrined in the laws and customs of the nations. May it effectively guarantee to all the sons and daughters of the Catholic Church the free and public profession of their faith and their religious convictions. This also entails for the Church the possibility of freely establishing educational and charitable programmes and institutions; moreover, these activities will benefit the interests of society as a whole. Christians see it indeed as their task to contribute to the safeguarding of sound morality in personal, family and social life. They see it as their duty to serve God in their brothers and sisters.'

Secondly, he points out that freedom is an inherent right and desire, and as such, one which will not tolerate being smothered for long. When he addressed the United Nations in 1979, he quoted at length from the Second Vatican Council's Declaration *Dignitatis Humanae*, emphasising the belief that 'the practice of religion of its very nature consists primarily of those voluntary and free internal acts by which a human being directly sets his course towards God. No merely human power can either command or prohibit acts of this kind. But man's social nature itself requires that he give external expression to his internal acts of religion, that he communicate with others in religious matters, and that he profess his religion in community.'

And thirdly, John Paul believes, again with disarming simplicity and conviction, that the fruits of religious freedom within any political community can only benefit that community in the long term. 'Those who are in charge of the common good,' he told a meeting of clerics in the Congo in 1980, 'cannot ignore that your Christian conviction is beneficial for the country. I do not doubt that they will continue to grant you the rightful religious freedom which you are recognised as having, and the possibility of working as good citizens, for the advancement of the nation.' And he developed the same line of reasoning during his visit to Guinea two years later, as he promised a useful partnership between Church and State. 'In offering this collaboration,' he assured his hosts, 'the Church wishes to serve the cause of the ennoblement of man in every aspect of his life. It lays claim to nothing more than the legitimate area of freedom, understanding and respect which renders possible the peaceful development of its spiritual and humanising mission. The well-known and painful events of the past, whose negative effects can still be felt in the ecclesiastical and social spheres, have not dulled the Church's will to continue sowing the seed of goodness.'

Despite the uncomfortable experience with the Communists – indeed, possibly because of it – developing diplomatic relations with the world at large has been a priority since John Paul's accession, and in the seven subsequent years some two dozen new understandings were reached with countries who before then had no, or only limited, diplomatic standing with Rome – including Greece, the Seychelles, Nepal, and the Knights of Malta. No fewer than thirteen such arrangements were concluded in one year – 1983 – alone. By the end of 1984, some 110 nations enjoyed diplomatic representation with the Holy See, including several socialist and non-Christian territories. Predictably, Soviet Russia and East Germany are not among them, nor are Israel, South Africa or Saudi-Arabia. Among the predominantly Catholic countries with no diplomatic status are Hungary, Czechoslovakia, Mexico and Poland, though the Pope was gratified to hear in June 1984 that his own native land was considering establishing some kind of concordat. He also welcomed the agreement, concluded in 1982, under which the three major Scandinavian countries – Norway, Sweden and Denmark – should resume full diplomacy with the Vatican (out of a desire to 'promote and develop mutual friendly relations') for the first time since the Protestant breach in the sixteenth century. This followed closely the pattern of events relating to Great Britain in the same year.

But perhaps the most significant development in this field was the restoration of ambassadorial status between the representatives of the Vatican and those of the United States of America, which occurred in January 1984 and which was seen as a most important progression of the Catholic Church's international influence. Formal relationships had lapsed in 1867, when the US prohibited the expenditure of federal funds on the maintenance of the American legation in the Papal States as a gesture of solidarity with the movement for Italian unification. Things remained in abeyance for over seventy years, until President Franklin Roosevelt appointed his own personal representative to the Vatican in 1939 – a move which, amid hopes of fuller relations, was aborted by the Protestant faction in America when President Truman later attempted to establish stronger diplomatic links. Like Presidents Johnson and Nixon before him, President Reagan had had several contacts with the Papacy, and many top-level meetings followed John Paul's visit to America in 1979. Renewed efforts in 1983, though welcomed by American Catholics, were opposed by members of other Churches on the grounds of religious favouritism, but eventually Pope John Paul II's aspirations were realised in full.

As the Head of the Roman Catholic Church, John Paul's relations with the nations of the world have not always been smooth. Emergent regimes in Africa and Central America have frequently proved less than willing allies in the cause of religious progress and the spread of the Christian Gospel. A long, edgy relationship with Guinea was brought to a satisfactory pass in 1980, when the Pope was able to appoint a new Archbishop of Conakry to replace Archbishop Tchidimbo, who had been released from nine years' imprisonment as part of a life sentence with hard labour after what the Guinea government feared

to have been an 'attempted invasion by dissidents and mercenaries against a democratic, secular and socialist republic'. The previous year, the Pope felt moved to protest against the expulsion of some five dozen Roman Catholic bishops and missionaries who had been bustled out of Burundi for allegedly endangering the security of the state 'by actions, gestures and words'. The bishops declared that they were quite unaware of the occasions on which they had so offended the Burundi government – an army-led revolutionary council – and the Pope hastened to express his solidarity 'with the Catholic congregations of Burundi and their religious ministers', as his own gesture of support for whose who remained, and who may have felt threatened. His move prompted the President of Burundi to restrict Roman Catholic prayer meetings to Sundays only, and to confine them 'to the parishes, not in the hills', and when four bishops had the temerity to demand his reasons for restricting their religious freedom, he accused them of 'spreading tracts, contributing to the division of the population', and of speaking out against any government decision to which they happened to take a dislike. The Church was described as 'constituting a hierarchy parallel to the state and the party', and several mission bank accounts were frozen.

John Paul II in Guatemala, March 1983.

The Pope was able to patch up, comparatively swiftly, his differences with the Burundi regime, and indeed with the Guinea government, to whom he paid a Papal visit in 1982, bearing assurances that 'the Church in Guinea desires to contribute loyally to the common good, offering its help for the moral advancement of its peoples, its work of reconciliation among men, and its service in the fields of education and assistance'. But the constant threat to his bishops and congregations abroad has never discouraged him from stating his case against unwelcome aspects of certain political regimes. He has expressed continual and total support for the Roman Catholic Church in its prolonged and severe criticism against, for instance, El Salvador's record on human rights, and in Archbishop Romero's successor, Mgr Rivera y Damas, he has one of the strongest protestors against human injustice in that area. The Pope also despatched to his bishops in Nicaragua a letter in August 1982 expressing support for their stand against what he derided as 'the absurd and dangerous' notion of a 'popular Church alongside, not to say against, the Catholic Church' – a reference to the kind of institution the Sandinista government was attempting to establish on the same lines as in Communist Europe.

Things became even more difficult in Chile when, during 1983, representatives of the Roman Catholic Church became increasingly identified with the political opponents of the extreme right-wing Pinochet government, whose arbitrary rule and vicious treatment of all critics had become a world-wide scandal. So much so that, late that year, the Pope publicly repeated a plea to General Pinochet, then celebrating the tenth anniversary of his rise to power, for four members of a revolutionary left wing movement accused of murdering an army officer, and who had sought refuge in the apostolic nunciature in Santiago, to be given safe conduct out of the country. The request was ultimately granted, but it did not stop the back-biting between the Church and the government. The clergy, for instance, were accused of organising a political demonstration that got out of hand, while their bishops continued to call for the abolition of a new military intelligence unit set up by the government.

Of course John Paul could, with some justification, opt for an easier, safer life and the quiet preservation of his Church world-wide, confining his efforts and restricting those of his representatives abroad to a purely theological, perhaps almost academically pastoral mission. Certainly that aim has a place in his plan. 'It is the mission of the Church to perform a religious and spiritual task in the world, not a political one,' he told the Austrian government in 1983. But, he continued, 'it is for the sake of the Gospel entrusted to it that the Church also proclaims, as the Second Vatican Council emphasises, the right of man. She acknowledges and greatly esteems the dynamic movements of today by which these rights are everywhere fostered. I refer not only to the orderly conduct of public life and to endeavours to safeguard fundamental human rights in one's own country, but also to the willingness of a nation to open its boundaries to people from other countries who are deprived of the freedom of religion, the freedom of speech and respect for human dignity.' In this respect, the Pope has taken his lead from Paul VI who, he once recalled, 'pleaded for greater respect for the right of the human person, for the dignity of the children of God, for greater awareness of the plight of the people on the part of civil and Church authorities.' Accordingly, as he explained to a civilian delegation in Portugal in 1982, 'the Church, carrying out her true spiritual mission and always wishing to maintain the greatest respect for the necessary and legitimate institutions of the temporal order, never neglects to appreciate and rejoice in everything that promotes the strength to live the intregral truth about man; she cannot neglect to congratulate the efforts that are made to safeguard and defend the rights and fundamental freedoms of every human person. She rejoices and thanks the Lord of life and history, when plans and programmes – of a political, economic, social and cultural nature – are inspired by love and respect for the dignity of man, in the search for the "civilisation of love"'.

The Pope asks a blessing on the people of Guatemala, and calls for an end to the bloodshed.

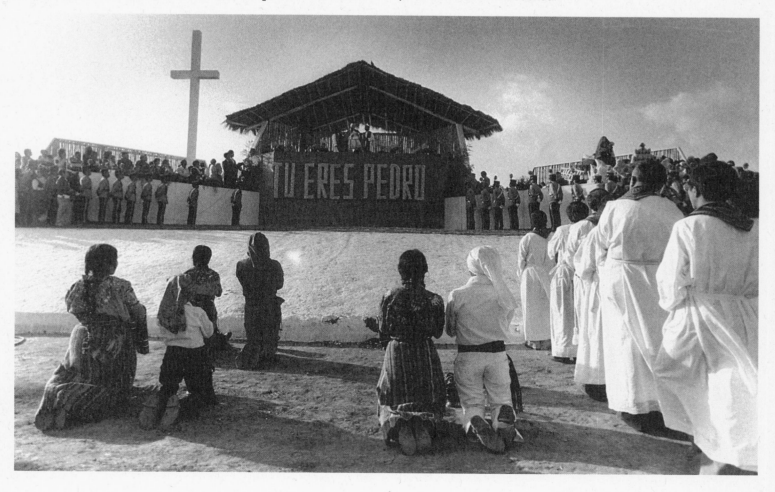

55

The Pope expanded this theme in some considerable detail the following year, with a reasoning that appears so logical and irrefutable that it can usefully be reproduced here at length. 'The Catholic Church,' he said, 'is always ready actively to support the commitment of states to promoting the well-being of men and nations. By reason of its all-embracing apostolic mission, the Church feels called upon to serve mankind publicly. The Church is not a political institution. It has no authority over technology or economic policy, and it does not thrive on power politics either. The Church respects the responsibility of the state, without interfering with its political tasks. Thus it derives even greater authority to bear the banner of true freedom, the banner of the inalienable rights of man, of his dignity and divine mission. In the name of true freedom and human dignity, the Church primarily has the task of standing up for moral conscience and responsible ethical action not only on the part of individuals but also in society. It is this permanent spiritual mission which motivates the Church, in co-operating with national governments, to deal resolutely with the comtemporary concerns of man, to advocate justice, peace, and co-existence in human dignity, and to uphold morality within both the family and society. This concrete task of the Church appears even more urgent at a time when blatant disregard for the fundamental human values erodes the very foundation on which our society rests, and endangers the innermost dignity of man. The modern pluralist state cannot forgo ethical standards in legislation and public life without causing severe damage to individual well-being and the good of society as a whole. This is true, in particular, in areas where cherished values such as respect for human life in all its phases must be protected. The Church expresses its solidarity with, and appreciation for, all of those who, out of personal conviction, defend the fundamental ethical values in present-day society and who especially seek to convince young people that this is a binding obligation for them.'

The faithful of Haiti listen to the Holy Father's address at Port-au-Prince, March 9, 1983.

In supporting the Church's right to participate in the formation and maintenance of a just and well-disposed world society, the Pope demands the concomitant commital from his own clergy. He told members of the Spanish priesthood in 1982 that it was the 'dimension of total self-giving and of permanent fidelity to love which constitutes the basis of your witness before the world. In fact, the world seeks from you a sincere lifestyle and a kind of work in keeping with what you really are. The witness is not simply a teacher who teaches what he has learnt, but he is one who lives and acts in conformity with a profound experience of what he believes in.'

That last thought is what effectively gives the priest the duty to look around him and take stock. Though the benefits of prayer and meditation in a more contemplative life are important, a more active involvement in practical realities of everyday existence is also imperative. The Papacy has come a long way since the days when it was

A rapturous welcome for John Paul II in Honduras.

seen to prefer a more submissive role to the dangers of speaking out and acting accordingly. Certainly the busy years of John Paul's reign to date have been of a character which more than justified his encouragement to Guatemalan children in 1983 to 'love this Church which, through the effort of its best children, contributed so much to shaping your personality and freedom; which has been present in the most glorious events of your history; which has been, and continues to be, at your side when destiny smiles on you or when sorrow oppresses you; which, through its schools, colleges and universities, has tried to banish ignorance by shedding the light of education upon the minds and hearts of its children; which has raised, and continues to raise, its voice to condemn injustices, to denounce acts of tyranny against the most poor and simple, not in the name of ideologies – under whatever banner – but in the name of Christ, of His Gospel, of His message of love and peace, of justice, truth and liberty.'

The Pope has never claimed – indeed he has refuted the idea – that the Church has, as he once put it, any 'worldly design, political or economic ambitions'. At the same time, he attaches great importance to the opportunity of maintaining contact with those who hold and wield civil power – a requirement for peace and understanding which was embraced within Catholic policy by the Second Vatican Council in its statement that 'the political community and the Church are autonomous and independent of each other in their own fields. Nevertheless, both are devoted to the personal vocation of man, though under different titles. This service will redound the more effectively to the welfare of all insofar as both institutions practise better co-operation. For man's horizons are now founded only by the temporal order; living on the level of human history, he preserves the integrity of his eternal destiny'.

Relying on this, the Holy Father made it plain during his 1980 African tour that, while 'the Catholic Church does not intend in any way to interfere with the specific responsibilities of the rulers, she likes to remember that in the spirit of her founder, the concept of power is inseparable from the concept of service, and that, in a way, all power being received from above, it must be exercised according to God.' His aim was therefore to concern himself with 'the desire to dialogue in the name of man taken in his integrality.' When in Upper Volta, for instance, he said that the Church had 'already collaborated loyally in the progress of the country. It continues to do so today as far as its possibilities permit, convinced of the importance of this task. I do not doubt that catechetical teaching is open, moreover, to life as a whole, so as to form in depth the man of the future, in the service of his country and of the most noble ideals.' The Pope reinforced this message more recently while addressing the North American Indians in Canada on the question of land and tribal rights. 'The Church does not intervene directly in civil matters,' he explained, 'but you know its concern for you and you know that it tries to inspire all those who want to live with the Christian spirit.'

The Church does not need an ideological system to inspire her; her own teachings compel her, as the Pope said on his first foreign tour, 'to love, defend and take part in the liberation of man: at the very centre of the message of which she is guardian and herald, she stands for brotherhood, justice and peace. She is against all forms of domination, slavery, discrimination, violence, attacks on religious liberty, aggression against man – everything which is against life'. The Church must preach 'to transform hearts and humanise the political and economic systems... to bring about liberation in its internal and deepest meaning'. The objective of the Church, which holds the truth concerning the nobility of man 'is to bring up the complete man who, guided by truth, becomes a mature member of society... A human person cannot develop and perfect himself apart from the search for the common welfare'. This was the case for freedom which John Paul twice took with him to his native Poland. Religious freedom is an inalienable human right and the Church will fight any organisation which denies it, in theory or in practice.

John Paul II has gone to great lengths to demonstrate that he is not a monarch in the sense that former popes were, even to the degree the Paul VI was. In an attempt to solve a number of problems, the Pope called, in November 1979, for an extraordinary meeting of 129 cardinals (some of them too old to vote in the conclave), to examine the Church's role in the modern world. The running of the meeting he left to three cardinals, in an effort to underline the importance of the Princes of the Church. Te principle of collegiality must prevail, but it is interesting to note that those who work in conjunction with him have little doubt that he would be prepared to brandish the Keys of Peter personally to devastating effect should he consider it necessary. Pope John Paul II comes, after all, from a tradition where the value of authority is greatly respected.

At the time of his election there were some who feared that a Polish pope might have difficulty in adjusting to Western secular mentality; that despite the talk of collegiality there was a danger of the Roman Catholic Church becoming more authoritarian. Certainly the latter prediction has proved in some ways to be justified. One aspect of religious doctrine in which John Paul was quick to assert his authority was the tendency to re-interpret the biblical texts in the light of the times. It is difficult to avoid the feeling that his first journey abroad – only three months after his accession – was made for the very purpose of declaring his opposition to this growing trend, and thus stamp his authority on the priesthood over whom he now presided. The occasion he chose was the third General Conference of the Latin American Episcopate, which took place in Mexico in January 1979. His thrust was direct and unequivocal, his attitude manfully uncompromising. 'Today,' he said, 'there occur in many places – the phenomenon is not a new one – 're-readings' of the Gospel, the result of theoretical speculations rather than authentic meditation on the word of God and a true commitment to the Gospel. They cause confusion by diverging from the central criteria of the faith of the Church, and some people have the temerity to pass them on under the guise of catechesis to the Christian communities. In some cases, either Christ's divinity is passed over in silence, or some people fall into forms of interpretation at variance with the Church's faith. Christ is said to be merely a 'prophet', one who proclaimed God's kingdom and love, but not the true son of God, and therefore not the centre and object of the very Gospel message.

'In other cases people claim to show Jesus as politically committed, as one who fought against Roman oppression and the authorities, and also as one involved in the class struggle. This idea of Christ as a political figure, a revolutionary, as the subversive man from Nazareth, does not tally with the Church's catechesis. By confusing the insidious pretexts of Jesus' accusers with the very different attitude of Jesus himself, some people adduce as the cause of his death the outcome of a political conflict, and nothing is said of the Lord's will to deliver Himself and of His consciousness of His redemptive mission. There is no doubt that all this is very demanding for the attitude of a Christian who wishes purely to serve his least brethren, the poor, the needy – in a word, all those who in their lives reflect the sorrowing face of the Lord.

'Against such "re-readings" therefore, and against the perhaps brilliant but fragile and inconsistent hypotheses flowing from them, evangelisation in the present and future of Latin America cannot cease to affirm the Church's faith: Jesus Christ, the Word and the Son of God, becomes man in order to come close to man and to offer him, through the power of His mystery, salvation, the great gift of God. Any

The Polish people pray with the Pope.

form of silence, disregard, mutilation or inadequate emphasis of the whole of the mystery of Jesus Christ that diverges from the Church's faith cannot be the valid content of evangelisation.'

Viewed in the light of these forceful declarations, the man who has expressed – and is well on the way to fulfilling – the intention of visiting every major Catholic population centre in the world, does not emerge quite as the simple pilgrim riding unawares on a wave of religion engendered by his own impressive personality. Latin America now includes the largest concentration of Roman Catholics; it is also the area where the Church is under the most pressure to enter the political arena and embrace the 'theology of liberation'. The Pope's major speech in Mexico was a masterpiece of diplomacy which brought comfort to both left and right wings of the Church. It was also the direct product of his humanism. By it, he dismissed 'liberation theology' as a 'false reinterpretation' of the Gospel: to interpret the Kingdom of God as mere political liberation was to empty it of its richness.

It has been suggested, however, that John Paul's stand on such a matter illustrates his failure to adapt to 'Western secular mentality'. If so, it is not so much because of his inability to do so but rather because of a deliberate rejection of what he sees as threatening the foundation of it, namely the fact that 'even where Christ is accepted there is at the same time opposition to the full truth of His Person, His mission and His Gospel'. In his retreat on the theme of the 'Sign of Contradiction' Cardinal Wojtyla outlined this danger. 'There is a desire to 're-shape' Him, to adapt Him to suit mankind in this era of progress and make Him fit in with the programme of modern civilisation – which is a programme of consumerism and not of transcendental ends. There is opposition to Him from those standpoints, and the truth proclaimed and recorded in His name is not tolerated (cf Acts 4, 10, 12, 18). This opposition to Christ which goes hand-in-hand with paying Him lip-service – and it is to be found also among those who call themselves His disciples – is particularly symptomatic of our own times'. This is the kind of thinking which lies at the heart of Pope John Paul's 'conservatism'.

The man whose self-confident celebration of his own vocation is so apparent and so reassuring has shown no relaxation on the status of priests, religious or nuns. One of

Hundreds of thousands of Poles greeted 'their' Pope with shouts of 'Solidarity' on his arrival in Warsaw in June 1983.

his first actions as Pope was to stop the laicisation of priests and others who wished to return to secular life. The concept of sacrifice for one's beliefs is understandably deep-rooted; the ideal of Maximilian Kolbe walks ever before him. To those priests who wished to lift the 1500-year-old ban on marriages, said by some to be one of the main causes for the steady defection of priests from the ministry, his reply was the firm reminder that "we must retain the sense of our unique vocation... We are in the world but we are not worldly'. To John Paul the reason for the defection is a 'crisis of identity'; the solution lies in the security offered only by solid spirituality and not in encouraging those who have taken vows of obedience and chastity in their 'refusal to be tested'.

To any who thought that his might be a stance built upon empty rhetoric, further and more practical proof of his authority was not long in coming. The Congregation for the Doctrine of the Faith, the papal organisation which once ran under the name of the Holy Office – began to adopt a noticeably more intransigent line with dissenters and questioners within the Church, and with such swift

response to the accession of John Paul that there was no doubting the source of influence which had put the steel into their counsels. Not long after his 'tightening-up' address to the Conference in Mexico, the Congregation brought a Dominican priest, the Belgian Eduard Schillebeeckx, to the Vatican to face interrogation. He had just published a book – *Jesus, an Experiment in Christology* – in which he sought to re-interpret long-held and fundamental beliefs in a way which served, as his opponents alleged, his own vehemently radical views. The German Professor Hans Küng also found himself on the receiving end of the Pope's disapproval when, in the same year, he questioned the doctrine of papal infallibility. Küng was stripped of his papal franchise to teach as a Catholic theologian, although he remained a priest and a member of the Roman Catholic Church.

Facing page: prayers at a Marian shrine in Altötting during the Pope's visit to West Germany, November 1980. Above: John Paul II in Warsaw, June 1983.

That first foreign journey as Pope gave John Paul the inspiration for a much expanded tour of Central America which took him, in March 1983, to no fewer than eight countries in as many days, and was potentially the most delicate and controversial of all the visits he has made to date – with the possible exceptions of those to Poland. The nature of many of the regimes which held and, in some cases, still hold sway there, the instability of a region which has increased in strategic importance almost week by week during the present decade, and the seemingly inherent violence associated with many countries in the area, made the trip a permanent headache for diplomats and security staff alike. Politically, for instance, there were serious doubts about the wisdom of including Nicaragua in the tour, since only a few months earlier the Pope himself had attempted – unsuccessfully – to have five priests removed from posts in government offices on the grounds that the tenure of political office in a pro-Marxist regime was inconsistent with the duties of ordained clergy. Meanwhile, El Salvador was in a virtual state of war – a continuation of the severe and apparently insoluble civil unrest which had already claimed the life of the Roman Catholic Archbishop Romero of San Salvador, at whose tomb Pope John Paul was now intending to pray. And in Guatemala the execution of six guerrillas on whose behalf John Paul had sent a special plea of clemency to the fiercely Prostestant president, nearly caused the papal visit be cancelled entirely.

Almost miraculously, it seemed afterwards, the entire programme proceeded pretty much as scheduled. Characteristically, the Pope did not tone down the sometimes fierce nature of his criticisms – both express and implied – on the record of some countries concerning their approach to fundamental human problems. This apart, the pastoral nature of his visit – for as such he described it prior to his departure from Italy – compelled him to warn his hosts that he would be near to those who 'suffer so

intensely, and who experience the scourge of division, war, hatred, worldly injustice, of ideological confrontations which cause turmoil in the world and find a stage for conflict among innocent peoples desirous of peace.' Indeed, he had chosen Lent as the season of his visit to emphasise 'the mystery of pain and hope, and the bloody tragedy of Good Friday, inseparable from the Easter joy of Christ's triumph over death and suffering.' Speaking of the frequency with which the image of God's love had been violated in the past, he said, 'I should desire ardently that my visit, by which I seek to share the Gethsemane and Calvary of your people, would foster, with its message of faith, fraternity and justice, an efficacious change especially of interior attitudes, capable of opening so many weary hearts to a well-founded hope of a better future.'

'During my visit,' said the Holy Father at the beginning of his tour, 'I intend to develop certain themes which I deem of top priority in this historic moment of your beloved Churches.' His main theme in a tour of enormously busy schedules turned out to be threefold – the question of the role, if any, of ordained priests in politics, social improvements, and the solution of political problems by non-violent means. It was clear that he anticipated the greatest difficulty in converting the last of these three themes into any degree of achievable success. 'Would that the prospect of this hope which enlightens the prayers of the entire Church for Latin America were without a shadow,' he said during a stopover in Lisbon. 'But even if my heart suffers with all the hearts wounded by the evil violence in every part of the world, confidence in God – rich in mercy – and love for mankind, redeemed by Christ, prevail. The journey that I am making, therefore, is one of Christian love and its sole aim is to be the reflection and proclamation of God's merciful love.

In this respect the tour began, somewhat perversely, on the most untypically hopeful note. Costa Rica, the Pope's first stop, has the unique and perhaps quaint distinction of being the only country, certainly in Latin America, to have abolished its army, as it did in 1948, condemning it as an unnecessary adjunct to a country which loved peace. Indeed, John Paul referred to Costa Rica on his arrival there as 'the land of fruitful history, the lover of peace.' Nevertheless, he added, 'my glance does not rest on this nation alone', and speaking of the remaining seven countries on his itinerary, he continued, 'There echoes in my mind with urgent emphasis the rending cry which arises from these lands and which invokes peace, an end to war and violent death; which implores reconciliation, with the end of divisions and hatred; which yearns for ample justice, until now futilely awaited; which wants to be called to a greater dignity without renouncing its Christian religious essence. Yes,' he went on, 'these nations have the capacity of progressively reaching the goals of achieving greater dignity for their sons and daughters. This must be done without returning to methods of violence or to systems of collectivism, which can turn out to be no less oppressive of man's dignity than a purely economic capitalism. It is the way of man, the humanism proclaimed by the Church in its social doctrine, which will be able to overcome deplorable situations which await suitable reforms.'

Violence – 'from whatever quarter it may come', as the Pope mentioned tactfully on his first day in Nicaragua – was much expanded upon during his time there. Though he professed that his visit was a religious mission, and commended it 'to the Virgin Mary so venerated by the faithful Nicaraguan people in her mystery of the Immaculate Conception', he made no secret of the fact that he had come to this troubled and perilous country 'to make my contribution so that the sufferings of innocent peoples in this area of the world may cease; so that bloody conflicts, hatred and fruitless accusations may end in order to make room for a genuine dialogue, a dialogue that may be a concrete and generous opportunity for a meeting of goodwill, and not a possible justification to continue to foment division and violence. I also come to launch an invitation to peace toward those who, inside or outside this geographical area – wherever they may be – promote in

John Paul II greets his fellow countrymen in Warsaw.

Warsaw during the Holy Father's second pilgrimage to Poland.

one way or another ideological, economic or military tensions which impede the free development of these peoples who love peace, brotherhood and true human, spiritual, social, civil or democratic progress.'

Bold and comprehensive though his approach was, it was not calculated to please a government which was already less than totally committed to the Christian message or to the Pope's enunciation of it. His welcome at Managua airport was decidedly cool and, as many observers had predicted, the left-wing Sandinista regime used the occasion for its own quite vitriolic political and diplomatic ends. The country was at the time ruled by a junta whose co-ordinator, Commander Daniel Saavedra, was delegated to greet the Pope. In doing so, he declared his country's desire for peace, but then attempted to justify his government's own revolutionary background by going directly against the Pope's teaching with the words, 'Our experience shows that one can be a believer and a consistent revolutionary, and that there is no contradiction between the two which cannot be overcome.' He went on to bring a blatantly political theme into his speech, which turned into a eulogy of the achievements of the Sandinista revolution which had expelled the right-wing General Somoza in 1979, and then into a harangue against the 'interventionist' policy then being pursued in the region by the United States of America.

The incident was followed by an even worse exhibition of the abuse of a pastoral occasion for political ends. John Paul later celebrated mass in the Nicaraguan capital, which was attended not only by scores of thousands of the faithful, but also by a huge number of contingents of government sympathisers who vociferously interrupted the proceedings with shouts calling for power for the people, prayers for 'the martyrs of the revolution', and 'a Church on the side of the poor.' There was prolonged

chanting, against which the Pope was powerless to proceed with the mass and which, added to several other more minor incidents on this ill-starred leg of the tour, contributed to making him 'very sad and very angry.'

Although neither the Nicaraguan stage of the Pope's Central American tour, nor his short subsequent visit to Panama, was considered – correctly as it turned out – potentially dangerous, the next stage – a twenty-four hour visit to El Salvador – had all the hallmarks of a possible disaster. Although the left-wing guerrilla movement (the FMLN) had announced its intention to observe a ceasefire for the duration, there was danger from the right-wing death squads who were thought to have been responsible for Archbishop Romero's murder three years before. Despite a tense, touchy prelude, the Pope's visit – which he afterwards described as 'unforgettable', and concerning which he singled out 'the pained face of this dear, faithful people, and the many sons and daughters who are suffering and weeping for various reasons' – was accomplished without incident. The only unexpected development was the promise by the interim President Magaña that elections would be held the following year, for the first time in half a decade. Pope John Paul seized on the possibility with a sense of vision and a word of warning. Anticipating the long-awaited chance for peace in a country torn by civil war, he said, 'I do not advocate an artificial peace which disguises the problems and ignores the corrupt mechanisms which must be reformed, but a peace for all, of all ages, conditions, groups, provenances and political opinions.' In the result, he was not even to see a ballot: a few months later the elections were summarily and indefinitely postponed.

Guatemala, which was next on John Paul's itinerary, was once sadly renowned for its proneness to natural disaster, but the circumstances of man-made disaster in which he found it caused him to perpetuate his theme of non-violence in the solution of problems. Describing it as a country which 'continues to suffer the scourge of fratricidal struggles which cause so much pain,' he called upon 'men of all positions and ideologies' to 'remember that every man is your brother, and be converted into respectful defenders of his dignity. And may the life of your brother, of every man, always be assured in the first place beyond any social, political, ideological, racial and religious difference.' And in a subsequent sermon, he advised a congregation of Indian peasants to 'organise associations for the defence of your rights and the realisation of your projects', but not to 'confuse evangelisation with subversion.'

The Pope's appeal against the recourse to political violence was repeated, with varying degrees of emphasis, throughout his tour, but one theme which hardly ever escaped his audience was his condemnation of social conditions, which he found particularly acute almost everywhere in Central America. Though he excluded Costa Rica from any criticism – 'I know the atmosphere of work and peace which distinguishes you, beloved sons and daughters of Costa Rica' – he pronounced a homily there in which he stated that the Church 'exhorts us to be committed to the elimination of injustice, to work for peace and the overcoming of hatred and violence, to promote man's dignity, to feel responsible for the poor, the sick, the alienated and the oppressed, the refugees and the exiles and the dispersed, just as for so many others whom our solidarity must reach.'

The 'promotion of man's dignity' as referred to in that string of committals, is one of John Paul's more resonant phrases substituting for 'human rights', and he found it especially appropriate that, during his visit, he was able to meet the judges of the Inter-American Court of Human Rights, whose headquarters are in Costa Rica's capital of San José. 'The establishment of the Court, which not without reason chose San José as its headquarters, marked a stage of special importance within the process of ethical growth and juridical development regarding the protection of human dignity,' he said. 'Certainly, this control of respect for human rights corresponds to the juridical system of each nation. However, greater sensitivity and a more assertive preoccupation concerning the recognition or violation of man's dignity and freedom have made us realise not only the convenience, but also the need for this protection and control exercised by each state to be complemented and reinforced by means of a supranational and autonomous juridical institution.'

In Guatemala a few days later, he spoke of the joint mission of the Church and universities in the defence of man, his rights and his freedom, and quoted Bishop Francisco de Marroquin, who well over a century earlier proclaimed the rights of man as one of the goals towards which learning should be aimed. 'For him' said the Pope, 'the university ought to be consecrated to the progress of divine and human sciences, and to the defence of man's rights. The Church teaches that the human person, created in God's image, has a unique dignity which must be

On June 18, 1983, John Paul II attended celebrations marking the 600th jubilee of the shrine of the Black Madonna at Jasna Gora.

defended against all threats, above all the present ones, which attempt to destroy man in his physical and moral being, both individual and collective. The university, which by vocation is an unselfish and free institution, appears to be one of the few institutions of modern society which along with the Church is capable of defending man in himself, without deceit, without other pretext and for the sole reason that man possesses a unique dignity and deserves to be esteemed for himself. This is the superior humanism taught by the Church.'

The theme of respect for the individual and for human rights in general was resumed by the Pope in Honduras – a country which has been under martial law for over fourteen years – when, in a homily delivered at a mass in Tegucigalpa, he appealed for the rejection of 'everything that is against the Gospel: hatred, violence, injustice, lack of work and the imposition of ideologies which suppress the dignity of men and women.' In Panama, he had already taken up the cause of the vast peasant population 'which has been frequently abandoned to an ignoble level of life.' And in Haiti, he commended the phrase, 'Something must change here', which was chosen as the theme of a Eucharistic Congress which he addressed. 'Things must indeed change,' he said. 'In preparing the Congress, the Church has had the courage to face up to the hard realities of the present, and I am sure that the same goes for all men of goodwill, for all who are profoundly attached to their fatherland. Certainly, you have a beautiful country, one with numerous human resources. In your case, one can speak of an innate and generous religious sentiment, of a vitality and of the popular character of the Church. But there are people who are packed together, without work, in the cities; there are displaced families; there are victims of various forms of frustration. But nevertheless, they are convinced that there are solutions in solidarity. The poor of every kind must regain hope. The Church maintains in this domain a prophetic mission, inseparable from her religious mission, and she demands the freedom to fulfil this. She demands it not in order to accuse, and not merely to take cognisance of the evil, but to contribute in a positive manner to its relief by engaging the consciences of all.

'In fact,' the Pope continued, 'there is certainly a profound need for justice, for a better distribution of goods, for a more equitable organisation of society, with more participation, a more disinterested conception of service among all those who hold responsibility. There is a legitimate desire, for the media and in the political sphere, for free expression respectful of the options of others and of the common good. There is the need for a more open and easy access to benefits and services which cannot remain the lot of the few; for example, the possibility of having enough to eat and of being cared for, housing, education, the overcoming of illiteracy, honest and worthy employment, social security, respect for family responsibilities and for the fundamental rights of man. In short, everything that would afford men and women, children and the elderly the possibility of leading a truly human life.'

In many other circumstances, words like these may have been criticised or dismissed as mere platitudes – pious hopes without real prospect of fulfilment, spoken by a man in a position of some privilege and considerable influence, and usually addressed more immediately to the well-fed peoples of the Western world who are more than able to look after themselves. It says much for John Paul that in a region of the world which somehow has often escaped global sympathies in respect of its poverty and oppression, his visit, not only to Haiti but also to the whole of Central America that year, should have embraced the squalor of shanty towns as well as the splendour of presidential palaces, and that his homilies should have lighted so boldly upon problems which many of his hosts might have preferred not to see exposed to the wider world. In striking out thus, the Pope demonstrated not only his sense of fundamental humanity, but also an enormous courage

crisis might be achieved, he pointed out that any attempt he made in his quest for a settlement 'would have no value if it did not truly represent the "first stone" of a general overall peace in the area, a peace that, being necessarily based on equitable recognition of the rights of all, cannot fail to include the consideration and just settlement of the Palestinian question.'

Confident in his abilities to provide the good example, the Pope has always insisted that his own priests, and the faithful who follow their teachings, must use every

John Paul II at prayer during his visit to Czestochowa.

which does not baulk at the prospect of personal danger or diplomatic discomfiture.

John Paul knows as well as anyone that humanity's withdrawal from the edge of the abyss of self-destruction by nuclear war is not a very likely prospect in the face of the aggression that manifests itself in present-day diplomatic intercourse. He therefore sees the role of any religious organisation in promoting peace, and in particular his own as head of the Roman Catholic Church, as of necessity little more than a perpetual plea, a constant encouragement, a repeated demand for the solution of international problems by non-violent means. This approach became obvious when he visited the United States of America at a time when the situation in the Middle East had recently worsened yet again. Hoping that a solution to the continual

opportunity to denounce and forgo violence if international peace is to be preserved. As recently as 1984, he was exhorting the clergy at the Latin-American Episcopal Conference to 'resist the anti-Christian temptation of those who do not believe in dialogue and reconciliation and resort to violence, and who substitute the power of arms or ideological oppression for political solutions.' In France in 1980, he delegated the burden of confronting the men of power to 'the great society of workers'. They, in the name of the moral power with which that world-wide association of labourers is endowed, must demand 'where, in what field, and why the bounds of this noble struggle have been

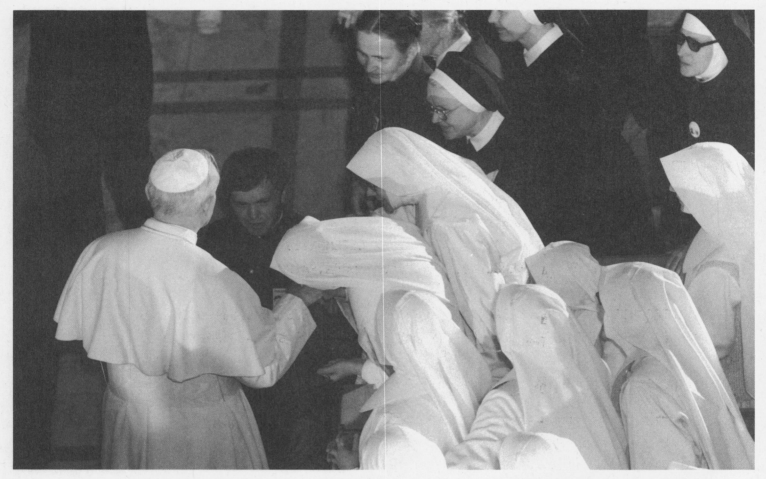

overstepped, the struggle for the good of man, in particular the most underprivileged and the neediest. Where, in what field, and why has this moral and creative power been turned into a destructive force, hatred, in the new forms of collective selfishness in which glimpses can be caught of the threat of the possibility of a struggle of all against all, and of a monstrous self-destruction? It is a categorical imperative of consciences: of every man, whole societies, and in particular of those on whom the main responsibility weighs for the present and for the future of the world. It is in this question that is manifested the moral power which is represented by the worker, by the world of work, and at the same time by all men.'

Above all, the constant theme runs through John Paul's many sermons on the question of war and peace that the ordinary man and woman should be aware of developments which have or may lead to conflict, and be prepared to stand up and campaign against their worst consequences. For the clergy, as he told an audience in Scotland in 1982, this can be a particularly solitary job. 'Do not,' he implored his listeners, 'let the sight of the world in turmoil shake your confidence in Jesus. Not even the threat of nuclear war. Remember His words: "Be brave; I have conquered the world". Let no temptation discourage you. Let no failure hold you down. There is nothing that you cannot master with the help of the One who gives you strength. Follow the example of Our Blessed Lady, the perfect model of trust in God and whole-hearted co-operation in His divine plan for the salvation of mankind.'

For the educationalists the challenge is equally daunting, particularly when the drive towards research or discovery involves progress towards the means of destruction. 'These dangers in the field of education,' he told a UNESCO audience in 1980, 'seem to threaten, above all, societies with a more developed technical civilisation. These societies are confronted with man's specific crisis which consists of a growing lack of confidence with regard to his own humanity, to the meaning of the fact of being man, and to the affirmation and joy derived from it, which are a source of creation. Modern civilisation tries to impose on man a series of apparent imperatives, which its spokesmen justify by recourse to the principle of development and progress. Thus, for example, instead of respect for life, we have the imperative of getting rid of life and destroying it. The marvellous results of researches and discoveries, especially in the field of the sciences of nature, have been and continue to be exploited – to the detriment of the ethical imperative – for purposes which have nothing to do with the requirements of science, and even for the purposes of destruction and death, and that to a degree never known hitherto, causing really unimaginable damage. Whereas science is called to be in service of man's life, it is too often a fact that it is subjected to purposes that destroy the real dignity of man and of human life. That is the case when scientific research itself is directed towards these purposes or when its results are applied to purposes contrary to the good of mankind. That happens in the field of genetic manipulations and biological experimentations as well as in that of chemical, bacteriological or nuclear armaments.'

Peace, of course, can be defined on many levels. It is not merely the absence of war, as the Pope said when confronted by the magnificence of the new Coventry Cathedral, that great British symbol of peace and regeneration. 'Peace involves,' he stated then, 'mutual respect and confidence between peoples and nations. It involves collaboration and binding agreements. Like a cathedral, peace has to be constructed, patiently and with unshakeable faith. Wherever the strong exploit the weak; wherever the rich take advantage of the poor; wherever great powers seek to dominate and impose ideologies, there the work of making peace is undone; there the cathedral of peace is again destroyed.'

Consequently, John Paul II has been at pains to intervene, by prayer and appeal, on every occasion when it has been practicable, and constitutionally possible, to make statements which effectively bring a problem to world-wide attention. 'I cannot address myself to you,' he broadcast to the peoples of Asia, from Manila in 1981, 'without touching on the most important issue of peace – the necessary condition for every nation and people if they are to live and develop. My heart is heavy when I think of the many parts of your continent where the sound of war has not yet died down; where the people involved might have changed, but not the reality of war; where weapons alone are thought to provide security; or where brother fights against brother in order to redress real or alleged injustices. I shall not cease to raise my voice to plead for peace. As I

John Paul II addressed the waiting crowds after celebrating Mass at the shrine of the Black Madonna, June 19, 1983.

have constantly done in public appeals and in private conversations with the leaders of the world, so now, again, I beseech each and every one to respect the values and rights of peoples and nations.' On one occasion – during a lengthy address in Poland in 1979 – he compared the problems of international peace with those of internal stability, stating that, 'as inward unity within each society or community, whether a nation or a family, depends on respect for the rights of each of its members, so international reconciliation depends on recognition of, and respect for, the rights of each nation. Chief of these rights are the rights to existence and self determination, to its culture and the many forms of developing it. We know from our own country's history what has been the cost to us of the infraction, the violation and the denial of those inalienable rights.'

On other occasions, the regulation of national rights and their recognition by other countries are referred direct to the Pope to resolve. It has long been a tradition with many Latin American countries, whose territorial squabbles seem never-ending, that their disputes are referred to international arbitration for resolution. In many cases, the overwhelming Catholic influence determines that the Vatican is the best arbiter, and John Paul II had an early taste of the role of the conciliator when, shortly after his reign began, he was asked to mediate in the Beagle Channel dispute, which threatened relations between Argentina and Chile. The request came after the Pope had personally appealed to the presidents of both countries to resolve their conflict peacefully, and had warned them of taking measures which could have 'unforseen consequences' – an appeal which followed a sudden and unexpected bombing of Chilean territory by Argentina. The Pope eventually sent Cardinal Antonio Samore – a former papal nuncio to Colombia and several other Latin American countries – to investigate in December 1978, and talks with the two opposing sides quickly began. It said much for the Pope's authority, and the protagonists' respect for it, that not only did the talks continue for over three years, but also that when, in early 1982, they seemed on the verge of breaking down, both governments reaffirmed their trust in the papal mediation team, which had itself been expanded in an effort to discharge the Pope's commission satisfactorily. By September of that year, John Paul intervened personally to urge Argentina to resurrect a ten-year-old arbitration agreement which she had abrogated on its expiry, and by the end of the next year, the Vatican was able to announce a significant narrowing of differences. A draft treaty was signed in March 1984, and ratified eight months later.

The Holy Father was disappointed at being less successful with regard to Argentina's other major international conflict in the early 1980s – that involving the sovereignty of the Falkland Islands. Indeed, the eventual outbreak of hostilities in mid-1982 between Argentina and Great Britain involved the Pope in terms not only of what he would say, but of what he would do. Since 1980, he had been scheduled to pay a pastoral visit to Britain, but – as with his visit to Northern Ireland three years earlier – he decided to cancel his journey after repeated appeals for the restoration of peace between the two nations proved unsuccessful. The idea of the head of the Roman Catholic Church visiting a country even then effectively at war with a predominantly Catholic state had assumed too many conflicting dimensions for it to be in any way possible. The news dismayed the British Catholics, and the Catholic archbishops of Westminster, St Andrews & Edinburgh, Liverpool, and Glasgow paid successive visits to Rome to negotiate for a change of heart. At the same time, archbishops from Argentina campaigned for the Pope to leave his acceptance revoked.

John Paul was ready to listen to them all. 'I first wished,' he later argued, 'to meet repeatedly with authoritative representatives of the episcopates of Argentina and of Great Britain in order to ask their opinion and advice on a problem of such importance for the concerned nations, and for the Churches which are located in them.' Eventually, the persistence of the British delegation to the Vatican – aided by an undertaking by the British Prime Minister, Mrs Thatcher, that in an effort to play down the possible political content of the papal visit, she would not meet the

Silent crowds at Czestochowa.

Poland, June 1983.

Pope during his tour as originally arranged – won through. But the Pope added an important rider to his agreement to visit Britain after all – namely that he would pay a short visit to Argentina as well, in order to show both communities that he was in the business of reconciliation and impartiality.

Indeed he proclaimed, as one of the aims of his visit to Britain, supplication for a just and peaceful settlement of the dispute in the South Atlantic, and no opportunity went by, as the tour progressed, without his offering prayers for peace, and for those already dead or wounded as a consequence of the hostilities. At Westminster Cathedral, for instance, he asked his congregation 'to join me at each step of my pastoral visit in praying for a peaceful solution to the conflict, praying that the God of peace will move men's hearts to put aside the weapons of death and to pursue the path of fraternal dialogue.' The saddening thought was with

him even as he prepared to celebrate Mass. 'My dear brothers and sisters,' he said, 'as we proceed to celebrate the mysteries of our faith, we cannot forget that an armed conflict is taking place. Brothers in Christ are fighting in a war that imperils peace in the world.' But he wisely and rightly avoided taking sides in a conflict in which – insofar as they were at war at all – both sides were strictly in the wrong. His coming, he emphasised, was 'as a herald of peace, to proclaim the Gospel of peace and a message of reconciliation and love.' As he was to insist at the end of both this and the Argentinian visit, 'I well knew that in directing my steps toward Great Britain – in carrying out a strictly pastoral mission which was not only the Pope's but the entire Church's – someone could perhaps have interpreted such a mission in political terms, deflecting it from its purely evangelical significance. In any case, I maintained that fidelity to my own ministry required that I should not halt in the face of possible inexact interpretations, but carry out the mandate to proclaim with gentleness and firmness the *verbum reconciliationis*.'

Young Solidarity supporters listen to the Holy Father at Czestochowa.

The Pope was careful to maintain much the same approach when, a few days after he had left the United Kingdom, he arrived in Buenos Aires, and addressed his hosts with the words: 'My stay on Argentinian soil, even though brief by well-known necessity, will be first of all an entreaty with you to Him from whom comes every fatherhood in Heaven and on earth, that He may fill the souls of everyone with feelings of brotherhood and reconciliation. In this spirit, permit me from this very moment to invoke Christ's peace on all the victims, on both sides, of this armed conflict between Argentina and Great Britain.' His condemnation of the hostilities might by now have become commonplace but for the relevance which it clearly bore to events then occurring, the sorrowful consequences of which made it all so painfully and simply true. 'These controversies,' he said, 'degenerate into local conflicts, always reprehensible for the loss of human lives, for the terrible destruction they cause, and for the feelings of enmity, often enduring, which they generate between nations. But they could even lead to more extended wars, with the risks of annihilation difficult to calculate. These controversies generally have serious foundations, but they assume such vastness because they are often embittered by very strong emotions, emotions which complicate

situations and prevent objective viewing of reality. The present meeting has an aspect and significance very different from the preceding ones. In a moment of anxiety and of suffering for this nation and its people, I felt pressed to undertake this unexpected journey. I was urged to come by that set of reasons which I wished to express to the sons and daughters of Argentina with the letter I sent to them, with much affection and faith, last May. I have come because I was pressed to confirm with my presence the deep affection which I nourish for you and to share with you my longing for peace and harmony with the entire world.' Furthermore, he cited the hostilities as an example of a whole series of conflicts in other parts of the world. 'Faithful to my position as a humble servant of the cause of peace and understanding among men,' he said, 'I cannot fail to extend my glance from here also over the entire world. The sad spectacle of the loss of human lives, with social consequences which will be prolonged for some time in the peoples who are suffering this war, makes me think with deep sorrow of the wake of death and desolation which every armed conflict always causes.'

Although, to the world at large, Pope John Paul's visit to Britain had been viewed in the context of the conflict in the South Atlantic, it carried a greater long-term significance which was swamped by the exigencies of the hour. It was, after all, the first occasion on which any Pope had travelled to the United Kingdom, and it marked the consummation of many years of effort to normalise relationships between Great Britain and the Vatican in the ever-rolling wake of the Reformation and the breach with Rome some four hundred and fifty years earlier. It was the outbreak of World War I which prompted the British government to rethink its historic distancing from the Vatican, and a diplomatic mission was established in Rome which paved the way for an official delegation in 1923. The recognition by Italy of the separate Vatican state under the Lateran Treaty of 1929 did not affect relationships between Great Britain and the Holy See, and it was not until the mid 1960s – following visits paid to successive Popes by Queen Elizabeth the Queen Mother, Princess Margaret and Queen Elizabeth II – that the possibility of full diplomatic relations seems to have been considered. With the impending visit of John Paul to British shores in May 1982, the process was speeded up, and by the previous January there was a United Kingdom legation at the Holy See enjoying full ambassadorial status. The Vatican likewise established a nunciature in London. So when the Holy Father arrived for his six-day visit, he had the full administrative support of a virtual papal embassy to smooth his path.

Everyone was careful to emphasise that this was not a political visit but a pastoral one, with Britain's six million Roman Catholics as the main beneficiaries. It was, therefore, appropriate that, on behalf of the Queen, the Pope should have been greeted at Gatwick Airport by the Duke of Norfolk, who enjoys not only the ceremonial

In June, 1983 John Paul II addressed a gathering of 400,000 people, mostly farmers, at Poznan.

position of Earl Marshal of England, but also the distinction of being the senior duke of the Roman faith. The Pope was overjoyed at this symbolic healing of a wound struck almost five centuries ago. Speaking that morning at Westminster Cathedral, he said, 'With heartfelt gratitude and love, I thank our Lord and Saviour Jesus Christ, that He has given me the grace of coming among you today. Today, for the first time in history, a Bishop of Rome sets foot on English soil. I am deeply moved at this thought. This fair land, once a distant outpost of the pagan world, has become, through the preaching of the Gospel, a beloved and gifted portion of Christ's vineyard.'

Nor did he hesitate to make full pastoral use of all the opportunities now afforded, with Masses being said not only at Westminster Cathedral, but also at Wembley Sports Stadium, Coventry Airport, and Knavesmire Racecouse near York, and meetings with bishops, religious workers, and huge gatherings of the faithful in all of the eight cities he visited. At Edinburgh Cathedral, for instance, he met local representatives of the Catholic Church, and encouraged them not to be tempted to see the changing social and political world as a reason for tampering with God's word – 'We must strive to apply the Good News to the ever-changing conditions of the world but, courageously and at all costs, we must resist the temptation to alter its content, or reinterpret it in order to make it fit the spirit of the present age' – nor to be dismayed 'if our message of conversion and life is not always well received.' At the city's Murrayfield Stadium, thousands of young people gathered to hear him talk about their futures, and advise them neither to think that they were alone in making career decisions, nor to make those decisions for themselves alone. At York, tens of thousands participated in a Mass during which the Pope delivered a comprehensive sermon on matrimony, emphasising 'the unbreakable alliance of total mutual self-giving – a total union of love', and the fact that despite the failure of some marriages, 'it is our duty to proclaim the true plan of God for all married love and to insist on fidelity to that plan as we go towards the fullness of life in the Kingdom of Heaven.' At Cardiff, he addressed the youth of Wales and England with a homily on the power of prayer and its contribution towards providing a personal sense of mission and a means toward international peace. At Coventry, he administered the Sacrament of Confirmation to twenty-six people during a mass held at the town's airport. It was the feast of Pentecost, and the Holy Father preached peace for a world 'disfigured by war and violence. The ruins of the old Cathedral constantly remind our society of its capacity to destroy. And today, that capacity is greater than ever. People are having to live under the shadow of a nuclear nightmare. Yet people everywhere long for peace.' And at Crystal Palace in South London, he spoke in front of an audience consisting of members of the Polish community in Britain – the sort of appointment he keeps with his countrymen in every one of his travels.

But there was no question that the issue of church unity was uppermost in most Christian minds when the Pope first landed in Britain, a preoccupation which was totally requited by the Holy Father's numerous meetings with Church leaders and his statements of reconciliation. This aspect of the visit was not an entirely happy one. Extreme Protestant groups were less than pleased, and their unease and anger at His Holiness' prospective meeting with the

Queen were not assuaged by the government's assurances that the encounter would be between Heads of State rather than between Heads of Churches – an assurance which had in any event to be retracted to avoid the political implications consequent upon the hostilities with the Argentinians. From the Free Presbyterian Church in Northern Ireland came the Rev Ian Paisley, together with members of the Orange Order, to stage demonstrations in London and elsewhere on what the Pope called his 'pilgrimage of faith', and there was an equal, if less vehemently expressed, concern at the recent publication of the Anglo-Roman Catholic International Commission's tentative proposal that the Pope might be recognised as a universal Primate.

Anti-papal protests were also strong in Liverpool and Glasgow, both of which cities have a long history of inter-denominational rivalry, and it was, correspondingly, at Liverpool that John Paul made his most eager plea for unity. He attended services at both the Anglican and Catholic Cathedrals there, and made it plain that 'restoration of unity among Christians is one of the main concerns of the Church in the last part of the twentieth century: this task is for all of us.' At Cardiff, he was quietly appreciative of the proposal of his young audience that 'since my visit to your city is brief, and we are able to meet together for only a few moments, those few moments should be devoted to a common prayer for unity. This is as it should be, for unity is God's gracious gift, and all our other efforts to do His will are vain if they are not rooted in change of heart, in holiness of life and in prayer for unity: these are the very soul of the ecumenical movement.' At Manchester, the Pope met with Sir Immanuel Jakobovits, the Chief Rabbi of the Commonwealth, and also met Jewish as well as Islamic leaders while in Edinburgh.

Nevertheless, it was clear that unity between Catholics and Anglicans took the lion's share of his time in Britain. Despite the Orange Order's denunciation of the Queen as a potential 'traitor to the Constitution', and an Ulster Unionist MP's opinion that it was 'constitutionally and logically impossible for England to contain both the Queen and the Pope', the Holy Father's forty-minute audience at Buckingham Palace on the first day of his tour set the tone for the entire undertaking. He had already stressed the importance of the theme of unity on his arrival at Gatwick, with expressions of gratitude for 'the ecumenical encounters which will take place during this journey of faith. The promotion of Christian unity is of great importance, for it corresponds to the will of our Lord and Saviour Jesus Christ. The sign of unity among all Christians is likewise the way and instrument of effective evangelisation. It is therefore my fervent prayer that the Lord will bless our efforts to fulfil His will: "that they may all be one"'. He reinforced that emphasis at Westminster Cathedral, describing his mission as one 'to mourn the long estrangement between Christians, to hear our blessed Lord's prayer and commandment that we should be completely one, and to remind all believers who today inherit the faith of their fathers that in each diocese the bishop is the visible sign and source of the Church's unity. I come among you as the visible sign and source of unity for the whole Church.'

But the ecumenical highlight of the tour was the service held in Canterbury Cathedral on the second day of John Paul's visit, and the talks which followed between the Pope, the Archbishop of Canterbury, and other British Protestant leaders. Pope John Paul had been looking forward to these meetings for some time. 'With grateful memories of our first meeting on African soil,' he wrote to Dr Runcie in a reference to a breakfast-time encounter two years earlier in Ghana, 'and with a renewal of the pledge we then made to work and pray for full unity in Christ, I assure you of the eagerness with which I look forward to embracing you again in the love of the Saviour.' The discussions resulted in a joint declaration which not only gave thanks for the work carried out hitherto (including that of the Anglo-Roman Catholic International Commission) to achieve unity, but also looked forward to 'the next stage of our common pilgrimage in faith and hope towards the unity for which we long.' This 'next stage', it was announced, would be the

Official farewell to Pope John Paul II at Krakow.

institution of a new commission to study outstanding obstacles to mutual recognition of ministries, and to recommend practical steps towards unity.

Despite the Pope's pronounced preoccupation with unity on this tour, the theme was by no means new either to the Holy Father himself, or to the millions who listen to his every word day by day and week by week. 'Live in unity,' he told followers during his tour of Africa in 1980. 'And to do so, banish all division. Membership of the same Body of Christ does not tolerate any exclusion, contempt or hatred. It calls for collaboration, peace and the brotherhood of love.' In his address to the people of Asia the following year, he saw the crusade towards Christian unity as a fundamental requirement in the twentieth century. 'The Catholics and the Christians of other Churches,' he said, 'must join together in the search for full unity in order that Christ may become ever more manifest in the love of His followers. The divisions that still exist between those who profess the name of Jesus Christ must be felt as an incentive to fervent prayer and to conversion of heart, so that a more perfect witness to the Gospel may be given. Christians will, moreover, join hands with all men and women of goodwill who share a belief in the inestimable dignity of each human person. They will work together in order to bring about a more just and peaceful society in which the poor will be the first to be served. Asia is the continent where the spiritual is held in high esteem and where the religious sense is deep and innate: the preservation of this precious heritage must be the common task of all.'

Furthermore, he widened his scope to cover all religions. The Church of Jesus Christ, he explained, 'pays homage to the many moral values contained in these religions, as well as to the potential for spiritual living which so deeply marks the traditions and the cultures of whole societies. What seems to bring together and unite in a particular way, Christians and the believers of other religions is an acknowledgement of the need for prayer as an expression of man's spirituality directed towards the Absolute.' And, speaking to the Episcopal Conference in Costa Rica in 1983, he showed how this unity was to be achieved – not, he insisted, by 'cunning and compromise, human wiles, unworthy transactions, nor by diluting our identity; neither is it a simple outward association for the sake of co-existence. Rather, unity in its fullest and most perfect form is offered as our model: that of the Son with the Father: unity of love, of communication, of self-giving. In a word, unity of love and of life.' Perhaps his most moving and articulate plea for unity was heard when he met leaders of the Lutheran Church during his 1980 visit to Germany. Mindful of the bloody struggle which the European breach with Rome had left in its wake, he told his audience, 'Today, I come among you as a pilgrim. We want to admit to each other our guilt: all have sinned. We are called to strive together, in the dialogue of truth and love, to full unity in faith. All the gratitude for what remains to us in common and unites us cannot make us blind to what still divides us. We must examine it together as far as possible, not to widen gaps, but to bridge them. We must leave no stone unturned: we owe it to God and the world.'

His Holiness greets the people of Vienna.

Seoul, May 1984.

in 1980, 'My words are meant to be words of love and peace for everyone; for Christians, and also for those who belong to the ancestral religions or to the large Islamic community of the country. We have religious values in common. We must therefore, with all the more reason, respect one another and recognise each one as having the right to profess his faith freely.' This sentiment tallied with what he had said only a few months earlier. 'The Church has also a high regard for the Moslems. They worship God, who is one, living and subsistent, merciful and almighty, the creator of Heaven and earth, who has also spoken to men. They strive to submit themselves without reserve to the hidden decrees of God, just as Abraham submitted himself to God's plan, to whose faith Moslems eagerly link their own. Although not acknowledging him as God, they worship Jesus as a prophet; his virgin Mother they also honour, and even at times devoutly invoke. Further, they await the day of judgement and the reward of God following the resurrection of the dead. For this reason, they highly esteem an upright life and worship God, especially by way of prayer, alms, alms-deeds and fasting.'

The Pope has also met Jewish leaders – not only in Britain, as we have seen – but also during his many other foreign journeys. In 1983, for instance, he met representatives of the Jewish community in Spain, and spoke of the 'spiritual patrimony' that Catholics and Jews have in common – 'The people of the New Testament, indeed the Church, feels, and is in fact, linked spiritually to the descendants of Abraham, our father in faith' – and of the fraternal dialogue, directed 'toward a greater understanding and appreciation between Jews and Catholics which the Second Vatican Council has promoted, and which is continuing and spreading even in spite of inevitable difficulties.' And in Switzerland the following year, he addressed a gathering of the Israeli community, speaking of the value of the work done by the Institute for Judaeo-Christian Research at the Department of Catholic Theology in Lucerne.

Indeed, right from the beginning of his Pontificate, John Paul has been insistent about the crucial quest for unity – a cause which had been championed by the Second Vatican Council in 1965, and which, in 1979, the Pope considered 'more urgent than ever. Great progress has been made,' he continued, 'but we cannot yet be content. We must carry out Christ's will fully.' He certainly had every intention of continuing with the effort for unity, particularly within the Christian Church, and there was no doubt that reunion with the Orthodox East was high on the list of his priorities. Within a year of his accession, he had set up his own lines of communication with the Patriarchate in Moscow, received numerous discreet visits from Athens, Constantinople and other parts of the Orthodox world, and had announced his decision to pay a three-day visit to Turkey, to meet the Patriarch of the Eastern Orthodox Church, which had broken with the Roman Catholic Church as long ago as 1054. Comparatively recent efforts to heal that breach included initiatives by Pope John XXIII, several reciprocal visits between Pope Paul VI and the Patriarch Athenogoras in the mid 1960s, and the joint declaration of 1965 by which the sentences of excommunication, which each Church had pronounced upon the other at the time of the schism nine hundred years before, were annulled.

Armed with the words of St John – 'I in them and thou in me, so that they may become perfectly one, so that the

Affinity with some faiths is fundamentally more difficult to achieve than with others, but two major faiths with which the Pope has been anxious to establish a dialogue are the Jewish and Islamic. For, as he once explained, 'faith in God, professed by the spiritual descendants of Abraham – Christians, Moslems and Jews – when it is lived sincerely, when it penetrates life, is a certain foundation of the dignity, brotherhood and freedom of men and a principle of uprightness for moral conduct and life in society.' His tours of Africa have brought him into close contact particularly with Islam, of which he said during his visit to Upper Volta

John Paul II conducts a ceremony for the canonisation of 103 South Korean martyrs in Seoul, May 1984.

world may know that thou hast sent me and hast loved them even as thou hast loved me' – the Pope met the Eastern Orthodox Patriarch Dimitrios, with whom he concelebrated Mass at the Patriarchal Church of St George in Istanbul – the Patriarch speaking in Greek, his guest in Latin. By the end of the following day, each had attended a Eucharist celebrated by the other, and had combined to produce a joint declaration in which they affirmed 'our resolute determination to do everything possible to hasten the day when full communion will be re-established between the Catholic Church and the Orthodox Church, and when we will at last be able to concelebrate the divine Eucharist.' They also announced the formal beginning of an inter-Church dialogue, named the members of each Church who would comprise the commission responsible for it, and looked forward to the time when it would contribute 'to the multiple dialogues that are developing in the Christian world in search of its unity. This purification of the collective memory of all the Churches,' the declaration went on, 'is an important fruit of the dialogue of charity and an indispensible condition of future progress. This dialogue of charity must continue and be intensified in the complex situation which we have inherited from the past, and which constitutes the reality in which our effort must take place today. We want the progress in unity to open up new possibilities of dialogue and collaboration with believers of other religions, and with all men of goodwill, in order that love and brotherhood may prevail over hatred and opposition among men. We hope to contribute in this way to the coming of true peace in the world. We implore this gift of Him who was, who is, and who will be, Christ our one Saviour and our real peace.' The journey to Turkey produced concrete results in accelerating the quest for unity between the Roman Catholic and the Orthodox Church. The motive behind the quest, it may be suggested, lies not only in the interests of

ecumenism but also in the furtherance of human rights. If Rome and Orthodoxy were to complete the healing of their schism, the Soviet state-sponsored church structures would collapse, and the struggle for religious rights in Russia would at last be brought into the open.

It is, of course, evident from the already enervating history of Solidarity and the Poles' struggle for basic freedoms that, as Pope, John Paul must remain a *symbol* of freedom rather than the means to its achievement. He suffers the disadvantages of distance, lack of political power, the despair of his followers, and an opposition supported by a master organisation which is nakedly aggressive and enjoys the experience of many decades spent crushing attempts to gain freedom within the Iron Curtain countries. Added to those distinct difficulties is the greatest drawback of all – the world-wide call on his services and his conscience. In his time as Pope, his official and personal sympathies have gone out in all directions. He has appealed for clemency for ex-President Bhutto of Pakistan, condemned to death and eventually executed in 1979 for conspiracy to murder an opponent. He has deplored the assassination of Earl Mountbatten, only a month before John Paul himself was scheduled to visit Northern Ireland, as 'an insult to human dignity'. And he has interceded for the lives of six alleged guerrillas during a state of siege in Guatemala – a plea which failed when the Guatemalan authorities shot them, then attempted to shift the blame onto their Vatican ambassador, whom they accused of delaying the communication of the Pope's appeal. John Paul was more successful in his appeal for the release of some seven dozen foreign hostages captured by the UNITA guerrillas in Angola: a few sick hostages were eventually given their freedom, and no harm came to the remainder, who were all released after many months of detention. He adopted a carefully considered attitude to the shooting down in August 1983 of a South Korean passenger airliner by the Russians, who justified their action on the grounds that the aircraft was spying over Soviet territory, and he restricted himself to mere expressions of shock at the incident and of sorrow and condolence towards South Korea and the families of the victims.

The reasons for his reticence were twofold and disarmingly simple. In the first place, there was no evidence, in those early days, concerning the intention of the Russians to do anything criminal, or concerning their belief in the purpose for which the plane had wandered into their airspace. Secondly, the incident itself called forth such a fury of claim and counter-claim, with everyone rushing to take sides according to their political sympathies, that for someone in John Paul's position a stance of neutrality, even if accompanied by expressions of horror, was the only decent alternative. It certainly did not imply a weakness in favour of the Russians, whose Marxist dogma he has consistently criticised. He had, after all, made his feelings well known during the 1979 Italian elections, when he insisted that, while Roman Catholics active in the Communist Party and other left-wing parties remained for him personally members of the Church, nevertheless 'their election cannot be seen to be in keeping with the principles of faith and morality.' It is a stand which owes its unyielding strength to his experience as a young priest who watched the Communists take over in Poland and threaten the Church as much as any other institution there. He does not automatically connect Marxism with workers. He has met and discussed philosophies with Marxists, and he knows the circumstances and aspirations of millions of workers. His conclusion is that the one is the avowed enemy of the other, and that by adopting Marxism as their creed – or merely submitting to it – workers will not only be disappointed but oppressed. His encyclical on work contains specific proposals dissociating any new economic order from the influence of extreme Marxism – or, indeed, extreme capitalism. Marxism has also been frequently attacked as an 'atheistic ideology' incapable of advancing individual well-being or promoting social justice. The liberation of the poor and oppressed, as he told the people of Brazil in 1980, for instance, must be in accordance with Christian, and not Marxist, concepts. Pronouncements like this were seized upon by Polish emigrants in London who opposed the Polish government's demand in 1981 to have the ashes of General Wladyslaw Sikorski restored to his homeland. Sikorski was working for the Polish resistance in Britain when his aircraft crashed off Gibraltar in 1943. His ashes are buried at Newark in Nottinghamshire. While the Pope has made no statement either in support of or against the demand, Polish patriots have, so far successfully, used Sikorski's known lifelong antipathy to Communism to justify supposed Papal support for their cause.

It is only to be expected that many of John Paul's pleas for clemency, tolerance, patience and good sense are bound to enjoy only mixed success in a world where diplomatic ears have a disconcerting habit of falling deaf at the wrong moment. But supposed inevitability does not, and should not, disqualify him from making his viewpoint known. He realises only too well the despairing consequences of remaining silent on important issues – a sin against the conscience as well as a betrayal of those who might be at risk. The role of the Papacy during the last war, for example, has often attracted criticism for passivity, and John Paul himself was harangued by the Ayatollah Khomeini when he appealed for the release of US hostages imprisoned in the American Embassy in Teheran in November 1979, on the premise that the Vatican could have spent its time more profitably protesting against 'fifty years of massacres and imprisonment under the most inhuman conditions' during the time of the Shahs.

More than 800,000 people filled the great Youido Esplanade in Seoul to greet the Pope in May 1984.

This was the sort of withering, caustic, and very final reply to which other modern-day Popes have rarely laid themselves open. Low profiles amid the cut-and-thrust of a harshly political world have characterised the attitude of an institution which has either restricted its outspokenness to matters of moral and spiritual moment, or has pronounced with a view to being all things to all men in an effort to please everyone and offend no-one. John Paul believes in decision, action and initiatives, and has the stomach for the consequences. In September 1982, he stunned much of the Western world by granting a twenty-five-minute audience at the Vatican to Yasser Arafat, the leader of the Palestinian Liberation Organisation, and by following this with a circumspect reiteration of papal support for 'a recognition of the rights of all people, and in particular those of the Palestinian people for their homeland, and of the Israelis for their security.' The Israeli government ignored that final placebo, and described the meeting between the head of the Roman Catholic Church and 'the leader of an organisation of murderers' as 'revolting'. Predictably, the Israelis resurrected the World War II ghosts with the reminder that 'the same Church which did not say a word about the massacre of the Jews for six years in Europe, and did not say much about the killing of Christians in Lebanon for seven years, is ready to meet the man who perpetrated the crime in Lebanon and is bent on the destruction of Israel – which is the completion of the work done by the Nazis in Germany.' John Paul eschewed the opportunity of a personal reply, and merely dismissed the accusation through a Vatican spokesman, as 'an outrage against the truth.' He might more justly have pointed out that, all of three years before, he had spoken without opposition in the United Nations of his insistence that an equitable recognition of the rights of all in the Middle East could not fail to include the consideration and just settlement of the Palestinian question, as well as international guarantees for the preservation of the particular, indeed unique nature of the city of Jerusalem.

Neither criticism of this nature, nor the prospect of making himself or the institution he heads unpopular, can deflect the Pope from one of his main concerns, namely governmental respect for human rights. Though much of his campaigning is of necessity done from a distance, he is not afraid to use his frequent and wide-ranging journeys to accentuate his insistence that injustice must at least be highlighted. One of his most celebrated brushes with his hosts came during his visit in 1983 to Haiti. Relations between its government, headed by President Duvalier, and the Vatican became noticeably strained the previous year, culminating in the arrest in December 1982 of a lay church leader for allegedly insulting the President's mother during one of his programmes as a Catholic radio station broadcaster. During his six weeks in detention, rumours of his torture led a group of Haitian bishops to issue a country-wide letter calling for prayers for the internee, and for the release of Haitians from 'torture and all forms of foreign domination'. The government had already warned – through the presidentially-appointed Archbishop of Haiti, who was also a relative of the President's wife – that further criticism would not be tolerated and left John Paul with no option, on his arrival for a short visit early the next year, but to condemn the country as full of 'division, injustice, excessive inequality, misery, hunger and fear.' He appealed for freedom of the press, and eventually curtailed a scheduled visit to the presidential palace – a move which embarrassed the President who, as a token of goodwill, had only just offered to forgo the prerogative of making his own episcopal appointments. The visit was widely reported to have unified the country's bishops in their opposition to the less desirable aspects of the Duvalier regime.

Pope John Paul had already made a forceful plea for the safeguarding of human rights, when he visited the Philippines in February 1981, in circumstances in which martial law – an oppressive fact of life for nine years under a president who had last been elected for a four-year term in 1969! – had only the previous month been lifted. The Pope refused to condone what he and his crusading archbishop, Cardinal Sin of Manila, knew to have been abuses of power. 'Even in exceptional situations which may at times arise,' the Pope said, 'one can never justify any violation of the fundamental dignity of the human person or of the basic rights which safeguard this dignity. Legitimate concern for the security of the nation, as demanded by the common good, could lead to the temptation of subjugating to the State the human being and his or her dignity and rights. Any apparent conflict between the exigencies of security and of the citizen's basic rights must be resolved according to the

Pope John Paul II in Seoul.

Above: on May 5, 1984 the Pope celebrated a Mass in Taegu stadium. Facing page: an attentive John Paul II in Vienna, September 1983.

fundamental principle – upheld always by the Church – that social organisation exists only for the service of man and for the protection of his dignity, and that it cannot claim to serve the common good when human rights are not safeguarded. People will have faith in the safeguarding of their well-being only to the extent that they feel truly involved, and supported in their very humanity.'

This extension of his philosophy regarding human rights, into the realm of personal involvement in governmental decision-making, may well have been influenced by the Pope's earlier and much more significant journeys to Ireland and the USA in the autumn of 1979. The visits were fraught with complications before they even got underway. There were those who imagined that he saw Ireland and Poland as victims of a common predicament, and John Paul was doubtless aware of the tendency to cast Britain and Russia in the same oppressive role, but as a Pole

he was aware too, of the dangers of such an analogy. No Pole can easily see Britain, the nation which remained the friend and ally of a conquered and occupied Poland, as an enemy of human rights. John Paul's message to Ireland was – as will become clear in the following paragraphs – that violence and terrorism had no part to play in human rights activity: 'Violence is a lie, for it goes against the truth of our faith, the truth of our humanity. Violence destroys what it claims to defend: the dignity, the life, the freedom of human beings. Violence is a crime against humanity, for it destroys the very fabric of society'. To deprive an individual of his life is to make the worst possible assault on his human rights. A British soldier and a policeman in the RUC have human rights like everybody else.

Originally, the papal itinerary in Ireland was confined to Eire, but John Paul eventually agreed to include the Northern Ireland town of Armagh in his schedule after persistent requests from both Catholic and Protestant leaders and groups to visit them. Only a month before the tour was due to start, Earl Mountbatten, and two members of his family, were assassinated and – on the same day – eighteen British soldiers were ambushed and killed at Warren Point. The Pope had no hesitation in condemning these 'barbarous crimes' which benefited no-one, least of all the people of Armagh, the acceptance of whose invitation he now felt obliged to revoke.

During his tour of Eire, the Pope made many references to the troubles in Ulster. In a monumental address at Drogheda he was quick and unyielding in his clearly-worded condemnation of those who perpetrated violence, excluding them by implication from the true fellowship of Christianity, while at the same time absolving Christianity as a whole from blame for the present state of affairs. 'The tragic events taking place in Northern Ireland,' he affirmed, 'do not have their source in the fact of belonging to different Churches and confessions; this is not – despite what is so often repeated before world opinion – a religious war, a struggle between Catholics and Protestants. On the contrary, Catholics and Protestants, as people who confess Christ, taking inspiration from their faith and the Gospel, are seeking to draw closer to one another in unity and peace. When they recall the greatest commandment of Christ, the commandment of love, they cannot behave otherwise.'

He was at pains to express his understanding of the frustrations and grievances which were effectively the root causes of the continuing violence: 'As long as injustice exists in any of the areas that touch upon the dignity of the human person, be it in the political, social or economic field, be it in the cultural or religious sphere, true peace will not exist.' But he denied the idea that any means to a desirable end was justified. 'What Christianity does forbid,' he warned, 'is to seek solutions to these situations by the ways of hatred, by the murdering of defenceless people, by the methods of terrorism. Let me say more: Christianity understands and recognises the noble and just struggle for justice; but Christianity is decisively opposed to fomenting hatred and to promoting or provoking violence or struggle for the sake of struggle. The command, "Thou shalt not kill", must be binding on the conscience of humanity, if the terrible tragedy and destiny of Cain is not to be repeated. It is Jesus himself who said: "All who take the sword will perish by the sword." This is the word of God, and it commands this generation of violent men to desist from hatred and violence and to repent.

'I join my voice today,' he continued, 'to the voice of Paul VI and my other predecessors, to the voices of your religious leaders, to the voices of all men and women of reason, and I proclaim, with the conviction of my faith in Christ and with an awareness of my mission, that violence is evil, that violence is unacceptable as a solution to problems, that violence is unworthy of man. I pray with you that the moral sense and Christian conviction of Irish men and women may never become obscured and blunted by the lie of violence, that nobody may ever call murder by any other name than murder, that the spiral of violence may never be given the distinction of unavoidable logic or necessary retaliation. Let us remember that the word

remains forever: 'All who take the sword will perish by the sword.'

Each phrase of this polemic was greeted with relieved applause, but the Pope was not finished yet. Violence, he added, was not only not the Christian way, it was the fruitless way: 'They attempt the impossible who thus seek to put an end to the intolerable.' He praised those who sought their redress peacefully, through 'efforts to walk the path of reconciliation', those whose 'courage, patience and indomitable hope have lighted up the darkness of these years of trial', and those whose 'spirit of Christian forgiveness' in the face of personal or family suffering 'have

Taegu stadium, Seoul.

given inspiration to the multitudes.' How different his serene contemplation of the peace-makers was from the heartfelt appeals he then made to all whom violence had tainted and might yet infect. One of John Paul's most passionate pleas ever was made at Drogheda that day, and the years between have neither obscured its simple, straightforward, Christian truth nor lessened its appeal to those who still seek peace in Northern Ireland. 'To all men and women engaged in violence,' he went on, 'I appeal in language of passionate pleading. On my knees, I beg you to turn away from the paths of violence and to return to the ways of peace. You may claim to seek justice. I, too, believe

experience of violence and hate.'

The readiness, indeed the ability of the young or their parents to respond to the Pope's plea was bound to depend upon the lead they were given from their mentors. Spiritual recognition of the essential worth of peaceful behaviour and the equally essential criminality of violence was one thing – the overwhelming influence of the IRA over its followers and those who felt powerless to disobey it was quite another. It was, therefore, with forlorn regret that, although the Protestant Ulster Volunteer Force agreed to stand down its military personnel if the IRA declared a ceasefire, the Pope received the news that the IRA had

in justice and seek justice. But violence only delays the day of justice. Violence destroys the work of justice. Further violence in Ireland will only drag down to ruin the land you claim to love and the values you claim to cherish. In the name of God I beg you, return to Christ who died so that men might live in forgiveness and peace.

'I appeal to young people who may have become caught up in organisations engaged in violence. Do not listen to voices which speak the language of hatred, revenge, retaliation. Do not follow any leaders who train you in the ways of inflicting death. Love life, respect life; in yourselves and in others. Do not think that courage and strength are proved by killing and destruction. The true courage lies in working for peace. Violence is the enemy of justice. Only peace can lead the way to true justice. And to you, fathers and mothers, I say: teach your children how to forgive; make your homes places of love and forgiveness; make your streets and neighbourhoods centres of peace and reconciliation. It would be a crime against youth, and its future, to let even one child grow up with nothing but the

The faithful of Seoul attend a canonization ceremony.

rejected his plea for an end to violence perpetrated by them in Northern Ireland. Pointing out that, when the Pope talked of 'men of violence', he should have embraced in his contemplation 'the 33,000-strong armed forces in the Six Counties, their repressive laws, the army forts, the proven cases of torture...', its leaders claimed that 'upon victory, the Church would have no difficulty in recognising us. Church leaders, politicians and establishments are bankrupt and have also failed to resolve the massive social and economic problems suffered by our people and created by British interference. Indeed, it would be correct to say that many of them haven't even examined possible ways of solving the problem. They lack the courage to honestly identify the problem. We have, and we will continue to deal with it, until the British dimension is withdrawn and a climate for real peace with justice can be created.'

The Pope is welcomed in Papua New Guinea, May 1984.

By that time, the Pope had left Eire for the United States, where he was to address the United Nations on the problems of peace and war and on the issue of human rights. As he told his congregation at Drogheda, it was entirely fitting that the visit to Ireland should precede his journey to New York, since many of the problems about which he would speak to the United Nations were crystalised within the troubled province which constituted Eire's nearest neighbour. But in many ways, John Paul's job in speaking to the United Nations was more difficult than it had been in Ireland, for instead of addressing himself to specific problems, specific acts, specific injustices, he was obliged to speak in generalities before an audience of mixed receptiveness. No definite charges could be made, no pointed criticism inferred, no identifiable examples instanced, for fear of unbalancing the thrust of his address or, more seriously, of giving offence and causing immediate diplomatic embarrassment.

This, however, did not prevent him from spelling out at the very beginning of his speech the corrosive effect of political interest on the concept of human rights as embodied in the Universal Declaration of 1948. 'If the truths and principles contained in this document,' he said, 'were to be forgotten or ignored, and were thus to lose the genuine self-evidence that distinguished them at the time they were brought painfully to birth, then the noble purpose of the United Nations could be faced with the threat of a new destruction. This is what would happen if the simple yet powerful eloquence of the Universal Declaration of Human Rights were decisively subjugated by what is wrongly called political interest, but often really means no more than one-sided gain and advantage to the detriment of others, or a thirst for power regardless of the needs of others – everything which by its nature is opposed to the spirit of the Declaration. "Political interest" understood in this sense, if you will pardon me, dishonours

the noble and difficult mission of your service for the good of your countries and of all humanity.'

Clearly, there was to be no cause for smugness among any of the delegates – a realisation that came sharply into focus when John Paul identified the threats to human rights. Those benelovent Western democracies who might have considered themselves largely free from blame were decisively disabused when the Pope condemned the continued inequality of the distribution of wealth as a contributory factor to the loss of human rights. 'People must become aware that economic tensions within countries and in the relationship between states and even between entire continents contain within themselves substantial elements that restrict or violate human rights,' he explained. 'Such elements are the exploitation of labour and many other abuses that affect the dignity of the human person. It follows that the fundamental criterion for comparing social, economic and political systems is not, and cannot be, the criterion of hegemony and imperialism; it can be, and indeed it must be, the humanistic criterion, namely the measure in which each system is really capable of reducing, restraining and eliminating as far as possible the various forms of exploitation of man, and of ensuring for him, through work, not only the just distribution of the indispensable material goods, but also a participation, in keeping with his dignity, in the whole process of production and the social life that grows up around the process.'

Although the Pope praised the 'remarkable progress' made in the last hundred years towards a greater sense of humanity, he condemned the 'frightful disparities between excessively rich individuals and groups on the one hand and, on the other, the majority made up of the poor and the destitute who lack food and opportunities for work and

John Paul II's symbolic act of greeting on his arrival in the Solomon Islands.

education, and are in great numbers condemned to hunger and disease.' Nor was it sufficient, in his opinion, to disclaim all blame by attributing the phenomenon of unequal wealth to unchangeable historical factors. He insisted that, while 'various forms of inequality in the possession of material goods, and in the enjoyment of them, can often be explained by different historical and cultural causes and circumstances, these circumstances can only diminish the moral responsibility of people today; they do not prevent the situations of inequality from being marked by injustice and social injury.' What was more, he proclaimed, any violation of human rights was a direct threat to peace. The United Nations could fulfil its role as peace-keeper only if it consistently applied its own 1948 Universal Declaration of Human Rights. Before a now silent assembly of delegates, some of whom were undoubtedly embarrassed or irritated, the Pope denounced the arms race: 'The continual preparations for war... mean taking the risk that some time, somewhere, somehow, someone can set in motion the terrible mechanism of general destruction.' Then with unfaltering conviction he went on to pray that 'every kind of concentration camp anywhere on earth may once and for all be done away with', condemning outright 'the various kinds of torture and oppression, either physical or moral, carried out... on the pretext of internal "security" or the need to preserve an apparent peace.'

Behind the endless appeals for an end to the conditions which lead to man's deprivation of other men's rights lies the uneasy knowledge that the abuse will continue as long as man puts his own interests before those of his soul. For a Christian, this means that relegating God, the teachings of His Son, and the doing of His works to second place behind personal, political or diplomatic aggrandisement, is a policy of doom for self as well and for others. It is one reason why Pope John Paul has aligned the Roman Catholic Church uncompromisingly with the quest for human rights. It

permits him, above all, to level direct criticism – in the name of God – at those who infringe the rights of others and who, because of their professed faith in and fear of the Almighty, should know better. He once defined 'evangelisation' abroad as 'preaching a message of hope, bringing the good news to all parts of society, and inviting individuals and communities to interior change' – a definition widely interpreted in the case of his subsequent visit to Nigeria, where he encouraged the young people of this newly emergent country with its new-found wealth, not only to be 'good citizens, to love your country, obey its laws, respect your leaders, pay your taxes,' but also to 'strive constantly to identify the ills of your society – in particular corruption, the parade of wealth, the neglect of the poor.'

If his denunciation of conditions in intensely Catholic Haiti provided a more striking example of this approach, his visit to Brazil in July 1980 provided the justification. He was speaking to a crowd of 150,000 workers in Sao Paulo, where the Church's declared support for a strike which had lasted for seven weeks in the metal-working industry had been strongly criticised by the Brazilian government. The Pope said then that 'the Church, when she proclaims the Gospel, also tries to ensure, without, however, abandoning her specific task of evangelisation, that all aspects of social life in which injustice is manifested should undergo a change towards justice. The common good of society demands as its fundamental requirement that society should be just. The persistence of injustice, the lack of justice, threatens the existence of society from within, just as it can be threatened from outside by everything that attacks its sovereignty or tries to impose on it ideologies and models, any form of economic or political blackmail, or any attack by force of arms.

'Force of arms' is anathema to John Paul. His pontificate began in one of the most internationally violent decades in history, and continues through another which threatens to surpass it in terror, deprivation, ugliness and depression. He has personally experienced, as we shall see, the horror of assassination attempts and has condemned and consoled in the wake of countless others – from that of his own Archbishop Romero of San Salvador, to that of Mrs Indira Gandhi. It is hardly surprising, therefore, that rarely a week has passed since those hectic days of late 1978 in which he has failed to emphasise the overriding need for peace. In doing so he has, of course, followed the enforced example of his own predecessors, notably John XXIII, whose great encyclical *Pacem in Terris* characterised the tone of his lamentably short reign, and Paul VI, whom John Paul has praised as 'a tireless servant in the cause of peace. I wish to follow him with all my strengh and continue his service.'

But with the potential horrors of war growing ever more devastatingly terrifying with each year that passes, the influence of John Paul II is indispensable in the struggle to deflect nations large and small from the path which may lead not only to local war but, through it, to a world-wide cataclysm. As he said very soon after his pontificate began, 'Let no-one have any illusions about the nature and the menace of political violence. The ideology and the methods of violence have become an international problem of the utmost gravity.'

The Pope's sentiments expressed in pursuit of international peace are simply founded. They emanate from what we have already seen as the inadmissibility of any form of violence by man against man, and the belief that, internationally as well as personally, men can compromise their differences honourably. 'Never think,' he implored political leaders during his visit to Ireland, 'that you are betraying your own community by seeking to understand, respect and accept those of a different tradition. You will save your own traditions best by working for reconciliation with others.' His statement there applied locally, but the wider implications were not difficult to detect. Events in Northern Ireland have sometimes come perilously close to armed conflict, and as the Pope said only a week later, 'We are continually troubled by the armed conflicts that break out from time to time.'

The fact that such conflicts, localised around the world, have not yet resulted in nuclear aggression is no reason for ignoring the reality of a growing world arsenal of weaponry which the Pope once described as exceeding in quality and size and destructive power anything that had ever been known before. 'Can we be sure, nowadays,' he said in France in 1980, 'that the upsetting of the balance would not lead to war, and to a war that would not hesitate to have recourse to nuclear arms?' In his address to the United Nations the previous year, he had declared himself unimpressed by political ploys by which nations sought to avoid their responsibilities. He condemned 'resistance to actual concrete proposals of real disarmament, such as those called for by this Assembly in special session last year'. Such resistance, in his opinion, merely showed that 'together with the will for peace that all profess and that most desire, there is also in existence – perhaps in latent or conditional form but none the less real – the contrary to and the negation of this will. The continual preparations for war demonstrated by the production of ever more numerous, powerful and sophisticated weapons in various countries show that there is a desire to be ready for war, and being ready means being able to start it. It also means taking the risk that sometime, somewhere, somehow, someone can set in motion the terrible mechanism of general destruction.'

Facing page: his Holiness in Canada, September 1984. Below: the Pope welcomed by Melanesian warriors and dancers on his arrival in Honiara, the capital of the Solomon Islands.

Furthermore, talk of reductions in arms was a potential danger, because it anaesthetised people against the reality that reductions involved only a tiny proportion of the destructive power of what already exists. The Pope has also boasted a healthy distrust of the philosophy that places in the existence of nuclear arms the hope of a permanent deterrent. Perhaps so, he told scientists at the UNESCO headquarters in Paris, but 'we may wonder at the same time if it will always be so. Nuclear arms, of whatever order of magnitude or of whatever type they may be, are being perfected more and more every year, and they are being added to the arsenal of a growing number of countries. How can we be sure that the use of nuclear arms, even for purposes of national defence or in limited conflicts, will not lead to an inevitable escalation, leading to a destruction that mankind can never envisage or accept?'

John Paul's revulsion at the mere concept of a nuclear war was graphically expressed when, in February 1981, he visited Hiroshima and Nagasaki as part of a twelve-day tour of the Far East. He described the Hiroshima Peace Memorial as the place above all others where the truths that 'war is the work of man; war is destruction of human life; war is death' imposed themselves upon human consciousness. 'To remember the past,' he continued, 'is to commit oneself to the future. I evoke before you the memory of 6th August 1945, so that we may better grasp the meaning of the present challenge. Since that fateful day, nuclear stockpiles have grown in quantity and in destructive power. Nuclear weaponry continues to be built, tested and deployed. The total consequences of full-scale nuclear war are impossible to predict, but even if a mere fraction of the available weapons were used, one has to ask whether the inevitable escalation can be imagined, and whether the very destruction of humanity is not a real possibility.' And over a year later, he repeated his pleas at the scene of another wartime disaster – Coventry, one of Britain's most severely damaged cities during World War II. He prayed that the lesson of the past might be that its tragedies should not be repeated: 'Today, the scale and horror of modern warfare – whether nuclear or not – makes it totally unacceptable as a means of settling differences between nations. War should belong to the tragic past, to history; it should find no place on humanity's agenda for the future.'

John Paul II greets the land of Switzerland in June 1984.

The passion for freedom expressed in a plea for peace, or justice, or human rights, is something which the Church as a whole can applaud, although its members may well be at variance over the methods by which such freedom should be achieved. In this respect, the quest for Church unity is remarkably similar. While ecumenicalism is an objective generally acknowledged to be 'a good thing' and one which John Paul has shown his intention of furthering – largely by the emphasis on collegiality – one of the principal stumbling blocks to unity between the Roman Catholic Church and, for example, the Anglican Church or the United States Episcopalian Church, had been the interpretation of the First Vatican Council of the role of the Pope. Vatican II's insight that the Petrine ministry does not exist in isolation reduced that stumbling block considerably. The Pope is not now seen over, against, or above his brother bishops but as one of them. His special role is not in any way diminished. He still has 'the solicitude of all the Churches' but he does not bear the burden alone. The requirement to other Church leaders to recognise the reigning pope as 'first among former equals' is not so contentious, and the former Archbishop of Canterbury, Dr Coggan, has agreed that on historical grounds he would accept that the pope was first among equals. Since then, the way has been opened for some of the divisions between Christians to be healed.

But, in addition to the disunity among the Churches within the Christian faith itself, the Pope inherited a few elements of rebellion among members of his own Catholic flock. The most serious example of this lies in China where for over thirty years there has been a division between Chinese Catholics whose ministry in the Church is recognised and blessed by the Vatican, and those whose appointments and work are not. The trouble began in 1951, when Mao Tse-Tung expelled all foreign (ie non-Chinese) bishops then working in China, and imprisoned a large number of native Roman Catholic clergy. Six years later, the Chinese government set up an All-Chinese Catholic Church, called the Patriotic Catholic Association, which elected and consecrated its own bishops in defiance of papal disapproval, and thus began a rival institution.

Seeing signs of a less rigid general policy in the wake of Mao's death in 1976, Pope John Paul II seized an opportunity, only ten months into his reign, to probe for a reconciliation, and announced publicly that the Vatican was prepared to use 'every possible means to restore the perfect union that once existed between it and the Chinese Church', even though he had already been told by the incumbent Bishop of Peking that he must not interfere in the Patriotic Catholic Association's internal affairs, and should recognise its independence. John Paul therefore sent to China an advisor on Chinese ecclesiastical matters, who reported back in September 1979 that there were several clergy and laymen who wished to retain allegiance to the Pope and 'who do not feel themselves to be represented by the Patriotic Church'. The following March, the Archbishop of Vienna paid a visit to Peking and concluded, after speaking with several Patriotic Church bishops, that 'for the moment, China is not interested in relations with the Vatican' – though he thought it possible that the future might bring about a gradual change. It encouraged the Pope to

make the first Vatican appointment to the post of bishop in twenty-five years, when Mgr Deng Yiming was created Archbishop of Guangdong. But the move proved premature. The Patriotic Church declared the appointment illegal, and described it as an intolerable and 'rude interference in the sovereign affairs of the Chinese Church.'

They proceeded, five months later, to depose Mgr Deng, and appoint their own replacement – one of a batch of new appointments effected at that time. By the end of 1981, things had got worse for the Pope, who in November heard with alarm that four priests had been arrested in Shanghai for allegedly 'having followed the wishes of the Roman Curia, engaged in criminal activities against China and the Chinese people, and tried to undermine the independence of the Chinese churches.' News also came that the Chinese government would be exercising stricter control on religious groups to ensure that traditional religious freedom was not being abused. The deteriorating position and the intolerable strain on relations between the two rival groups – one American observer reported in May 1982 that 'loyal Catholics and Patriotic Catholics are turning on each other with mounting rancour' – prompted the Holy Father to try to begin talks. The Chinese again refused to have any truck with him. Catholics loyal to the Vatican retaliated by absenting themselves from Masses held at churches in Shanghai which the government had recently allowed to be reopened and run by patriots, while Vatican-appointed priests urged them to cut their ties with the government-sponsored branch. Vatican messages were transmitted to Jesuit priests, urging them to oppose the Patriotic Church and set up a loyal Church in opposition – going underground if necessary. Many priests did so, and held clandestine services in private homes, using ordinary

King Bhumibhol Adulyades and Queen Sirikit welcomed the Pope during his visit to Thailand in May 1984.

bread for the Host, grape-juice for wine, and wearing other than ecclesiastical vestments. When a Hong Kong report was published alleging that the new movement had effectively undermined the credibility and authority of the official Chinese Church, two leading Jesuits were imprisoned for five years for subversion.

The atheist Chinese government made a great show of extending tolerance not only to their own tame brand of Patriotic Catholics, but also to the Protestants whose churches, now restored after the excesses of the cultural revolution of 1966, were gradually allowed to reopen. By the end of 1982, the first two seminaries run by Patriotic Catholics were opened – one in Shanghai, another in Peking. As if to emphasise the point, two Roman Catholic priests were arrested on charges of running an underground Catholic Church organisation loyal to the Pope, and maintaining clandestine contacts with the Vatican. Early in 1984 they were sentenced to ten years' imprisonment by the State Religious Affairs Bureau. Practically helpless to effect any sort of relief for his beleaguered clergy, John Paul met a group of Taiwanese bishops the following month and called on the Church in Nationalist China to mediate in the matter on his behalf. At the same time, he held out an olive branch to the Chinese government – who had been campaigning for the reunion of Taiwan with the Chinese mainland for many years – by declaring that the Roman Catholic community in Taiwan belonged to 'a unified reality'. The sentiment led to beliefs that the Vatican would soon withdraw its recognition of the Taiwanese government, and indeed a spokesman in Rome described reports to that effect as 'concrete – not invented.'

Half-way through the third year of his reign, John Paul suffered the horror of the first, and most famous attempt on his life. The event is still the subject of controversy, rumour and investigation, though at the time it all seemed terrifyingly simple in both execution and explanation. The scene in which it took place was familiar enough. It was a sunlit, early evening, and the Holy Father, robed in white, was benignly acknowledging the plaudits and protestations of love from over ten thousand pilgrims as he toured St Peter's Square in an open jeep. He slowed at various points to speak to and bless groups of children and nuns in the crowd. It was during one of these pauses, conveniently lengthy for any assailant to do his work, that a series of pistol shots suddenly rang out. The unforgettable terror of the moment seems to have frozen the instant in time. For what seemed like an age, the Pope stood motionless against the split-second silence of a crowd that had hardly collected its thoughts. Then he slumped back; a heavy, helpless figure in white amid the posse of black-suited bodyguards that rushed to surround him, as others in the jeep – primarily his secretary – struggled to settle him against all the odds into a position of relative comfort. An equally helpless, patently startled driver looked anxiously over his shoulder, first towards the Pope, then towards the knot of tangled humanity in that part of the crowd from which the shots had come, as police leapt the barriers to investigate. Then the order was given to make straight for the Vatican, and the driver sped the jeep dramatically round the Square at a pace which alerted those mystified onlookers hitherto ignorant of the incident to the desperate realisation that the worst may have happened. Drama of this order lends itself to all kinds of misconceptions, though in the wake of the subsequent news that the Pope had been given the Last Rites, almost any misconception was forgivable.

An ambulance was waiting at the Vatican, and when the Pope had been transferred from the jeep he was taken to the Gemelli Hospital where one of the bullets which struck him was found to have entered his abdomen, and others to have wounded him in the right arm and left hand, splitting open a forefinger. The limb injuries were easily dealt with, but the body-wound required a five-hour operation to remove parts of the Pope's intestine. Thankfully, an anxious public, which by now comprised the whole waiting world, received the news that no damage had been done to any vital organs, and that the operation to repair the wound had been successful. The patient's blood loss – less than a litre – was not serious, while the risk of infection was judged to be minimal in a man of his standard of health. His bemused reaction to the incident, as he had struggled with his failing consciousness, had given way to calm understanding and immediate forgiveness for the would-be assassin.

The recipient of the Pope's historic expression of indulgence was a twenty-three-year-old Turk, Mehmet Ali Agca. Less than two years earlier, he had confessed to the murder of a Turkish newspaper editor, and had escaped from subsequent imprisonment just before the Pope's visit to Turkey. At that time, he had sent a letter to that same newspaper, explaining that his only reason for escaping from prison was to enable him to assassinate John Paul – whom he called 'the commander of the masked Western

The Pope is met by a guard of honour at Fribourg.

88

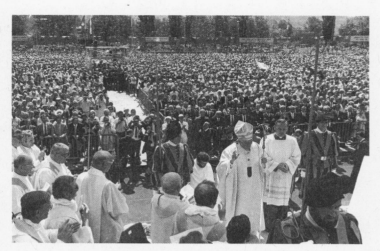

On June 12, 1984 John Paul II celebrated Mass at Lugano stadium for a congregation of 50,000.

imperialist crusaders' – if the papal visit were not called off. The threat never materialised. Agca fled to Iran, returning to Turkey to pick up false papers, and crossed into neighbouring Bulgaria. His gypsy existence throughout the countries of Europe ended in Italy late in 1980, though by this time he was truly on the run. The Turkish authorities had been able to alert the Italian police of their certain knowledge that Agca was in Italy where, save for a brief trip to Spain in April and May, he managed to remain undetected until the time of the attempted assassination.

The police experienced no difficulty in arresting Agca once the deed was done. At his trial two months later, he admitted trying to kill the Pope but refused to attend most hearings on the ground that the Italian courts had no jurisdiction to try an offence committed within the politically independent territory of the Vatican. He also alleged that he had been tortured in prison. The trial proceeded in his absence, and during the three-day hearing it was confirmed that Agca had planned three other assassinations, including that of Queen Elizabeth II. He was found guilty and sentenced to life imprisonment, of which the first year was to be spent in solitary confinement to purge his guilt in respect of other crimes. His lawyer asked in vain for a reduction of the sentence, on the plea that Agca was psychologically not responsible for his actions.

That plea was rejected, but not before it had touched on the question as to whether Agca had acted alone (as his defence had argued), and this aspect of the case has exercised legal and diplomatic minds ever since. Before long, and on information eventually volunteered by Agca himself, the Italian authorities were in little doubt that the Soviet Union and Bulgaria – who, it was believed, regarded the Pope's support for the Polish trade union Soliditary as a major spiritual force behind the current unrest in Poland – had instigated the attempt, and the arrest in Rome of a Bulgarian airline executive late in 1982 on suspicion of involvement led to a brief diplomatic breach between Italy and Bulgaria. This was worsened by Italian investigations into alleged Bulgarian plots to kill Lech Walesa, and the discovery of Bulgarian gun-running, drug-smuggling, and military espionage in Italy.

Eventually, Italian persistence prevailed, and by mid-1983 Bulgaria and Italy were coordinating judicial measures to bring suspected conspirators to book. One of them was the already identified Bulgarian airline executive; four others were Turkish. The Bulgarian's health declined in prison, and twice – once on the express wish of the Pope, who described his detention as 'a pitiable ordeal which cannot leave me indifferent', he was let out under house arrest. John Paul also interceded with the Italian authorities for a speedy decision about whether to bring the accused to trial – an unusual move prompted by a sense of mercy for which he was already becoming famous. Only a few months before, he had visited Agca – by now halfway through the third year of his term – to talk face to face with his assailant, though the details of their conversation have remained secret.

How far the Holy Father guessed or cared to guess at the implications of the attempt on his life, as he lay recovering from his wounds, can only be speculated upon. By the end of his first week in hospital he was able to sit up and take food by mouth. By then, his surgeons had invited an international team of specialists to examine and treat him. They found 'the emergency care most complete and effective; the surgical care excellent.' The Pope was declared out of danger ten days after the incident, and spent another ten days in the hospital – appearing at regular intervals, fully robed, at his window to receive the good wishes of the crowds – before being allowed back to the Vatican. On that occasion he emerged from the hospital's Polyclinic looking slightly wasted, a little stooped and inestimably saddened. The unknowing observer would have attributed this to the experience of three weeks before, but the real reason was made clear in an address he gave the following Sunday. One of his oldest and closest colleagues, Cardinal Stefan Wyszinski, had died. For all that his passing could have been anticipated, it seemed a cruel duty that now set the debilitated Pope about the business of calling for ultimate prayers for the soul of a man whose life had run so much in tandem with his own. Wyszinski – who had interrupted John Paul's canoeing session to tell him he was auxiliary Bishop of Krakow twenty-three years before; who had first campaigned, even ten years before that, against the Polish government's treatment of the Roman Catholic Church; who had emerged from a three-year internment to galvanise the Polish people against the injustice of the Gomulka and Gierek administrations in a movement which had already been seen as heralding the introduction of reforms in the 1980s; and to whose encouragement and example John Paul himself owed the consistency of his Marian devotion – was a hero of earlier years and of earlier hardships. John Paul was quickly learning that his own cross was to grow heavier as time wore on.

For, less than three weeks after his discharge from hospital, the Pope suffered a relapse. Cytomegalovirus, an infection of the lungs and liver, had taken hold and caused his condition to deteriorate markedly. On 20th June, he was readmitted into the Gemelli Clinic, and nursed back to health again. But the interruption to his progress meant that an operation which had been due for the end of that month to reverse the colostomy performed on the day of the assassination attempt had now to be postponed. For safety's sake, the Pope was kept under observation throughout the period of that postponement, and the final operation took place early in August. By the middle of that month he was again out of hospital, stronger, impatient to resume his duties, and with the memory of the incident which had taken him there well and truly behind him.

Unhappily, things did not stay like that for long. On the eve of the first anniversary of the attempt on his life, Pope John Paul II was in Portugal, on what he had termed 'a pilgrimage to the land of Mary.' He made a special journey to the shrine dedicated to the Blessed Virgin at Fatima, to give thanks for his preservation twelve months before. While there, a Spanish priest, Fr Juan Krohn, suddenly rushed through the crowd shouting 'Down with the Pope; down with Vatican II', and brandished a bayonet as he made for the Pope. He was apprehended before he came close enough to use it, and was taken away to be interrogated. He turned out to be a member of an extreme Catholic dissident group, the Sedevacanists, who claimed that the Papacy had been vacant since the death, in 1958, of Pope Pius XII, whose successor John XXIII had convoked the Second Vatican Council, which in 1965 had propounded fundamental – and, to the Sedevacanists, unacceptable – ecclesiastical reforms. Fr Krohn's seminary condemned what it called his 'act of blind terrorism', while the Sedevacanists ventured the blunt opinion that he must have lost his head. But this did not prevent him from being charged with attempted murder, an offence carrying a maximum sentence of twenty years in prison. He pleaded 'guilty and unrepentant' at his trial five months later, making use of the attendant publicity to denounce the Pope for destroying the Catholic Church, betraying the Polish trade union movement, and being the cause of 'Western Communism, and all the evils of the world.'

The Pope's anniversary jinx continued into 1983. In May of that year, he was to pay a pastoral visit to Milan, but the previous February another Turk, Mustafa Savas, was arrested on suspicion of involvement in what appeared to be another plot against the Pope's life. The arrest followed allegations made by members of a narcotics cartel that they had been offered money by Savas to assist in an attempt to kill the Holy Father in Milan, and police uncovered detailed plans for such an attempt.

Lugano stadium, June 1984.

'The event of 13th May 1981,' as the Pope has euphemistically, and somewhat dramatically described and identified the first attempt on his life, is still a live, and much-researched issue. At the time, it spawned a new consciousness and sense of appreciation of his work, as well as a more critical look at the nature and direction of his pontificate. It was quickly seen that, for all the Pope's uncompromising support for the more traditional fundamentals of the Church's teaching, he has shown not so much a liberal as a progressive sympathy with many of the world's social problems, which are often blamed on those who hold traditionalist or reactionary views. One of John Paul's most graphic pleas, for instance, has questioned the use and abuse of private property. Sometimes, his suggestions involve a delicate balance of expression, as when, during his 1979 visit to Mexico, he insisted that 'the Church does indeed defend the legitimate right to private property, but she also teaches no less clearly that there is always a social mortgage on all private property, in order that goods may serve the general purpose that God gave them. And if the common good requires it, there should be no hesitation even at expropriation, carried out in the due form.' The defence of private property in principle is one to which Paul VI subscribed, but which he claimed must be subordinated to the principle that 'God intended the earth and all it contains for the use of every human being and people. Thus as all people follow justice and unite in charity, created goods should abound for them on a reasonable basis.' Pope John Paul has taken this argument further, linking it to that most favourite theme – the satisfaction of human rights. 'The landowners and the planters,' he said during an address to proprietors and workers on a reclamation project in the Philippines, 'should not let themselves be guided in the first place by the economic laws of growth and gain, nor by the demands of competition or the selfish accumulation of goods, but by the demands of justice and by the moral imperative contributing to a decent standard of living and to working conditions which make it possible for the workers and for the rural society to live a life that is truly human and to see their fundamental rights respected.'

This in turn introduces the much more urgent question of poverty – one reason, the Pope stated at the beginning of his pontificate, why 'the voice of the Church, echoing the voice of human conscience, and having not ceased to make itself heard down the centuries in the midst of the most varied social and cultural systems and conditions, deserves and needs to be heard in our time also, when the growing wealth of a few parallels the growing poverty of the masses.'

The subject is a touchy one for, to the unthinking observer, there is nothing more glaringly unjust than the untold wealth of the Vatican and its satellites world-wide, compared with the poverty that exists among so many of the Pope's faithful. It is a misleading antithesis, of course, since the impoverishment of the Church would do little or nothing for the poor of Asia or Africa. 'Why is it,' the Pope asked a Ghanaian audience in 1980, 'that such initiatives encounter such difficulty and fail to achieve tangible and lasting results? The answer is to be found primarily, not in the economic or monetary spheres, but in an area of much

John Paul II addressed professors and students at the Miséricorde University in Fribourg, June 1984.

deeper dimensions – in the domain of moral and spiritual imperatives.' But at the same time, the apparent inconsistency is not one to which John Paul has taken fright. 'I want to come here just because it *is* a poor area,' he told a crowd of Dominican peasants in 1979. In the Philippines two years later, he was emphasising the gesture with the consummate yet simple oratory of conviction: 'Preference for the poor is a Christian preference! It is a preference that expresses the concern of Christ who came to proclaim a message of salvation to the poor, for the poor are indeed loved by God, and God it is who guarantees their rights. The Church proclaims her preference for the poor within the totality of her mission of evangelisation that is directed to all people. No area of her pastoral mission will be omitted in her concern for the poor.'

At other times more than a hint of political sting has characterised his addresses to the less fortunate. Recalling a visit to South America made by Paul VI, Pope John Paul told peasants in Mexico in 1979 that, like his predecessor, he wished to be in the company of people who are 'nearly always abandoned at an ignoble level of life, and sometimes harshly treated and exploited', in order 'to be in solidarity with your cause, which is the cause of humble people, of the poor. In view of the situation that continues to be alarming, not often better and sometimes even worse, the Pope wishes to be your voice, the voice of those who cannot speak or who are silenced, in order to be the conscience of consciences, an invitation to action, in order to make up for lost time which is often time of prolonged suffering and unsatisfied hopes. The depressed rural world, the worker who with his sweat waters also his affliction, cannot wait any longer for full and effective recognition of his dignity, which is not inferior to that of any other social sector. He has the right to be respected and not to be deprived.'

Despite his constant encounters with poverty in some of its most harrowing forms, and his frequent references to it as an evil which must eventually be overcome, the Pope is not content with a policy of merely placating its victims. In his many visits to developing countries he has carefully linked the potential problem of poverty with that of national development, and has urged the leaders and people of those countries not to fall into those sins of omission of which the rich northern hemisphere civilisations are so often guilty. 'Let us remember,' he said in Guatemala, 'that you can make your brother die little by little, day by day, when you block his access to the goods which God created for everyone's benefit and not just for the advantage of the few.' He believes, more fundamentally, that development is the new name for peace, and his memory of the ways in which European humanity has developed – ways which have brought more than their fair share of war, deprivation, prejudice, and depression – has led him freely to denigrate those intolerable aspects of his own civilisation, when he speaks to the people of emergent nations. 'There is a great danger,' he commented while in the Ivory Coast in 1980, 'of wanting just to copy or import what is being done elsewhere, for the mere reason that it comes from so called 'advanced' countries: but advanced towards what? What claim have they to be considered advanced? Has not Africa too, more perhaps than other continents which were formerly in control of it, the sense of interior things called to determine man's life? How I would like to contribute to defend it from invasions of every kind, views of man and society that are one-sided or materialistic, and which threaten Africa's way towards a really human and African development.'

A year later, he had cleverly combined the theme of Western capitalist influences with that of hunger and privation when he became the first Pope ever to address a regular Food and Agriculture Organisation conference – the one held in Rome in November 1979. In his address, he pointed out that the development and use of resources should serve the basic needs of all. 'The time of illusion is past,' he continued, 'when it was thought that the problems of under-development and difference in growth amongst countries could automatically be solved by exporting the industrial models and ideologies of developed countries. The time is past when it was thought that the right of all people to food could be granted by aid programmes made possible by the gifts of surpluses, or by emergency aid programmes in exceptional cases.'

The Pope has always been at pains not to protest too much. It has become extremely fashionable in the last thirty years to knock colonialism for all it is worth in defence of the new, breezier atmosphere which surrounds many independent countries today, but John Paul does not deny that the empires of the recent past have been able to boast certain achievements even though they may also stand convicted of many abuses. But he acknowledges also – and seems to approve of the fact – that 'the world rejoices that this period is now drawing to a final close', and that the citizens of Africa, Asia and Central America are now, for the most part, sovereign peoples, 'the true masters of their own land and the helmsmen of their own destiny.' Accordingly, as he told his Ivory Coast audience, the task of tackling the problems of self-government boils down to 'creating an orderly whole, in which none of the best products of the past are denied, while drawing at the same time fom the modern world what can help to elevate man, his dignity, his honour. There is no real development, no real human or social progress outside that.'

What blights his hopes and expectations, however, is the self-interest which prompts the developed and politically aware nations to offer a cynical hand of friendship – with strings attached. He took up the point in Ghana, which has not been noted for its placid post-independence history. 'It is with astonishment mingled with sadness,' he said there, 'that we see that this continent is marked by influences directed from inside and outside, often under cover of economic aid, but actually in the perspective of an interest that has nothing really humanitarian about it but its label. If only the different nations that compose it can live and grow in peace, without becoming involved in ideological or political conflicts that are alien to its deep mentality.' And on the last day of his 1980 African tour, he said farewell to the peoples of that continent with the following plea: 'There is a great temptation to demolish instead of construct, or else to succumb to the intoxication of profit for the benefit of a privileged class. Do not get caught up in this disastrous mechanism, which has really nothing to do with your dignity as creatures of God, or with what you are capable of. You should not imitate certain foreign models, based on contempt of man or on interest. You should not run after artificial leads which will give you an illusory freedom or which will lead you to individualism, whereas the community aspiration is so strong in you. Nor should you delude yourselves about the virtues of ideologies which hold out bright prospects of complete happiness, always postponed to tomorrow.'

A papal blessing, Canada.

Before the tour had ended, however, he had dwelt on the theme again in Kenya, listing those evils which were particularly pertinent to public and private life in Africa at the time, and he left his listeners – indeed his hosts on that occasion – fully aware of the need for a change of course in order to eliminate what were fast developing into not only bad habits, but also accepted bad habits. 'The State, the justification of which is the sovereignty of society, and to which is entrusted the safeguarding of independence, must never lose sight of its first objective, which is the common good of all its citizens – all its citizens without distinction – and not just the welfare of one particular group or category. The State must reject anything unworthy of the freedom and of the human rights of its people, thus banishing all elements such as abuse of authority, corruption, domination of the weak, the denial to the people of their right share in political life and decisions, tyranny or the use of violence and terrorism. Here again, I do not hesitate to refer to the truth about man.' He drove the point home two years later in Nigeria, where the specific abuses he mentioned were – and still are – particularly rife. 'In pursuit of progress – total progress,' he explained, 'anything must be rejected that is unworthy of the freedom and the human rights of the individual and of the people as a whole. Thus are rejected such elements as corruption, bribery, embezzlement of public funds, domination over the weak, callousness towards the poor and handicapped. Participation in the political life of the country, freedom of religion, of speech, of association, the protection of a well-functioning judiciary system, respect for and promotion of things spiritual and cultural, love of truth: these are the ingredients for progress that is truly and fully human. I have no doubt that the authorities and the people of Nigeria are fully aware of these challenges and values. I trust that they will always work together in the pursuit of the true economic and social development of the country.'

The Pope's pleas in this connection are founded – like many of his arguments – upon the incontrovertible truth that there is a fundamental equality in all human persons which must be the starting point for any state's appreciation of popular aspirations. This is also the basis for his persistent warnings about the injustice of racism. It may come as some surprise that the Vatican began its own campaign against racial discrimination in the pre-war days of Pope Pius XI, and that both John XXIII (in his encyclical *Pacem in Terris*) and Paul VI (in messages to the African people in 1967, and in an address to the Ugandan parliament two years afterwards) championed the rights of racial minorities. To them and to John Paul himself, racism is anti-evangelical in nature, the means by which division and bitterness are instigated, and an affront to human rights. As such it 'cannot lead to anything but violence, and gives the latter an endemic character: an open violence, which sets nations or ethnic groups in opposition to one another, and a more subtle, because less visible, violence which affects even morals.' Indeed, he has perceived an unequivocally strong mission in supporting the cause of racial equality. The problem impels him to speak out; it 'demands from me that I shall do so with deep and strong conviction', as he said in Kenya: 'I cannot abstain from exposing instances of institutionalised discrimination before world opinion.' In Zaire a few days later, he was even more forthright. 'In my opinion,' he stated, 'it is by struggling against this scourge of racism that I intend to act to promote respect for these rights.'

John Paul II greets the indigenous peoples of Canada.

Tempting though it is to dwell at length on the issues – mostly newsworthy to a secular audience – upon which the Pope is likely to elicit world-wide comment, his more fundamental theological beliefs and their consequences upon his attitudes to moral values must not be forgotten. It is almost negative to say that Pope John Paul has never made any secret of his personal veneration of the Blessed Virgin Mary. His love for her goes back to his very earliest years and his worship of her had become an intrinsic part of his spiritual integrality long before he became Pope. On his accession, he quartered his papal coat-of-arms with the letter M to indicate his reliance upon the Marian doctrine. The Virgin is an object of faith which he has never allowed to become overwhelmed by the many other issues on which he has felt inspired to speak. For the Pope, Mary is the figure to whom successive generations have confidently turned in the belief that in her alone reside the power and the qualities of the only woman who could truly purge and compensate for the errors of Eve. She is, as John Paul described her during his visit to Ephesus, 'the first among the humble and the poor who have remained faithful, and who are waiting for Redemption. She is again the first among the redeemed, who in humility and obedience welcome the coming of the Redeemer.' She was, and remains, the only means by which Christ could help man – by becoming His earthly mother so that He could become Man Himself. In this way, she became the link between the Saviour of mankind, and mankind itself – a fundamental mission which she willingly assumed and expressed in the *Magnificat*. For, in the words, 'He hath holpen His servant Israel, as He promised to our forefathers, Abraham and his seed for ever', she accepted the motherhood not only of Christ, but of the totality of the universe of man. From that time, as St Anselm maintained, Mary began to bear us in her womb.

For the Pope, the most important aspect of her sanctity is the faith in which her life as the prospective and eventual mother of Christ was conducted. He likes to recall that 'she received the Word in her heart as well as her body' – that she conceived in an act of faith, and believed in Him to whom she gave birth. She lived her growing faith with the deepening and progressive discovery of its efficacy and spiritual refreshment, in spite of those darker times. Though she witnessed the crucifixion of her Son, she committed herself unconditionally to Him and to His Father, living out her life and surviving its hardships by listening to and obeying the word of God. By the fervour of her faith, and by her consequent Assumption into the company of Heaven she experienced complete victory over the death of body and soul. 'Today, too,' said John Paul in one of his homilies, 'we, with the same filial fervour and the same deep trust, have recourse to the Blessed Virgin, greeting in her the Mother of God, and entrusting to her the destinies of the Church'.

The Holy Father's devotion to the Virgin Mary and her own divine destiny accounts for his persistent praise of women in their role as mothers. This in turn explains a growing degree of hostility towards his attitude by today's feminists, who have long been campaigning for an end to what they see as the prejudiced, inborn vision of women whose lives are restricted to usefulness within the home.

The Pope, aware of the movement long before he became Bishop of Rome, made specific reference to the role of women in his encyclical *In Exercise of Work*. He contended that there was a certain role in motherhood beyond the act of childbearing, which cannot be fulfilled by men. Women can fulfil it, however, and in so doing they maintain the status quo in society. That statement hardly placated the feminists who felt that his insistence upon this narrow interpretation of feminine usefulness effectively disapproved of women working outside the domestic sphere – even though the Pope had been careful also to say that a woman's domestic role 'does not exclude fulfilment outside the house.' What, perhaps, marks out the justice of the feminists' campaign – at least by secular standards – is the fact that the Pope, like most of his predecessors, has remained adamant about the confined role which women may adopt within the Roman Catholic Church itself.

It was of little comfort, for instance, to many women religious workers that the new canon law code promulgated in January 1983 – the result of eighteen years of consideration by a commission originally established by Pope John XXIII – eased restrictions formalised in 1917 only to the extent that women could serve on ecclesiastical courts and diocesan commissions if a severe shortage of priests made it inevitable, or could perform priestly duties subject to the approval of their bishops, and in any event were excluded from taking Mass or hearing confessions. Although many of the commission's rulings were not influenced by the present Pope, he has strongly defended this part of the code. It is part and parcel of an innate doctrinal conservatism on his part that has disappointed many, but which has also heartened many others who find the material temptations of the world difficult enough to cope with spiritually, without having to assimilate confusing and possibly inconsistent concessions from the Church.

Of all the traditional bastions of the papacy, infallibility is certainly not one which Pope John Paul is inclined to modify, far less dispense with. His argument goes back to the one he used in connection with re-readings of the Gospels: papal infallibility, like the Holy Bible itself, is a gift of Christ to the Church on earth. To condense or limit it is a nonsense of inconsistency for a Church whose establishment is founded and maintained on a consistent lore and a doctrine of faith bestowed upon it from above. 'When this essential basis of faith is weakened and destroyed,' the Pope told German bishops only six months after the Küng incident, 'the most elementary truths of our faith begin to collapse.' So too, of course, do the fundamental human rights and obligations to which Catholic dogma is irrevocably attached – the right of an unborn child to life, the right of each child to a happy and secure upbringing, and the prerequisite obligation upon all wedded couples to maintain a faithful and dignified marriage.

Indeed it is the issues of abortion and divorce which have forced themselves very much upon the Pope, who knows how wide the gap is between the Church's teaching and popular practice both within the Church and outside it. In 1981, for instance, he spearheaded a campaign in Italy – 'a holy cause', he called it – against abortion, taking as his main target the controversial legislation, passed by the Italian government in 1978, which allowed the termination of pregnancies in certain circumstances. The Pope's attitude was, as always, uncomfortably straightforward and brooked no equivocation: abortion was, for him, an offence against human rights and a violation of the commandment not to kill. He was criticised from many quarters, on both the content and the tone of his utterances and, as far as the Italian government was concerned, for having effectively interfered in a matter of civil authority. So widespread, indeed, was the unease felt by his contribution to the argument at a time when a national referendum on the subject was being held, that even the attempt on his life, which occurred four days before the ballot, did not produce the expected sympathy-support for his views, and the voters chose not to repeal any substantive part of the law already in force. It did not, of course, stop the Holy Father from reiterating his point when offered the opportunity to denounce this 'evil which we have not yet found the right way to curb, and the horrible nature of which far too few people have yet come to understand.' He recently insisted that 'Whoever denies protection to the most innocent and weakest human person, to the human person already conceived even though not yet born, would commit a most serious violation of the moral order. The killing of an innocent child is never

Young Canadians meet the Holy Father.

legitimate. Such would undermine the very foundation of society.' Little wonder that of the seven of the original forty-two offences which, under the new canon law, continue to involve automatic excommunication, abortion is still one.

Coupled with abortion is the growing problem of divorce – one of the elements which, as the Pope said during a visit to Austria, puts 'marriage and the family in grave danger today.' Not that he had failed to give ample warning of the looming disaster. 'There are signs of an alarming degeneration of fundamental values,' he had said two years earlier: 'an erroneous conception of the mutual independence of the partners in marriage; grave misconceptions with regard to the relations of authority between parents and their children; the concrete difficulties frequently experienced by families when they try to pass on lasting values to their children; the increasing number of divorces; the widespread evil of abortion.' He sees part of the problem as an inability or an unwillingness on the part of married couples to appreciate their irreplaceable mission in today's world. 'The generous love and fidelity of husband and wife offer stability and hope to a world torn by hatred and division. By their lifelong

John Paul II in Switzerland, June 1984.

perserverance in life-giving love, they show the unbreakable and sacred character of the sacramental marriage bond. At the same time, it is the Christian family that most simply and profoundly promotes the dignity and worth of human life from the moment of conception.'

The failure to achieve this ideal, he contends, often stems from a misguided concept of freedom seen, as he put it in one of his apostolic letters, not as 'the capacity to realise the divine plan for marriage and the family, but rather as an autonomous force of self-realisation, selfishly aiming at one's personal well-being and frequently directed against one's fellow human beings.' They are tendencies which may be totally personal, but yet which derive their support from public opinion in its questioning of the institution of marriage and its constant attempts to justify alternatives. Accordingly, John Paul II has followed the teachings of his predecessors – particularly the eloquent John Paul I, who commended the holiness of the Christian family as 'indeed a most apt means for producing the serene renewal of the Church: through family prayer, the *ecclesia domestica* becomes an effective reality and leads to the transformation of the world.' In his own *Familiaris*

Consortio, the present Pope said, 'To bear witness to the inestimable value of the indissolubility and fidelity of marriage is one of the most precious and most urgent tasks of Christian couples in our time.' Thus, as he had already written in his very first encyclical, *Redemptor Hominis*, in 1979, 'married people must endeavour with all their strength to persevere in their matrimonial union, building up the family community through the witness of love and educating new generations of men and women capable in their turn of dedicating the whole of their lives to their vocation – that is to say, to the 'kingly service' of which Jesus Christ has offered us the example and the most beautiful model.'

Not surprisingly, another mark of John Paul's papacy has been a halting of the tide of sexual permissiveness which at one time threatened to engulf even Roman Catholicism. The Vatican and United States ecclesiastical authorities are now disowning the notorious *Human*

Sexuality: New Directions in Catholic Thought, a study commissioned by the Catholic Theological Society of America. The report takes a very liberal attitude towards fetishism, transvestism, 'sex clinics', sex-change operations, sex-therapy, pornography, fornication for 'divorced singles', 'involuntary singles' and widows, and towards homosexual acts. For John Paul this kind of activity is a degradation of the human personality and an assault on man's dignity. Sexual permissiveness is a contradiction of his concept of human rights, for it is based upon a separation of love and sex and the responsibility which is part of love. Like the concentration camps of Auschwitz, it reduces the human body to the status of an object. Similarly, it is difficult to imagine how this Pope will ever accept the radical interference with human biology involved in the contraceptive pill.

The Pope made his clearest rejection of artificial birth control since his election to the papacy, in Chicago during his visit to America. With characteristic deftness he praised 350 American bishops for their support of the controversial encyclical letter of Pope Paul VI, *Humanae Vitae*, which spelled out the prohibition. He said that the bishops themselves had, in a pastoral letter, rightly spoken against both the ideology of contraception and contraceptive acts. As an inevitable parallel to his reaffirmation of 'the right to life and the inviolability of every human life, including the life of unborn children', he has endorsed the view that euthanasia – or mercy killing – is a 'grave moral evil'. It was an announcement which was entirely consistent with his earlier teachings, (some well-informed Church sources have suggested that Wojtyla's *Love and Responsibility* was one of the prime inspirations for Paul VI's *Humanae Vitae*), and with his vision of the family which 'carries with it the most fundamental values of mankind' as the archetypal and natural expression of human solidarity. It was also the direct product not, as some would claim, of his inexperience of such matters as a committed celibate, but rather of his first-hand pastoral experience in Poland. During his years in Krakow he had founded a Family Institute and placed in charge of it a gifted woman psychiatrist, a survivor of Ravensbruck, who had served as a guinea-pig for numerous hideous medical experiments. Through work in the Institute, Wojtyla acquired a wide knowledge of divorce, alcoholism, wife-beating, poverty and sexual problems. His decisions on contraception and abortion arise not from an obliviousness to human problems but at least in part from a compassionate desire to protect the sanctity of the family unit from threats which he cannot help seeing as not dissimilar to the 'operations' conducted in Nazi camps.

This was small comfort, however, for the increasing number of Roman Catholics who had hoped for a more liberal approach to sexual matters. Many were bitterly disappointed and yet, miraculously, the crowds continued to cheer. In Philadelphia the Pope closed the door to women in the priesthood in a reaffirmation of 'the prophetic tradition'. Some among his listeners received the news stony-faced but, with one or two exceptions among the Women's Liberation Movement, they joined enthusiastically in the rousing ovation which accompanied John Paul's departure. The Pope attacked the materialism of American society and hundreds of thousands of Americans – Catholics and non-Catholics, religious and atheist – applauded. He left America as he had already left Mexico, Poland and Ireland and as he has left dozens of other countries in the ensuing six years – to the sound of cries of joy and affection.

Inevitably, the fact that so many express love and respect for the man while suggesting the impossibility of applying some of his teachings, more obviously those on contraception, to their own lives, provokes the question of whether the enthusiasm which greets his every move is merely a personality cult. In one address *Urbi et Orbi* at the conclusion of the conclave which elected him, John Paul stated with great determination: 'Our own life, which so unexpectedly brought us to apostolic service, has scant value. Our personality, we wish to emphasise, must vanish through the heavy task we are called upon to perform'. But has it – and indeed should it? John Paul's charisma has earned him the nickname of 'Superstar'. One banner among the multitude that flew in the crowds assembled in St. Peter's Square once greeted him as 'the John Travolta of the Holy Spirit', and like John Travolta he too has been involved in the 'pop scene'. Shortly after his election, the 'Wojtyla Disco Dance' heralded him with the somewhat dubious but no doubt well-intentioned eulogy: 'He's the groove, he's the man, the new pope in the Vatican'. Needless to say the Vatican, after some hesitation, banned it. This was not quite sort of 'Superstar' they had in mind.

Yet the personality is little short of overwhelming. It is in no way to detract from the sincerity of John Paul to suggest that his dramatic training has shown him how most effectively to convey what he himself sincerely believes. He has a perfect sense of dramatic timing and of how best to employ a fascinating baritone voice, but over and above all this he is transparently a man in whom the four vital functions of mind, heart, soul and body are perfectly balanced. He has an easy and effective relationship with the physical, he has a first-class rational mind, he has a real and in no way sentimental sense of compassion and a profound awareness of the spiritual, the transcendant dimension of all existence. This is what makes John Paul II so impressive. Like Christ his master, he is a symbol of the fully-developed man, a symbol of something which every man must strive to become – which is why he constantly exhorts all men to become 'kings' in their own inner kingdom.

The following of such a personality can surely only be good. Just as John Paul's papacy cannot really be divorced from the life that laid the foundation for it, so the personality cannot be divorced from the values which have shaped it, and to which it in turn is committed. Does the respect for such a personality point to a deep-rooted and enduring recognition of values much older than consumerism, and to a confirmation of Cardinal Confalinieri's assertion that what drew the crowds was a deep hunger for the nourishment of solid spirituality? John Paul's comprehensive attentions to life's problems and his audiences' cheerful, appreciative acceptance of his suggested solutions which spurn the easy way out imply that the answer is 'Yes'. One thing is certain. The imprint of conquered suffering on Wojtyla's face at rest, and the love which radiates from his ready smile, have restored to the splendour of the See of Peter the ancient figure of the suffering servant. It is a figure which has been almost lost to the affluence of Western Europe and of North America but it is one which best bears witness to the spirit of Jesus Christ.

Pope Paul VI died on the evening of 6th August, 1978. His funeral was, in accordance with his own wishes "pious and simple" and the cardinals who attended *above* and *center right* wore red vestments…not a color of mourning…and miters that stressed their role as bishops. His body finally came to rest *below* in the crypt of St. Peter's.

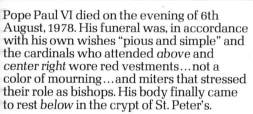

Left: In Krakow, Cardinal Wojtyla celebrated a Requiem Mass for the pope whom he had loved and respected.
Far left: Cardinal Wojtyla and Cardinal Wyszinski photographed in Rome before the August conclave.
Above right: John Paul I, the man whose thirty-three day pontificate was so abruptly concluded.
Below right: The body of John Paul I lying in state in St. Peter's.

While the body of John Paul I lay in St. Peter's *left*, an apparently endless procession of mourners filed past, many of them weeping openly.

For the second time in less than two months the college of cardinals assembled in Rome, among them Cardinal Ursi *top*, Cardinal Pironio *above* and Cardinal Colombo *below*. Once more the Mass 'for electing the pope' was held *above right*, and once more the doors of the Sistine Chapel were sealed on the 111 cardinals, to ensure the secrecy of the conclave *center and below right*.

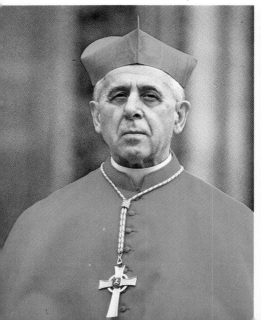

Seven times the smoke rising from the famous chimney in a cornice of St. Peter's turned slowly black, indicating to the crowd waiting in the square below that no decision had been reached, but at 6.18 pm on 16th October, as the smoke began to rise again *below*, it was indisputably white.

When the new pope appeared for the first time before the world *above* and *left*, it was to break with tradition. Before giving the customary Latin benediction *urbi et orbi*, he chose first to speak in Italian, thereby winning the hearts of the Roman crowd.

The inauguration of John Paul II on 22nd October, 1978 was attended by numerous heads of state, diplomats and foreign dignitaries. Many among the colorful congregation came in national dress, including groups from Poland who flocked with great pride and affection to witness the inauguration of the first Slav pope. Characteristically the Pope had asked that the ceremony be held at ten rather than later in the day, in order to avoid keeping the Italian fans from their televised football match in the afternoon.

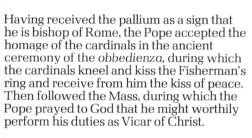

Having received the pallium as a sign that he is bishop of Rome, the Pope accepted the homage of the cardinals in the ancient ceremony of the *obbedienza*, during which the cardinals kneel and kiss the Fisherman's ring and receive from him the kiss of peace. Then followed the Mass, during which the Pope prayed to God that he might worthily perform his duties as Vicar of Christ.

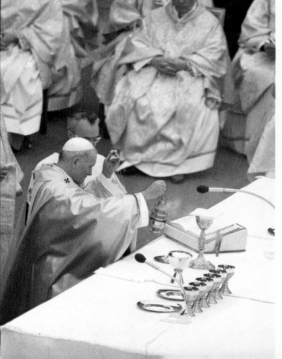

Having concluded the Mass, John Paul mingled with the 250,000 people assembled in St. Peter's Square. Millions of people too, had watched the live transmission of the service on television sets throughout the world.

His inauguration was greeted with the enthusiasm that was to follow him on the many visits that he was soon to make throughout Italy.

John Paul II began his 'ministry of love' as he intended it to continue. In his first speech to journalists *below*, he assured them: "You can count on my understanding and I permit myself to expect the same from you" and, as in defiance of protocol, he walked among the crowd, the same 'understanding' was everywhere apparent.

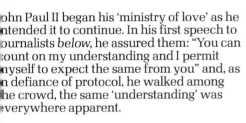

113

The life of John Paul II bears constant witness to his reverence for the dignity of man as a revelation of the 'mystery of Christ'. He has always made time for people and Vatican officials were initially disconcerted by his refusal to be separated from the surrounding crowds.

On 25th January, 1979 the Pope made his first journey outside Italy since becoming Pontiff. En route to Mexico, where he was to take part in the third international meeting of the Bishops' Conference of Latin America, he visited the Dominican Republic and was received with overwhelming exuberance.

Vast crowds gathered in Independence Square to attend an open-air Mass celebrated by Pope John Paul II on the following day, and before leaving for Mexico His Holiness was also able to meet and talk with President Guzman *below right*.

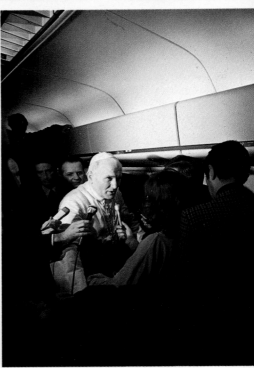

For the Pope, who is renowned for the fact that he seldom stops reading or writing, even in the back of a car, a 'plane journey *above* provides an opportunity to work or to meet with journalists.

Even a dawn earthquake could not halt the swarming pilgrimage to greet him in Mexico. The reception at the airport was so tumultuous that John Paul II could not reach microphones for an arrival speech and it took some considerable time to gain the open, truck-like vehicle that was to take him into the city.

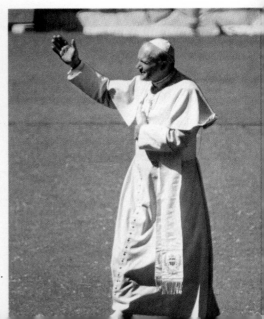

At least 5 million people packed into Mexico City to see the Pope, who won them over shortly after his arrival by accepting a proffered Mexican hat and clapping it onto his head. Riding through the crowds he scored a symbolic victory in a country which is officially anti-clerical and the only one in Latin America to shun links with the Vatican.

Mexico City's huge central square was packed for the Pontifical Mass which John Paul celebrated on the day of his arrival. So too, were the surroundings of the Shrine of Our Lady of Guadalupe *above*, which lies twenty minutes outside the city and which the Pope was also to visit.

Right: Pope John Paul II at Oaxaca.

Despite his expressed intention not to do so, President Jose Lopez Portillo did go to the airport to meet the Pope and when, on 29th January, John Paul flew the 300 miles to Oaxaca, it was in the president's 'plane. There half a million Roman Catholic Indians, many of them colorfully dressed in traditional costumes, were waiting to catch a glimpse of the Holy Father.

The packed streets of Mexico were festooned with flowers and portraits of the Pope for the duration of his visit and every public appearance he made was greeted with delighted enthusiasm.

Below: On 30th January the Pope paid a brief visit by helicopter to Santa Cecilia.

The reception throughout John Paul II's time in Mexico had been unquestionably warm and while his essentially conservative views expressed to the Conference of Latin American Bishops had left some uneasy feeling within the Church, it was clearly apparent that to the people at large, his visit had done much to dispel half a century of bitterness.

On Good Friday, almost exactly six months after his election, the Pope walked along a route marked by the Stations of the Cross, himself bearing a cross, from the Colosseum to the terrace of the Temple of Venus on the Palatine Hill.

The meditation and prayers at the Stations of the Cross formed part of the Easter celebrations, in the course of which John Paul II made an impassioned appeal for world peace.

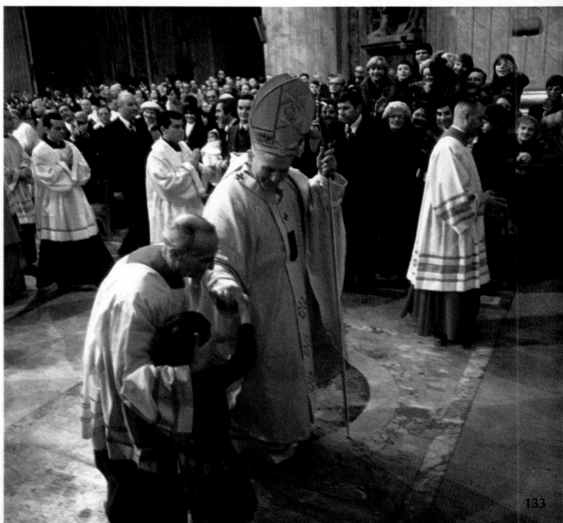

On 2nd June, 1979 Pope John Paul II returned to his native land as the first Roman Catholic Pontiff ever to visit a communist country. The occasion was striking evidence that Poland is a land where two powerful ideologies have to some extent accepted the need for peaceful coexistence; it was also the homecoming of a dedicated patriot and, as the Pope stepped from his papel Boeing 727 at Okecie military airport to be greeted by Poland's Primate, Cardinal Wyszinski, it was a moment of great joy and profound emotion. For members of the Roman Catholic Church in particular, his visit was a source of great encouragement.

BŁ. RADZYM GAUDENTY PIĘCIU BRACI POLSKICH
YKT BŁ.BOGUMIŁ ŚW.STANISŁAW SZCZEPA
A BŁ. KINGA BŁ. JOLANTA ŚW. JACEK ODI

A human tidal wave appeared to converge on Warsaw, to line the motorcade route from the airport into the city and when, during the afternoon, the Pope celebrated an open-air Mass before the Tomb of the Unknown Soldier in Victory Square, it was for a crowd of more than 250,000 people.

Paradoxically, approximately 90 percent of the population of this communist-ruled country are practicing Roman Catholics. It is small wonder then, that the state's attempts to prevent too obvious an outpouring of joy, failed miserably. The Pope's return meant a reunion with fellow churchmen. Above all, however, it meant a rapturous meeting with people from all parts of Poland.

When John Paul finally left Warsaw to fly westwards by helicopter to Gniezno, the ancient city from which Poland had emerged as a nation and embraced Christianity more than 1,000 years ago, it was to be greeted once more with flowers and cheers of enthusiasm.

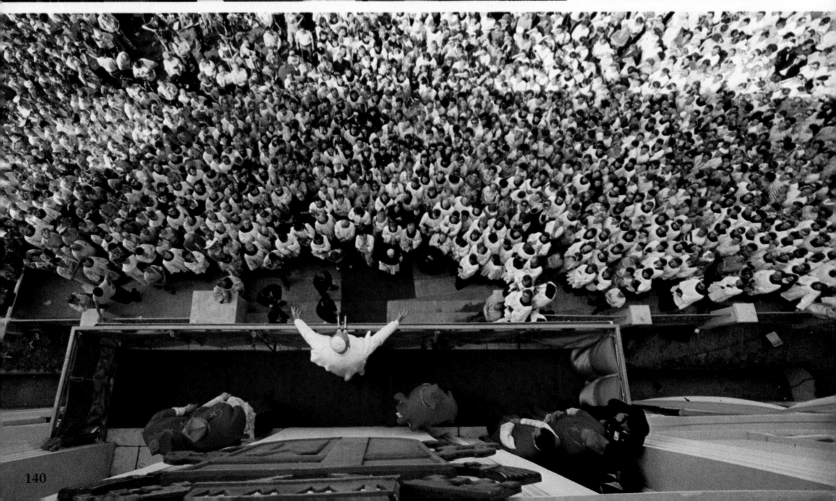

On Monday, 4th June, the Pontiff journeyed to Czestochowa where, for three days, he stayed at Jasna Gora (Bright Mountain) monastery, Poland's most popular religious shrine.

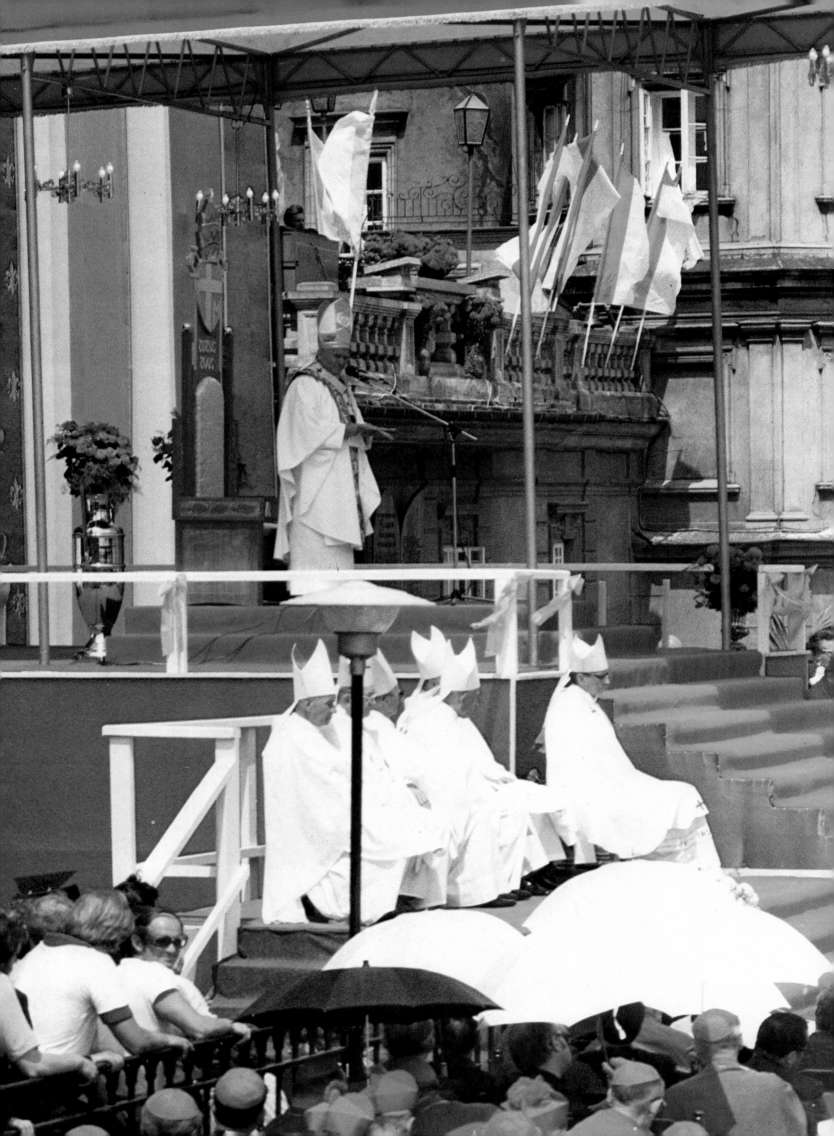

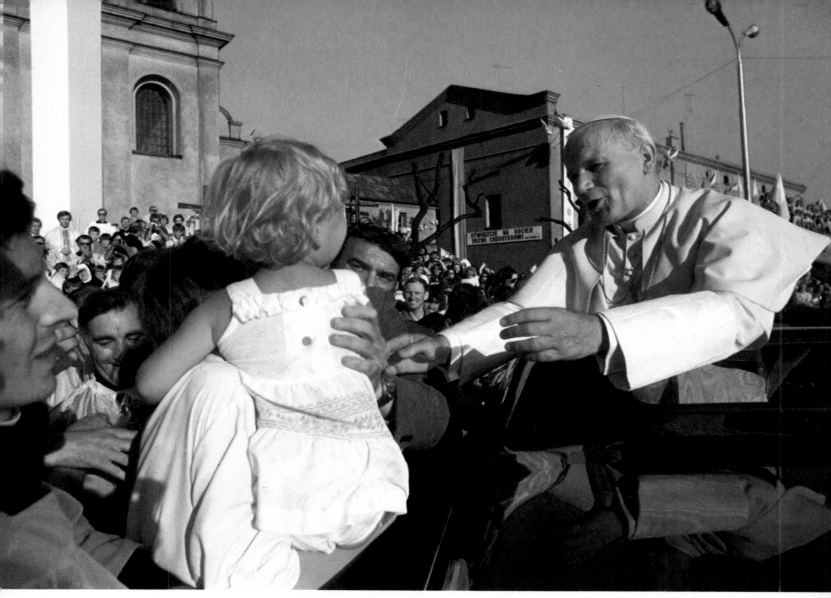

The Pope stirred an outpouring of faith and affection that no political leader in the contemporary world could hope to inspire, let alone command. When he draws children to him, it is not the calculated action of one who desires to impress but rather one which is striking only for its obvious warmth.

At Czestochowa, where the famous painting of the Black Madonna is enshrined, the Pope led approximately half a million pilgrims in a carefully compiled consecration of Poland and the universal church to Mary, 'Queen of Poland'. The veneration of the Mother of God is deeply engraved upon the consciousness of the Polish people.

Outside the monastery of Jasna Gora, Pope John Paul II, accompanied by Cardinal Wyszinski, met with the same enraptured response. Many among the pilgrims remarked upon the fact that His Holiness seemed to convey an almost tangible sense of strength and joy; joy in adversities overcome, joy in being a Christian and joy in being human.

On the evening of the 6th June, the Pope returned to Kraków *left and above and below right*, the community he had served for twenty years as bishop and archbishop. Here he was greeted with special affection.

On the following day he paid an emotional visit to his home-town of Wadowice *above*, now proudly flying both the Polish and the Vatican flags. Then, from the site of many fond memories, the Pope made a sorrowful journey to the death-haunted railyards of Birkenau *below*.

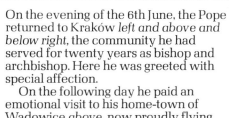

At Auschwitz, John Paul II made the first pilgrimage of any pope to the Nazi death factories and visited the cell of the beatified Franciscan priest, the Blessed Maksymilian Kolbe, who sacrificed his own life to save a fellow prisoner. Accompanied by some of the few survivors of the camp, the Pope remembered before God, the four million people who were herded from the cattle trucks to the gas chambers.

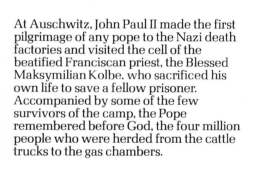

Possibly the most moving moment of the Pope's Polish visit was a Mass held among the barbed-wire fences, prison blocks and watch-towers of what he termed "a place built on hatred and contempt for man". To the hundreds of thousands among the congregation at this Mass, concelebrated by priests who had themselves been prisoners in the camp, Auschwitz must act as a reminder of the ultimate expression of human hatred. "It is necessary to think with fear of how far hatred can go, how far man's destruction of man can go, how far cruelty can go."

In preparation for the Pontiff's visit, the state had split the country into quadrants round Warsaw, Gniezno, Czestochowa and Kraków and citizens were directed to attend ceremonies only in their zone. Workers, students and schoolchildren were warned against absenting themselves during his stay. Yet despite such efforts and despite the failure of Polish television to show any sizeable crowds, the crowds were indisputably there.

By the time, on 10th June, the Pope's visit drew to its conclusion, his pilgrimage had been witnessed by an estimated 18 million people, leaving with them encouragement to challenge for freedom with all the strength of their Christian faith.
Below left: Pope John Paul II with Polish Communist Party Leader Edward Gierek.

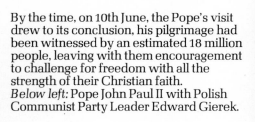

On 29th September, Pope John Paul II once more ventured outside Italy, this time to undertake what in Italy, *La Stampa* described as "A trip to the edge of a volcano". The Pontiff's visit to Ireland was considered one of the most potentially explosive journeys ever to be undertaken by a pope. Yet John Paul remained undaunted. "Peace must be announced and proclaimed everywhere …It must be announced especially where it does not exist". As he told journalists who accompanied him during his flight, his mission was to be one of peace, of reconciliation and of prayer.

The reception at Dublin airport was possibly a little more restrained than that in, for example, Mexico City. The crowds of faithful were held at a distance by strict security controls. Nevertheless he was received with military honors and as the first reigning pontiff ever to visit Ireland stepped from his Aer Lingus Jumbo, St. Patrick, to be greeted by Cardinal Tonas O'Fiaich, Archbishop of Armagh, it was a moment of obvious joy and pride for the people of Ireland.

Ireland Welcomes Pope John Paul II

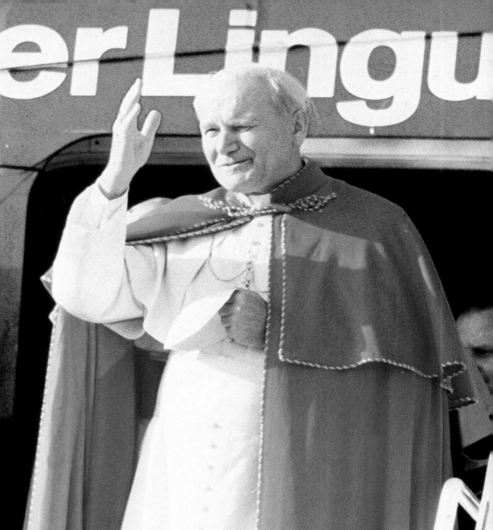

In Dublin's Phoenix Park, the Bishop of Rome and Pastor of the whole Roman Catholic Church joined in the celebration of the Eucharist with hundreds of thousands of Irish men and women. Calling to mind how many times across the centuries the Mass had been celebrated in this land, Pope John Paul urged for the continuance of acts of faith in these troubled times of prevailing materialism. "I am living a moment of intense emotion," he said; it was a moment shared by an immense crowd of people who had travelled from far and wide to catch a glimpse of their Holy Father.

Overleaf: In the celebrated 'Popemobile', the Pope made his way through a sea of waving flags and dancing and cheering people.

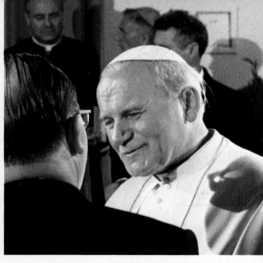

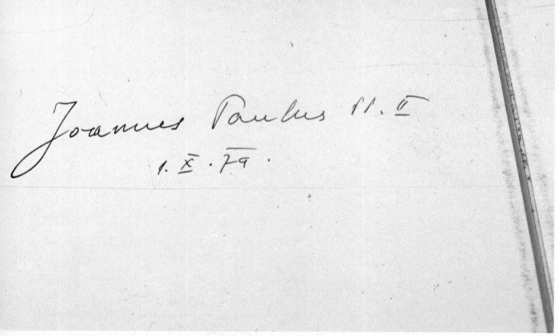

Joannes Paulus II. P.

1. X · 79 ·

The crowds at Phoenix Park were an indication of the numbers and the atmosphere that were to follow the Pope throughout his three day visit to Ireland. Cheers, singing and a general air of festivity followed his repeated call for peace. "Peace cannot be established by violence; peace can never flourish in a climate of terror, intimidation and death" ... "on my knees I beg you to turn away from the paths of violence and to return to the ways of peace."

Overleaf: Galway Racecourse was miraculously transformed by countless young people, assembled for a Pontifical Mass.

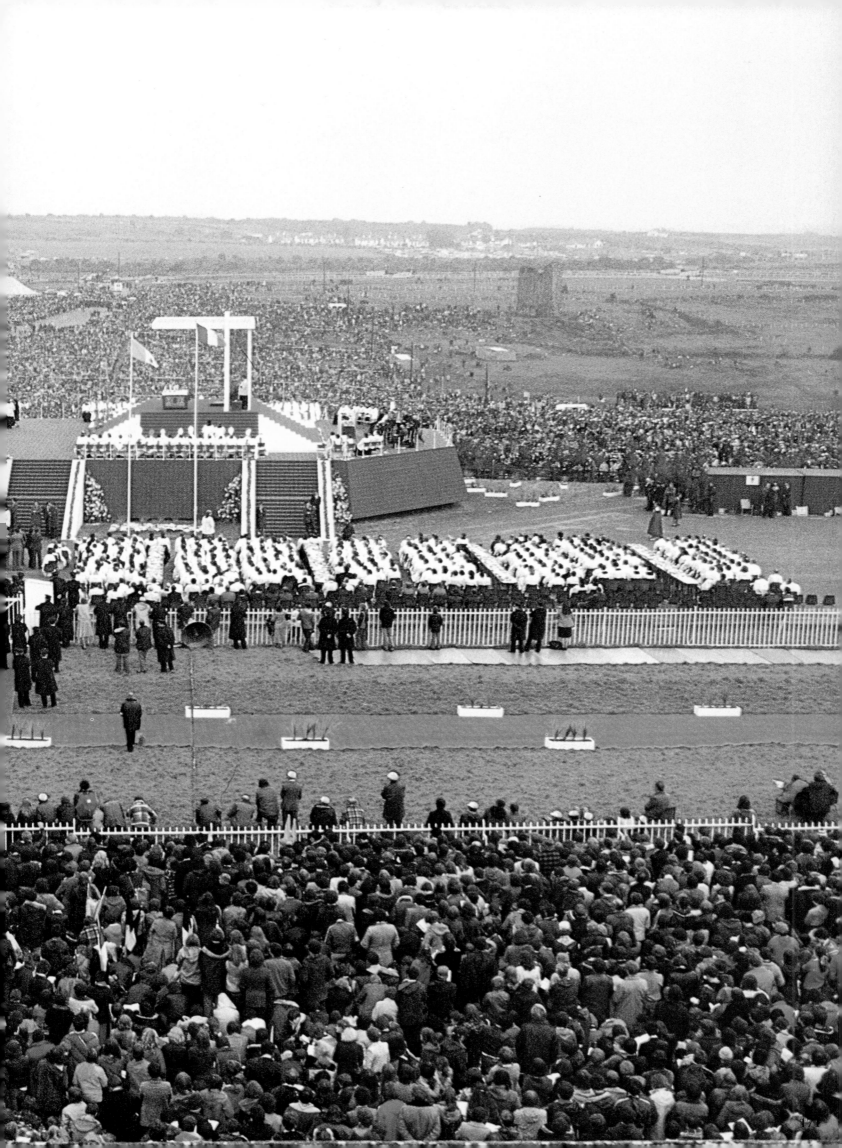

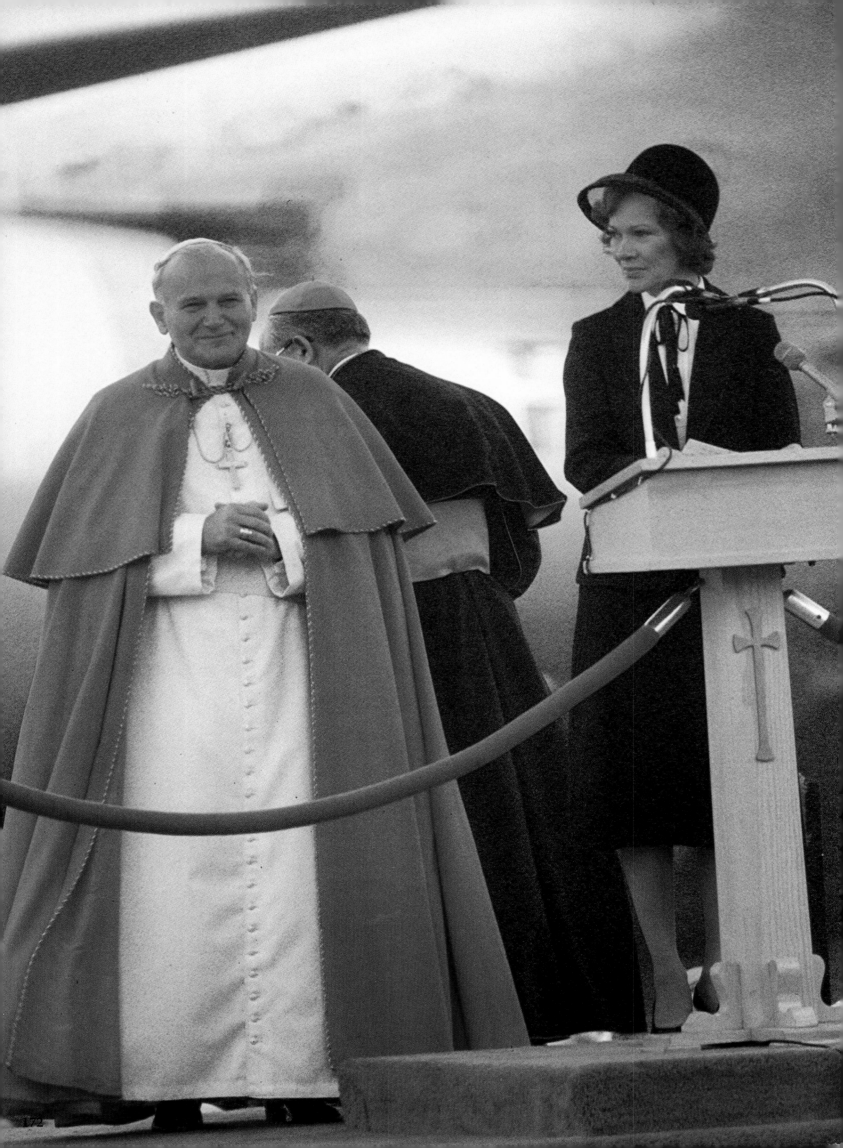

When John Paul II left Ireland, leaving behind him a vision of renewed hope, it was to fly directly to America. For the first time as Pope, he was visiting a country in which the majority of the population were not Roman Catholics but this did not appear to temper the warmth of his reception. At Logan International Airport, Rosalynn Carter, acting as her husband's personal emissary welcomed him with the words: "Americans of every faith have come to love you in a very special way," and the crowds straining to see him through the Boston rain added poignancy to her speech.

One of the primary objectives of the Pope's visit to America was to give an address to the United Nations Assembly. Having been warmly welcomed by Dr. Kurt Waldheim, the Secretary General, the Pope proceeded to deliver a speech lasting 61 minutes, which reflected a disconcertingly powerful intellect and which contained a defiant challenge to delegates of countries which still practice persecution in the name of security. John Paul's main theme was that peace is threatened by any violation of human rights anywhere, and that the U.N. can fulfil its peace-keeping mission only if it remembers and applies its own 1948 Universal Declaration of Human Rights.

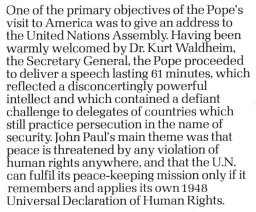

A crowd of approximately 75,000 waited impatiently for the Pope in New York's Yankee Stadium and when he finally arrived in his white reconstructed Ford Bronco, the rhythmic clapping, and flashing of cameras, gave him the reception of a superstar. Yet his homily during the mass was to warn against the hedonistic values of the superstar culture, against what he described as "the frenzy of consumerism".

Overleaf: Undaunted by the weather, eager New Yorkers packed the streets for John Paul's motorcades.

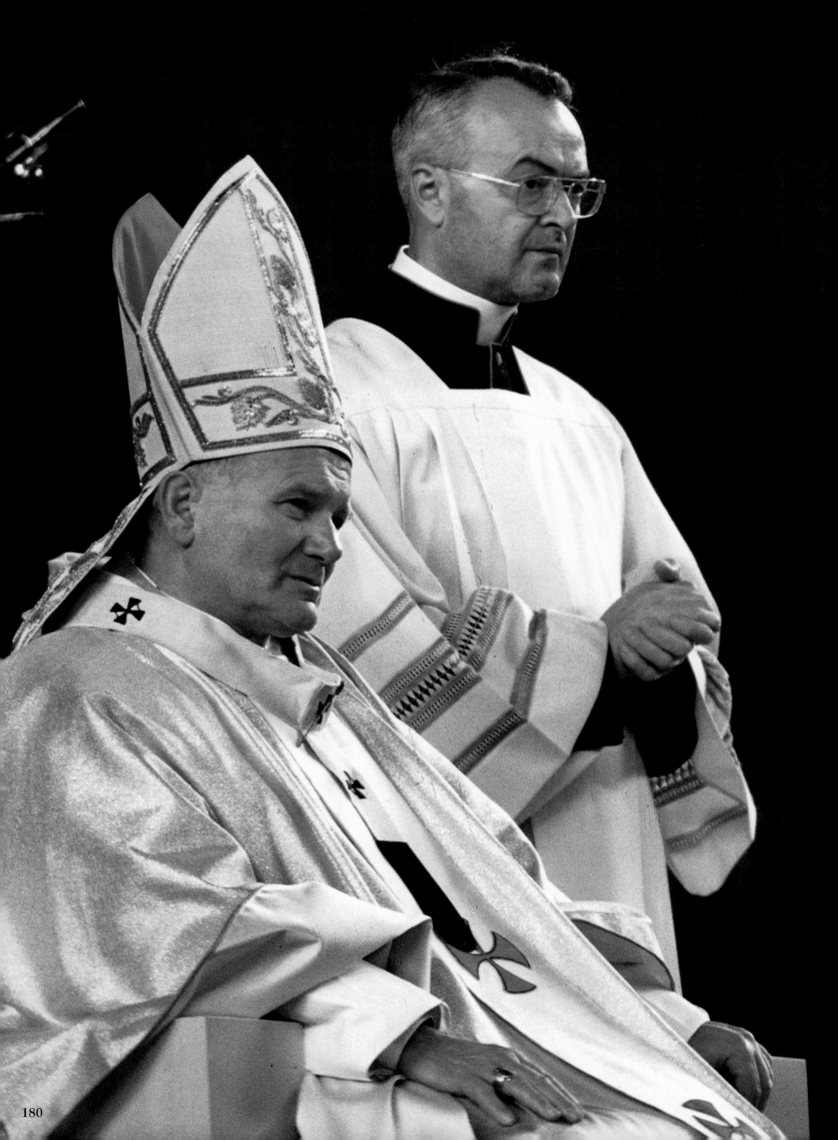

The Pope had come to America tired from an emotional and demanding stay in Ireland. Yet even at the point of exhaustion at the end of each marathon day, he radiated warmth, humor and strength. By the second day in New York, he was visibly at his ease, smiling and waving with delight en route to a morning service at St. Patrick's Cathedral and characteristically embracing any children he encountered.

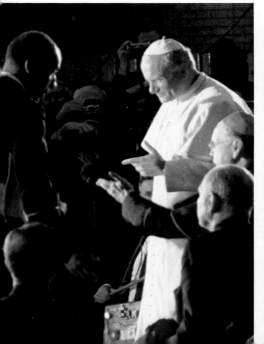

At Shea Stadium, 60,000 people were present for the Pope's final New York appearance. Despite the weather, they listened attentively to his words of farewell: "Above all, a city needs a soul if it is to become a true home for human beings. You, the people must give it soul, by loving each other."

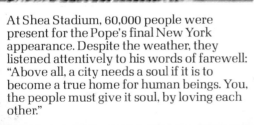

In Philadelphia the Pope celebrated Mass for a huge and enthusiastic congregation in Logan Circle. It was in Philadelphia also that John Paul chose to make a direct and highly controversial pronouncement reaffirming traditional doctrine to 12,000 priests, nuns and seminarians in the Civic Center. Here the Pontiff insisted on the celibacy and the permanency of priesthood and rejected the idea of the ordination of women.

People came by every conceivable means of transport from throughout the Midwest and from as far away as Florida and New Mexico to wait for the Pontiff in a 600-acre expanse of farmland near Des Moines. On first hearing of the Pope's intended visit to America, Joe Hays, a local farmer, had written a note to invite John Paul to Iowa, and so, characteristically, the Pope had arranged to pause here in rural America.

In an address to an extraordinary convocation of 350 U.S. Roman Catholic Bishops in Chicago, the Pope issued the most unequivocal statement of his papacy on artificial contraception. He condemned both the ideology of contraception and contraceptive acts and went on to reiterate the Church's rejection of abortion, of divorce, of homosexual practice and of non-marital sex. Inevitably those who had hoped for more radical views were disappointed but amazingly, the cheering continued.

Pope John Paul II's visit to Washington and his meeting with President Carter were to mark the approaching conclusion of his stay. Throughout his visit he had extolled the freedom which America represented but together with his obvious affection for this land, there was also criticism. His traditional stance had raised many questions but perhaps the greatest mystery lay in the spectacle of countless Americans…Catholics and non-Catholics, religious and atheists… applauding the Pope's attacks on consumerism. It was a tribute to the man and significantly, a tribute to values older than materialism.

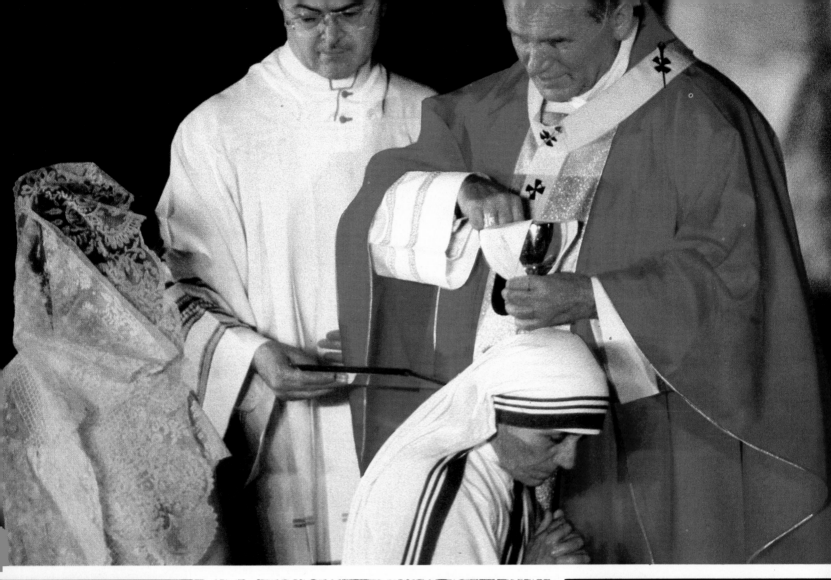

John Paul administers Holy Communion to Mother Theresa (top), founder of the Missionaries of Charity; and offers comfort to compatriot Lech Walesa (above) during the Polish Solidarity crisis. A wider audience (left) heard him in Turkey in 1979, when he celebrated Mass (opposite, top) during his ecumenical tour. (Right) greeting West German cardinals when visiting the Federal Republic in 1980.

195

Kissing the ground wherever he goes symbolises the Pope's embrace of all mankind: John Paul thus honours (left) the Ivory Coast and (above) Kenya. (Top picture) a more expansive gesture in Zaire, where he administered the Sacrament to Kinshasa's police.

(Above) jubilation from Brazil's youth during the Pope's busy, twelve-day visit in July 1980. (Left and top) a compassionate Pope comforting a young girl at Bahia, where his itinerary included a visit to a centre for the care of lepers. (Overleaf) spectacularly colossal settings for the celebration of Mass. On one occasion over a million people packed Rio de Janiero's Flamengo Waterfront Park to see him administer the Sacrament.

Blue skies, bunting and festive crowds greeted the Pope in the Philippines during his 1981 Far Eastern tour. 'Long Live the Holy Father' is a message which finds a place in every capital city he visits, as it did (top picture) in Manila. (Left) a trio in white: John Paul, President and Mme Marcos on a balcony bedecked with flowers and ribbons in Vatican colours.

Japan provided a sharp contrast in climate as the Pope continued his Far Eastern tour (left and top). The spiritual focus of his visit were pilgrimages to Hiroshima and (right) Nagasaki – both apt settings for his uncompromising speeches against the continuing arms race. (Above) a welcome from President Zia on the Pope's arrival in Pakistan.

(Previous pages) the Holy Father befriends the young innocents of Nigeria during his second visit to the African continent with its plethora of emergent nations. A heartfelt hug for a baby and Confirmation for a teenage boy express his emotive concern for their upbringing as products of an uncertain future: 'This afternoon, the Pope belongs to you,' he announced to another young audience at Onitsha. His Holiness' arrival at Lagos marked the beginning of his first foreign tour since the attempt on his life nine months earlier, and as a special mark of appreciation, fifty-six Nigerian priests concelebrated Mass before over a hundred compatriot clergy and laity in Rome shortly before the Pope left the Vatican. Among those whose privilege it was to see and hear him during this tour were these Nigerian choristers (right), their formal white surplices and blood-red cassocks contrasting strongly with their well-worn and practical footwear; and the Polish community who provided a special welcome for him as he travelled to Lagos Stadium to celebrate Mass (opposite top). He repaid their loyalty with a meeting for Polish community delegates at the papal nunciature. During the same tour, the Pope ordained over a hundred Nigerian priests in an impressive outdoor ceremony at Kaduna (above and overleaf), where Nigerian national flags alternated with crucifixes showing Nigeria's vision of Christ.

'The Holy Father,' said the Vatican-based Fr Boniface Asuzu, shortly before the Pope left Rome for Lagos, 'is putting into practice the commission to preach the Good News to all nations, and it is as comforting as it is praiseworthy that this apostolic zeal of the Holy Father impels him to leave the Vatican several times a year to proclaim the liberating Good News to all races and cultures.' No more compelling evidence of the immensity of the Pope's audiences could be imagined than the vast crowds that hailed him in the heat and dust of Lagos, as he made his way to the Stadium in a Land Rover which his hosts had painted in the distinctive and brilliant colours of the Vatican national flag. (Overleaf and subsequent pages) a Pope by turns smiling and contemplative, serene and eventually slightly dishevelled after a busy and enervating first day in Lagos. His five-day visit to Nigeria took him to five major towns and involved the celebration of five Masses. 'I would ask you,' he told President Shagari on his arrival, 'to consider me one of your own, for indeed I come to this land as a friend and a brother to all its inhabitants.' He looked forward to a time when Nigeria would 'astound the world by its achievements', but be able also to 'share its wisdom and sense of life.'

Contrasting moods during the Pope's visit to Portugal, May 1982. (Right) a sobering homily at the Catholic University in Lisbon and (above and top) a tumultuous welcome in the centre of the capital as he arrived to celebrate Mass (left and overleaf).

A moment of history – John Paul II (left) became the first Pope to bring his blessing upon his Catholic flock in the United Kingdom to them in person, in the first reciprocal act of its kind to the many visits made to the Vatican by British sovereigns and government representatives since the breach with Rome in the sixteenth century. Though it was primarily a visit to British Catholics – 'In this England of fair and generous minds,' the Pope said, 'no-one will begrudge the Catholic community pride in its own history' – the tour had wider and more controversial overtones. It very nearly didn't happen at all, and only frantic efforts to find acceptable formulae prevented the Anglo-Argentinian conflict over the Falkland Islands from causing a cancellation of the Holy Father's visit. It was well worth those efforts: crowds overflowed Wembley Stadium in North London where he came to celebrate Mass (right), and the ecumenical visit to Canterbury Cathedral was paralleled in Edinburgh where, in addition to meeting priests of his own religion in the Cathedral (above), the Pope also conferred with Scotland's Jewish, Protestant and Islamic leaders. At Southwark Cathedral in London, His Holiness presided at a moving para-liturgical ceremony for the sick and disabled (overleaf, left) and spoke to the thousands outside the Cathedral beforehand (overleaf, right).

'My visit,' the Pope said while in England, 'takes place at a time when the world's attention has been focused on the delicate situation in the South Atlantic. In a world scarred by hatred and injustice, and divided by violence and oppression, the Church desires to be a spokesman for the vital task of fostering harmony and unity, and forging new bonds of understanding and brotherhood.' So it was that, in a hastily-arranged pilgrimage of impartiality, the Pope visited Argentina less than a fortnight after his departure from the United Kingdom. He was greeted at the Casa Ronda in Buenos Aires by President Galtieri (left) and members of his junta (right), before appearing in front of a huge and ecstatic crowd (above), who made no secret of their welcome for him or of the hopes they vested in him for peace. 'The Father of Reconciliation' was how one banner described him (overleaf, bottom left) in a visually even-handed sentiment. A local version of the ubiquitous 'popemobile' took him from place to place under a yellow and white canopy, while the proud azure and white of Argentina's national flag fluttered about him and draped the balconies from which he spoke. The visit had a pastoral purpose too, since his last day in Argentina brought him to a meeting with the representatives of the Latin American Episcopal Conference.

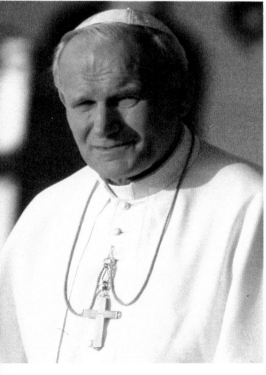

The Pope arriving at Madrid Airport on his first visit to Spain (right), and (left) meeting the King and Queen at St Jaime Cathedral. Nuns gave him an enthusiastic reception at Alba de Tormes (above), where he listened attentively (overleaf, left) to a formal welcome. (Overleaf, right) elevating the host at an open-air Mass in Avila.

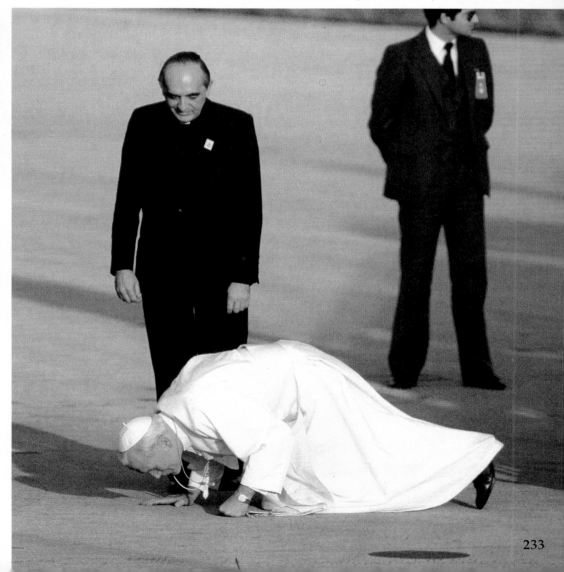

The Pope is always assured of a huge
following in Italy, and whole cities respond
to his frequent pastoral visits throughout
the length of the country. These scenes
were photographed during his November
1982 visit to Sicily, where a service with
the Orthodox Church (right) extended his
quest toward Christian unity.

A monumental tour of Central America in 1983 took John Paul II to eight countries in eight hectic days. He timed the visit to take place during Lent, 'the season which leads us to Christ in its history of pain and of hope, in the bloody tragedy of Good Friday, inseparable from the Easter joy of his triumph over death and suffering.' It was his seventeenth apostolic mission outside Italy, and his theme of peace, justice and brotherhood took its example from his first port of call – Costa Rica. Despite an unfortunate tumble as he stepped from his aircraft (right) he seemed more than usually content to be in a country which loves peace so profoundly that it has long since abolished its own army. He was greeted by President Luis Monge, his wife and daughter (opposite, below) after a triumphal motorcade procession through the main streets of San José in a vehicle which paraded his papal coat of arms as well as the Costa Rican national flag (left). The transparent happiness of that visit was in stark contrast to the tensions of many other Central American nations, especially Haiti where he denounced the injustice and abuse for which that country has long been well known, and curtailed a visit to President Duvalier who had greeted him on his arrival (overleaf, below right).

(Top) the Pope at the opening of the conference of Latin American bishops, Port-au-Prince Cathedral, Haiti. (Left) a gentle greeting to crowds in Honduras and (opposite top) in Guatemala City. (Right) the welcoming message writ large at Panama Airport.

'I come as a messenger of peace, as a sustainer of hope, as a servant of faith... to fill souls with sentiments of brotherhood and of reconciliation.' Thus, Pope John Paul II on his arrival in Nicaragua. He described his host country as 'a land of lakes and volcanoes', but it was into a political and diplomatic volcano that he had come. A virulently left-wing government had taken power three years earlier, and was still stridently campaigning to maintain an order which admitted no rival except poverty and squalor. The Pope's short visit to Leon and Managua, therefore, brought him past dilapidated, gutted buildings (above), victims of the recent struggles for power, and into contact with a war-weary people who clung to their Catholic faith as if it were the only thing left to them. The Holy Father's addresses – indeed the services he conducted – were given against an overpowering backdrop of political images and ideological messages (right), and one Mass was so effectively fragmented by the shouting of party slogans that he felt moved to express his disappointment and anger. At Leon he allowed himself to look patently saddened as he left the war-scarred Cathedral (left), despite a huge placard way above its West Door which bore his portrait and the words 'Leon loves and acclaims you'.

A pilgrim amongst pilgrims, John Paul II spent an unforgettable twenty-four hours at the Shrine of Our Lady of Lourdes – unforgettable both for him, for the citizens of Lourdes, and indeed for the people of France. President Mitterand was at Tarbes Airport to welcome him (below), and to express his pleasure at meeting 'the man who has made himself the apostle of great causes'. Huge bouquets of flowers, predominantly yellow and white, were presented to the Pope (left) by the children of Tarbes, before he travelled to nearby Lourdes, with its profusion of narrow streets packed with admirers and full of the sound of church bells. His destination was the grotto of Bernadette (overleaf and subsequent pages), the girl to whom the Virgin Mary had appeared eighteen times a century and a quarter earlier. The Pope paid a later, evening visit to the grotto to say the Rosary in front of the pale blue and white image of the Madonna, and was afterwards joined by thousands of the faithful in one of the most spectacular acts of prayer to the Virgin, and demonstrations of loyalty to the Church and its Pope – a huge candlelit procession (following pages) in which John Paul himself carried a lighted torch as a symbol of unity with his flock and of devotion to the singular mission of the Church.

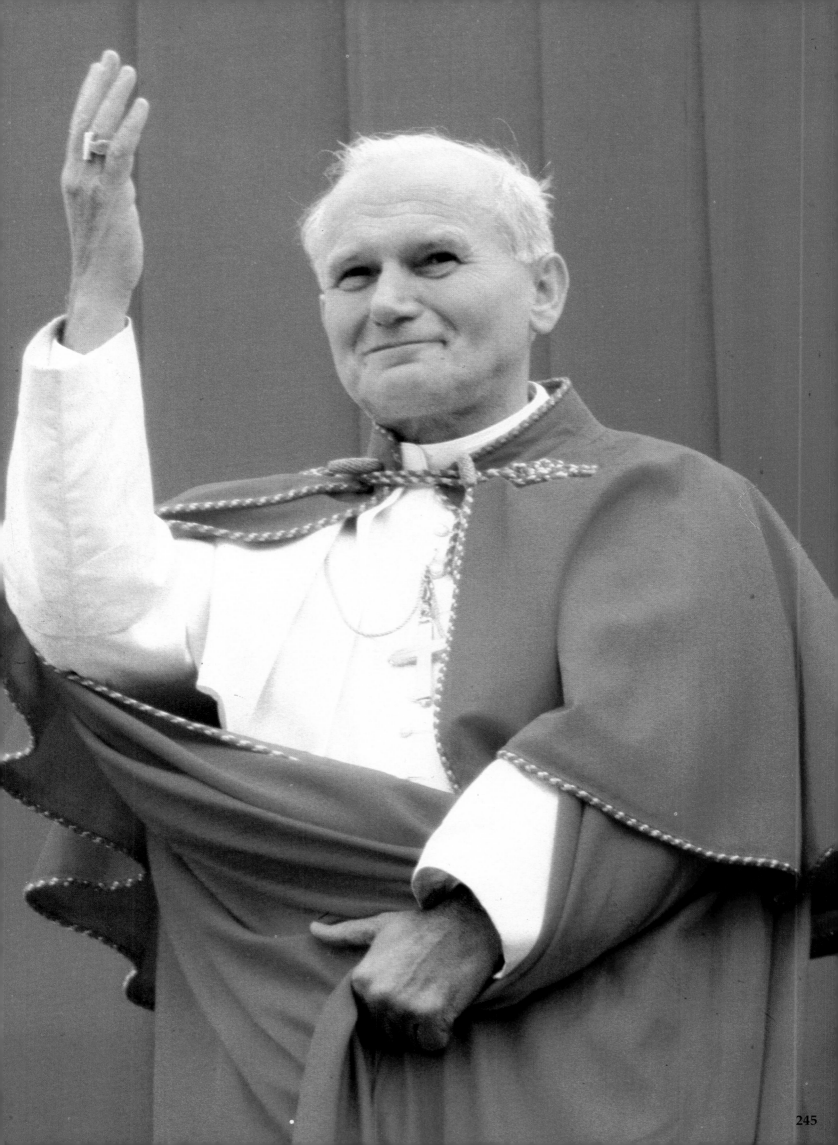

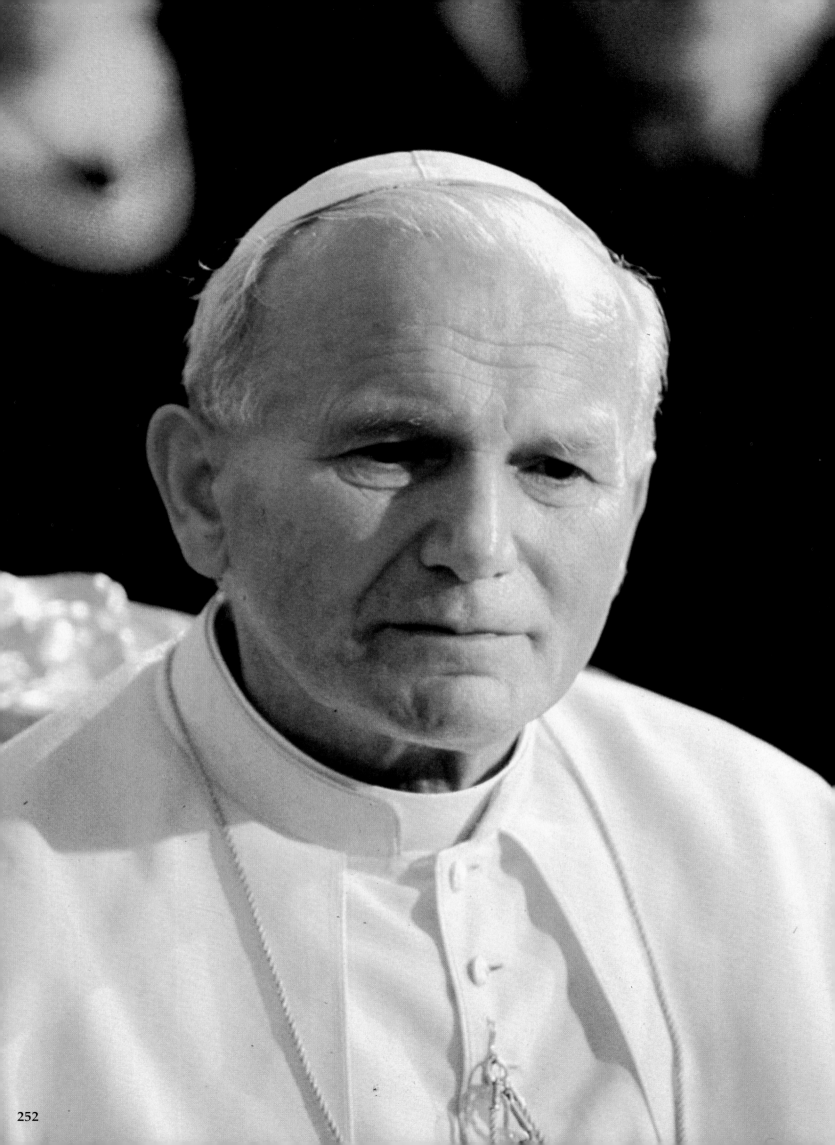

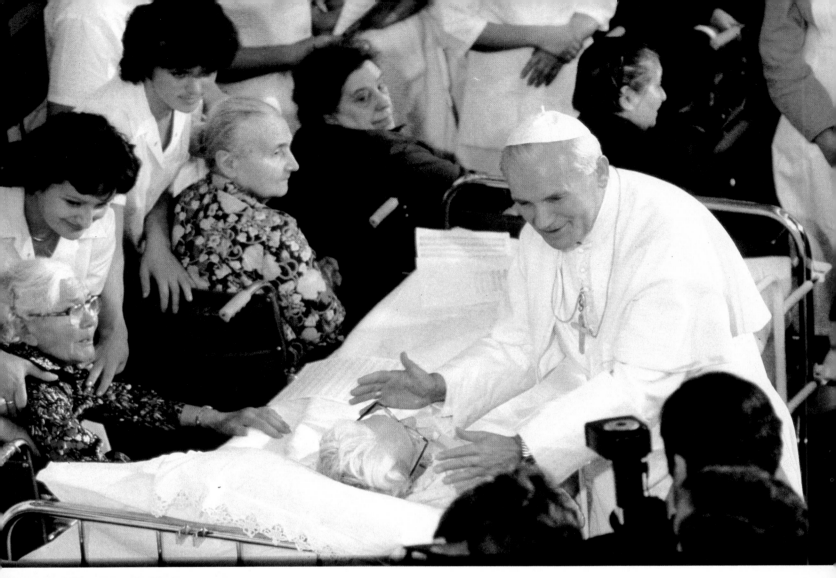

Personal moments in Austria in September 1983: (above) the Pope with a young Viennese girl; (top) visiting the sick on his first full day in Austria; (right) about to attend Mass at St Stephen's Cathedral in Vienna.

253

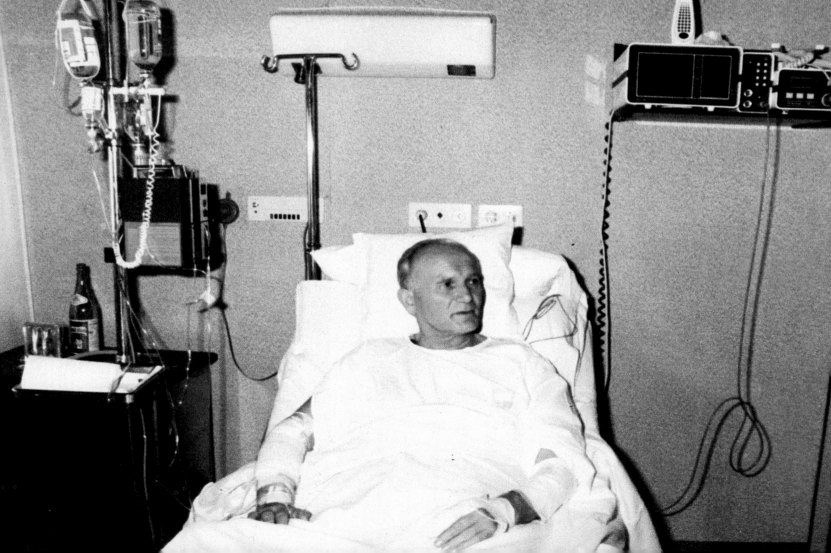

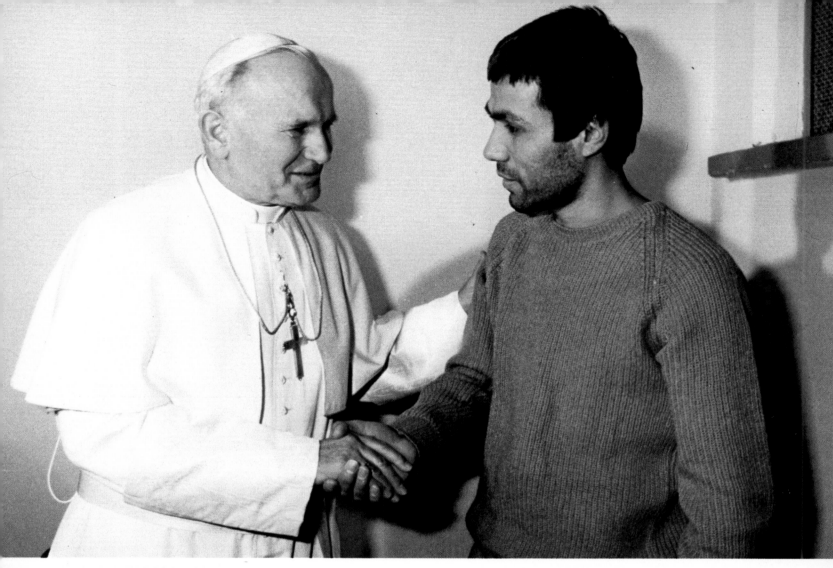

Hatred turned to friendship. (Opposite page, top) the dramatic moment of the assassination attempt against the Pope in May 1981; the Holy Father slumps back as scuffles in the crowd direct horrified faces towards the assailant. (Opposite page, below) the Pope recovering in the Gemelli Hospital – his right arm and left hand heavily bandaged. (Above) John Paul leaving the Rebibbia Prison after his historic meeting with the would-be assassin, Mehmet Ali Agca, in his cell (right) – a meeting of explanation, forgiveness and ultimate reconciliation (top).

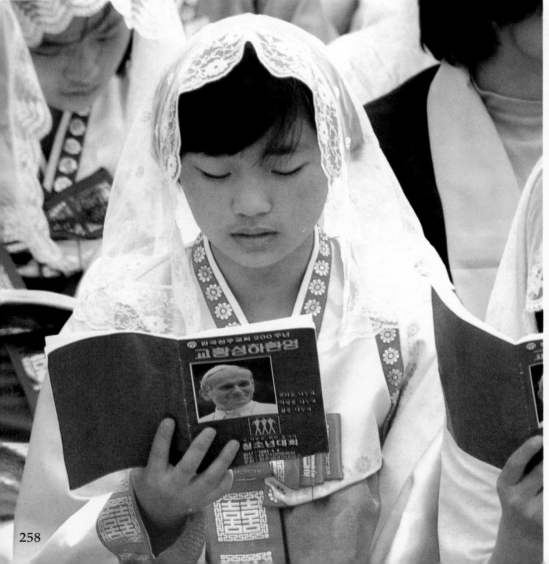

(Top, right, and previous pages) a brilliant setting for the Pope's visit to South Korea. (Left and overleaf) sections of the crowds who came for a glimpse or a blessing.

(Previous pages) the Pope confirming young Koreans during ceremonies in Seoul. (These and following pages) a riot of traditional colour to complement the dazzling effect of acres of flowers, the brightly-covered stands and the massive white symbols of the Christian faith standing against the perfect blue skies: choirs, audiences of the adult faithful, and immense crowds of schoolchildren who shouted for him, waved flags at him, or joined in his devotions, made every stage of Pope John Paul's South Korean pilgrimage a memorable one.

From Korea, the Pope travelled to Papua New Guinea on the second leg of his second Far Eastern tour. At Port Moresby, he kissed the ground (opposite page, top) as his first act of homage, and enjoyed an unusual kind of walkabout (left) as he met lines of welcoming tribesmen.

(Previous pages) the whole of Mount Hagen seemed to be out to greet John Paul as his endless motorcade took him to a huge park on the outskirts of this Highland centre. Thousands of tribesmen from up to a hundred miles away had made the journey on foot to welcome him with traditional dances. For them all, it was their first sight of this white-clad figure from the West, and flags (above) and booklets (right) helped to create the sense of occasion. A simple garland gave the Pope great pleasure (opposite).

(Above and left) the Holy Father deep in public, and private, prayer on two occasions during his visit to the Solomon Islands, having arrived in Honiara from Papua. Alongside the inevitable Catholic ceremonies (right) were more local rituals, such as painting-in the eye of the Chinese dragon (overleaf).

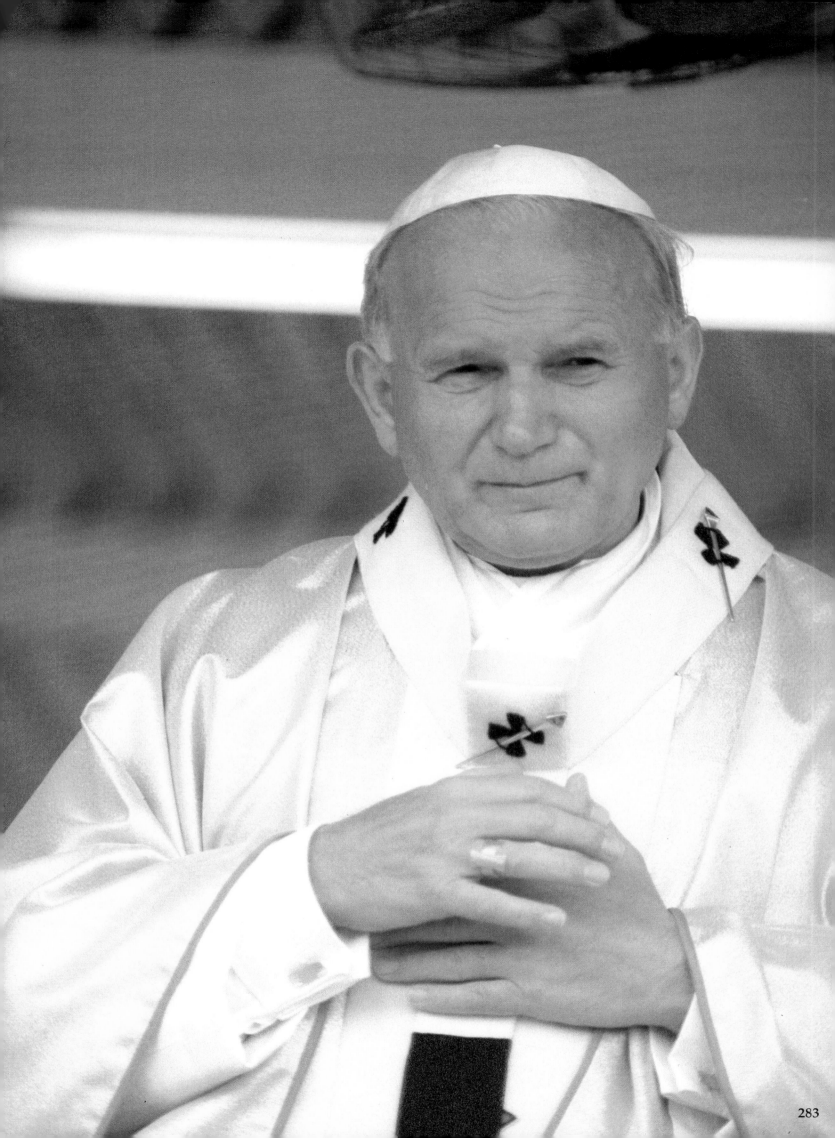

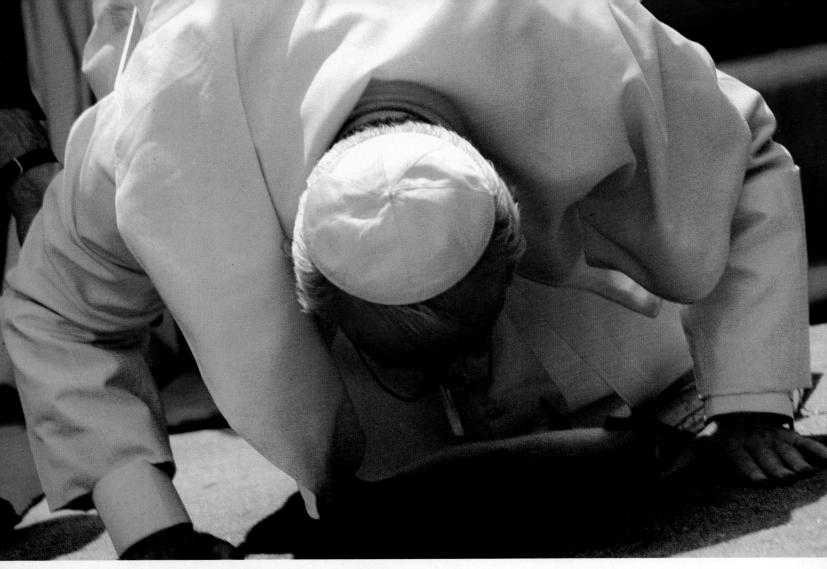

The last stage of the nine-day Papal tour of the Far East took John Paul to Thailand where, on arrival at Bangkok (above), he was garlanded with a decoration of beads, and officially welcomed by the country's Crown Prince (right). On his crowded itinerary were an ordination Mass at Sanpran, a meeting with members of the Thai government and the diplomatic corps at Bangkok's Government Palace, an address to the Thai Episcopal Conference at St Louis' Hospital Chapel, Bangkok, and a meeting with clergy and laity at the capital's Cathedral of the Assumption. The splendour of one of Thailand's sumptuous Roman Catholic temples (overleaf, left) contrasted with a brief, depressing, but significant visit to the refugee camp at Phanat Nikhom, the temporary home of seventeen thousand otherwise homeless victims of the wars in neighbouring countries, who had sought asylum in Thailand. The setting for a Mass which the Pope celebrated in the centre of Bangkok was magnificent and expansive (overleaf, top right) as were the surroundings of the royal palace where His Holiness met King Bhumibhol, Queen Sirikit, and members of their immediate family (overleaf, bottom right).

Pope John Paul visited Switzerland for six days in June 1984.
Impeccable hospitality (above) greeted him everywhere, and the
skills of the local alpenhorn experts provided interest and
entertainment for him (top). There were more serious moments,
however: the earnestness of the Papal blessing (opposite page,
top); the concentration of prayer at a Mass in Fribourg (right);
and contact with the sick at Einseideln (opposite page, bottom).

A contrast in styles. The Pope with his Swiss cardinals at Zurich Airport (left), and combining mission with his love of sport in the Swiss Alps in July 1984 (this page). Two months earlier (overleaf) the Pope met President Reagan in Alaska.

(Previous pages) one of the most spectacular ceremonies of the Pope's tour of Canada in September 1984 – a combination of secular festivity and religious devotion in which fifty-five thousand young people participated at Montreal's Olympic Stadium. Interspersed with the hymn-singing, the prayers and the Holy Father's address was a programme of music and dancing, the orchestrated fluttering of white scarves, and this display by religious workers standing in formation to spell out 'John Paul' in front of his dais. Earlier, in the first ceremony of its kind in Canada, he had beatified Mother Marie Leonie Paradis, New Brunswick's founder of the Little Sisters of the Holy Family a century before. In his address on that occasion, the Pope talked of the role of women in the Church, though he made no mention of their ordination, an issue on which his conservative views had caused considerable discontent among Montreal's female Catholics. (These pages and overleaf) more memorable scenes from the Pope's 12-day visit, of which perhaps the most picturesque interlude was his voyage along the Rideau Canal (left and right) on his last day in Ottawa. He travelled in a bullet-proof boat which looked, according to one observer, like a spruced-up version of *The African Queen* with a huge cross instead of a chimney! Large crowds greeted the Pope everywhere, as (above) at Edmonton, Alberta.

(Previous pages) more examples of the colossal gatherings that Pope John Paul's Canadian tour involved, whether at airports on the outskirts of major cities (bottom left), or in the vast parks within (top left). Part of his itinerary took in the Maritime Provinces: his famous 'popemobile' was almost engulfed by crowds during a seven-hour visit to Moncton (bottom right), while at the little fishing village of Flatrock, near St. John's, a much smaller local congregation watched him bless some four dozen fishing smacks and skiffs, which bobbed in the water nearby (top right). During this part of the tour, the Pope met fifteen crew members of a Polish sail-training ship which had made a detour to Newfoundland to pick up provisions, and he gave them a rosary each to take home to their families. (These pages) the Pope (left) with Canada's Governor-General, Mme Jeanne Sauvé, and the newly-elected Prime Minister, Mr Brian Mulroney at Government House, Ottawa, on his penultimate day in Canada. All are evidently happy that the feared cancellation of the visit because of state elections was ultimately avoided. Much of His Holiness' time was devoted to the North American Indians, whose compounds he visited (below) in order to share their tribal ceremonies and listen to their long-standing grievances (overleaf) concerning land rights and the preservation of their heritage.

More encounters with Canada's Indians.
At the shrine of St Anne de Beaupré, near
Quebec (top), they presented the
Pope with beaver skins, caribou hide boots,
and even a leather mitre.

The Pope's visit to the Beaupré Indians was the first of three such meetings. The shrine there is dedicated to St Anne – 'the grandmother of the Catholic Indians' – and is festooned with the discarded crutches and trusses of those who have been cured there. The Pope honoured the Blessed Kateri Tekakwitha, an Indian girl persecuted in the seventeenth century for her Christian beliefs. (Left) maple-leaf and fleur-de-lys flags alternate with the Papal standards.

(Previous four pages) Pope John Paul attending a Mass in Winnipeg. (Left and right) the Pope delivering an address, despite the assaults of the weather, during an outdoor Mass at the Basilica of Notre Dame at Lebreton Flats, just beside the Ottawa River. It was the final day of the tour which had taken him to all but two of Canada's provinces – his twenty-third visit outside Italy, and his longest stay in any one country. It was marked by huge and consistent enthusiasm on the part of the Canadians and, for the Pope's own part, a concentration on the themes of economic and military policies. In Newfoundland he had denounced the 'blight of unemployment' and attacked fishing monopolies. At Edmonton, he warned of the growing rift between rich and poor nations. In Quebec, he spoke of the lessons to be learned from what he admitted as the Roman Catholic Church's initial blunders on first encountering Indian civilisations four centuries ago. And on this occasion in Ottawa, he urged a reaction against 'the breathtaking spiral of armaments presented as being at the service of world peace'. Nor did he forget the Polish community in a country with scores of ethnic groups. As the photograph (overleaf) shows, emigrant Poles welcomed him with redoubled vigour to remind him that, however cosmopolitan he has become, John Paul II is still very much a son of Poland.

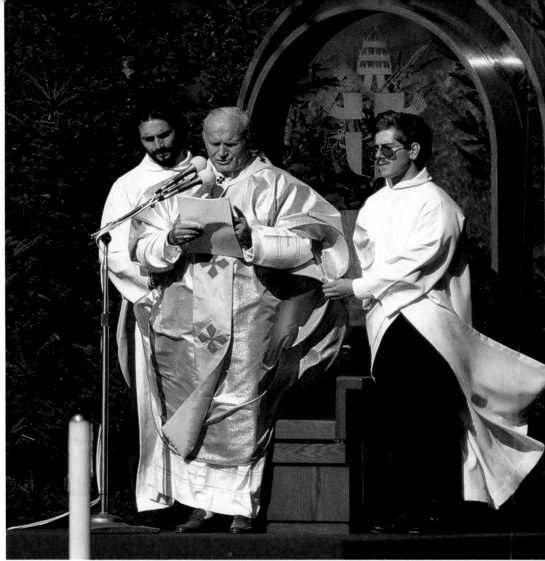

PASTORAL VISITS

The Dominican Republic and Mexico

January 25 to 31, 1979

On Monday, January 29 Pope John Paul II arrived at Cuilapan in Mexico, where over half a million Indios from the regions of Oaxaco, Chiapas and other parts of the country had gathered to meet with him. The following is an extract from the Pope's address on this occasion.

'Before this imposing spectacle reflected in my eyes, I cannot but think of the identical picture that my predecessor Paul VI contemplated, ten years ago, in his memorable visit to Colombia and, more concretely, in his meeting with the peasants.

'I want to repeat with him – if it were possible in an even stronger tone of voice – that the present Pope wishes "to be in solidarity with your cause, which is the cause of humble people, of the poor". The Pope is with these masses of the population that are "nearly always abandoned at an ignoble level of life and sometimes harshly treated and exploited".

'Adopting the line of my predecessors John XXIII and Paul VI, as well as that of the Second Vatican Council, and in view of a situation that continues to be alarming, not often better and sometimes even worse, the Pope wishes to be your voice, the voice of those who cannot speak or who are silenced, in order to be the conscience of consciences, an invitation to action, in order to make up for lost time which is often time of prolonged suffering and unsatisfied hopes.

'The depressed rural world, the worker who with his sweat waters also his affliction, cannot wait any longer for full and effective recognition of his dignity, which is not inferior to that of any other social sector. He has the right to be respected and not to be deprived, with manoeuvres which are sometimes tantamount to real spoliation, of the little that he has. He has the right to be rid of the barriers of exploitation, often made up of intolerable selfishness, against which his best efforts of advancement are shattered. He has the right to real help – which is not charity or crumbs of justice – in order that he may have access to the development that his dignity as a man and as a son of God deserves.

'Therefore it is necessary to act promptly and in depth. It is necessary to carry out bold changes, which are deeply innovatory. It is necessary to undertake urgent reforms without waiting any longer.

'It cannot be forgotten that the measures to be taken must be adequate. The Church does indeed defend the legitimate right to private property, but She also teaches no less clearly that there is always a social mortgage on all private property, in order that goods may serve the general purpose that God gave them. And if the common good requires it, there should be no hesitation even at expropriation, carried out in the due form.

'The agricultural world has great importance and great dignity. It is just this world that offers society the products necessary for its nutrition. It is a task that deserves the appreciation and grateful esteem of all, which is a recognition of the dignity of those engaged in it.

'...An evil that is quite widespread is the tendency to individualism among rural workers, whereas a better co-ordinated and united action could be of great help. Think of this too, dear sons.

'...On your side, leaders of the peoples, powerful classes which sometimes keep unproductive lands that hide the bread that so many families lack, human conscience, the conscience of peoples, the cry of the destitute, and above all the voice of God, the voice of the Church, repeat to you with me: it is not just, it is not human, it is not Christian to continue with certain situations that are clearly unjust. It is necessary to carry out real, effective measures – at the local, national, and international level... It is clear that those who must collaborate most in this, are those who can do most.'

Poland

June 2 to 10, 1979

On the morning of Saturday, June 2 Pope John Paul met the leaders of the Polish Government in the Belvedere Palace in Warsaw. The following is an extract from his address on this occasion.

'We Poles feel in a particularly deep way the fact that the raison d'être of the State is the sovereignty of society, of the nation, of the motherland. We have learned this during the whole course of our history, and especially through the hard trials of recent centuries. We can never forget that terrible historical lesson – the loss of the independence of Poland from the end of the eighteenth century until the beginning of the twentieth. This painful and essentially negative experience has become as it were a new forge of Polish patriotism. For us, the word 'motherland' has a meaning, both for the mind and for the heart, such as the other nations of Europe and the world appear not to know, especially those nations that have not experienced, as ours has, historical wrongs, injustices and menaces.

'... the Church... everywhere and always strives to make people better, more conscious of their dignity, and more devoted in their lives to their family, social, professional and patriotic commitments. It is Her mission to make people more confident, more courageous, conscious of their rights and duties, socially responsible, creative and useful.

'For this activity the Church does not desire privileges, but only and exclusively what is essential for the accomplishment of Her mission. And it is this direction that orientates the activity of the Episcopate... In seeking, in this field, an agreement with the State Authorities, the Apostolic See is aware that, over and above reasons connected with creating the conditions for the Church's all-round activity, such an agreement corresponds to historical reasons of the nation, whose sons and daughters, in the vast majority, are the sons and daughters of the Catholic Church. In the light of these undoubted premises, we see such an agreement as one of the elements in the ethical and international order in Europe and the modern world, an order that flows from respect for the rights of the nation and for human rights. I therefore permit myself to express the opinion that one cannot desist from efforts and research in this direction.

'I desire at the end to renew once again my cordial thanks to you and... I add the expression of my regard for all of you, the distinguished representatives of the Authorities, and for each one in particular, according to the dignity you hold, as also according to the important part of responsibility that is incumbent on each one of you before history and before your conscience.

In the afternoon of the same day the Pope celebrated Mass in Victory Square in Warsaw for a gathering of hundreds of thousands of the faithful. The following is an extract from the homily he delivered on this occasion.

'It is... impossible without Christ to understand the history of the Polish nation – this great thousand-year-old community – that is so profoundly decisive for me and each one of us. If we reject this key to understanding our nation, we lay ourselves open to a substantial misunderstanding. We no longer understand ourselves. It is impossible without Christ to understand this nation with its past so full of splendour and also of terrible difficulties.

'... We are before the tomb of the Unknown Soldier. In the ancient and contempory history of Poland this tomb has a special basis, a special reason for its existence. In how many places in our native land has that soldier fallen! In how many places in Europe and the world has he cried with his death that there can be no just Europe without the independence of Poland marked on its map! On how many battlefields has that soldier given witness to the rights of man, indelibly inscribed in the inviolable rights of the people, by falling for "our freedom and yours"!

'... I wish to kneel before this tomb to venerate every seed that falls into the earth and dies and thus bears fruit. It may be the seed of the blood of a soldier shed on the battlefield, or the sacrifice of martyrdom in concentration camps or in prisons. It may be the seed of hard daily toil, with the sweat of one's brow, in the fields, the workshop, the mine, the foundries and the factories. It may be the seed of the love of parents who do not refuse to give life to a new human being and undertake the whole of the task of bringing him up. It may be the seed of creative work in the universities, the higher institutes, the libraries and the places where the national culture is built. It may be the seed of prayer, of service of the sick, the suffering, the abandoned – "all that of which Poland is made".

'... I cry – I who am a son of the land of Poland and who am also Pope John Paul II – I cry from all the depths of this Millennium, I cry on the vigil of Pentecost:
Let your Spirit descend.
Let your Spirit descend,
and renew the face of the earth,
the face of this land.
Amen.'

Ireland

September 29 to October 1, 1979

On Saturday, September 29, 1979 Pope John Paul II travelled to Killineer near Drogheda, in the Archdiocese of Armagh, where he delivered an address to a gathering of about three hundred thousand people. The following is an extract from this strong appeal for peace and reconciliation in Ireland.

'... the tragic events taking place in Northern Ireland do not have their source in the fact of belonging to different Churches and Confessions... this is not... a religious war, a struggle between Catholics and Protestants. On the contrary, Catholics and Protestants, as people who confess Christ, taking inspiration from their faith and the Gospel, are seeking to draw closer to one another in unity and peace. When they recall the greatest commandment of Christ, the commandment of love, they cannot behave otherwise.

'But Christianity does not command us to close our eyes to difficult human problems. It does not permit us to neglect and refuse to see unjust social or international situations. What Christianity does forbid is to seek solutions to these situations by the ways of hatred, by the murdering of defenceless people, by the methods of terrorism. Let me say more: Christianity understands and recognizes the noble and just struggle for justice: but Christianity is decisively opposed to fomenting hatred and to promoting or provoking violence or struggle for the sake of 'struggle'. The command, 'Thou shalt not kill', must be binding on the conscience of humanity, if the terrible tragedy and destiny of Cain is not to be repeated.

'... This is my mission, my message to you: Jesus Christ who is our peace. Christ "is our peace" (Eph. 2:11). And today and for ever He repeats to us: "My peace I give to you, my peace I leave with you" (John 14:27).

'... peace cannot be established by violence, peace can never flourish in a climate of terror, intimidation and death. It is Jesus himself who said; "All who take the sword will perish by the sword" (Matt. 26:52). This is the word of God, and it commands this generation of violent men to desist from hatred and violence and to repent.

'I join my voice today to the voice of Paul VI and to my other predecessors, to the voices of your religious leaders, to the voices of all men and women of reason, and I proclaim, with the conviction of my faith in Christ and with an awareness of my mission, that violence is evil, that violence is unacceptable as a solution to problems, that violence is unworthy of man. Violence is a lie, for it goes against the truth of our humanity. Violence destroys what it claims to defend: the dignity, the life, the freedom of human beings. Violence is a crime against humanity, for it destroys the very fabric of society. I pray with you that the moral sense and Christian conviction of Irish men and women may never become obscured and blunted by the lie of violence, that nobody may ever call murder by any other name than murder, that the spiral of violence may never be given the distinction of unavoidable logic or necessary retaliation. Let us remember that the word remains for ever; "All who take the sword will perish by the sword" (Matt. 26:52).

'... I wish to speak to all men and women engaged in violence. I appeal to you, in language of passionate pleading. On my knees I beg you to turn away from the paths of violence and to return to the ways of peace. You may claim to seek justice. I too believe in justice and seek justice. But violence only delays the day of justice. Violence destroys the work of justice. Further violence in Ireland will only drag down to ruin the land you claim to love and the values you claim to cherish. In the name of God I beg you; return to Christ, who died so that men might live in forgiveness and peace. He is waiting for you, longing for each one of you to come to Him so that He may say to each of you: your sins are forgiven, go in peace.

'... To all who bear political responsibility for the affairs of Ireland, I want to speak with the same urgency and intensity... Do not cause or condone or tolerate conditions which give excuse or pretext to men of violence. Those who resort to violence always claim that only violence brings about change. They claim that political action cannot achieve justice. You politicians must prove them to be wrong. You must show that there is a peaceful, political way to justice. You must show that peace achieves the works of justice, and violence does not.'

The United States of America

October 1 to 7, 1979

On Tuesday, October 2 His Holiness John Paul II delivered an appeal for peace and the protection of human rights to the General Assembly of the United Nations in New York. The following is an extract from this address.

'Now, availing myself of the solemn occasion of my meeting with the representatives of the nations of the earth, I wish above all to send my greetings to all the men and women living on this planet, to every man and every woman without any exception whatever. Every human being living on earth is a member of a civil society, of a nation, many of them represented here.

'... towards the end of the terrible Second World War, the Charter of the United Nations was signed and on the following 24 October your Organisation began its life. Soon after, on 10 December 1948, came its fundamental document, the Universal Declaration of Human Rights, the rights of the human being as an... individual and of the human being in his universal value. This document is a milestone on the long and difficult path of the human race. The progress of humanity must be measured not only by the progress of science and technology, which shows man's uniqueness with regard to nature, but also and chiefly by the primacy given to the spiritual values and the progress of moral life.

'... This Declaration was paid for by millions of our brothers and sisters at the cost of their suffering and sacrifice, brought about by the brutalization that darkened and made insensitive the human consciences of their oppressors, and of those who carried out a real genocide. This price cannot have been paid in vain! The Universal Declaration of Human Rights... must remain the basic value in the United Nations Organisation with which the consciences of its members must be confronted and from which they must draw continual inspiration.

'... Fourteen years ago, my great predecessor, Pope Paul VI, spoke from this podium, he spoke memorable words which I desire to repeat today: "No more war. War never again. Never one against the other, or even one above the other, but always, on every occasion, with each other."

'Paul VI was a tireless servant of the cause of peace. I wish to follow him with all my strength, and continue his service. The Catholic Church in every place on earth proclaims a message of peace, prays for peace, educates for peace. This purpose is also shared by the representatives and followers of other churches and communities and of other religions of the world, and they have pledged themselves to it.

'... I consider that the famous opening words of the Charter of the United Nations – in which the peoples of the United Nations, determined to save succeeding generations from the scourge of war, solemnly reaffirmed faith in fundamental human rights, in the dignity and worth of the human person, in the equal rights of men and women and of nations large and small – are meant to stress this dimension.

'... An analysis of the history of mankind, especially at its present stage, shows how important is the duty of revealing more fully the range of the goods that are linked with the spiritual dimension of human existence. It shows how important this task is for building peace and how serious is any threat to human rights. Any violation of them even in a peace situation is a form of warfare against humanity.

'... I would now like to draw attention to a second systematic threat to man in his inalienable rights in the modern world, a threat which constitutes no less a danger than the first to the cause of peace. I refer to the various forms of injustice in the field of the spirit.

'Man can indeed be wounded in his inner relationship with truth in his conscience, in his most personal belief, in his view of the world, in his religious faith, and in the sphere of what are known as civil liberties. Decisive for these last, is equality of rights without discrimination on grounds of origin, race, sex, nationality, religion, political convictions and the like.

'... For centuries, the thrust of civilization has been in one direction – that of giving the life of individual political societies a form in which there can be fully safeguarded the objective rights of the spirit of human conscience and of human creativity, including man's relationship with God.

'... It is a question of the highest importance that in internal social life as well as in international life, all human beings in every nation and country should be able to enjoy effectively their full rights under any political regime or system.

'Only the safeguarding of this real completeness of rights for every human being, without discrimination, can insure peace at its very roots.

'... I hope that each person will live and grow strong with the moral force of the community that forms its members as citizens. I hope that the state authorities, while respecting the just rights of each citizen, will enjoy the confidence of all for the common good.

'I hope that all the nations, even the smallest, even those that do not yet enjoy full sovereignty, and those that have been forcibly robbed of it, will meet in full equality with the others in the United Nations Organisation. I hope that the United Nations will ever remain the supreme forum of peace and justice, the authentic seat of freedom of peoples and individuals in their longing for a better future.'

Turkey

November 28 to 30, 1979

On the morning of Friday, November 30, the Feast of St Andrew, the Pope was present at the Byzantine Liturgy of St John Chrysotom, concelebrated in the Greek Orthodox Cathedral of St George at Phanar by the Ecumenical Patriarch, His Holiness Dimitrios I, and the Holy Synod. The following is an extract from the discourse given by Pope John Paul II at the end of the Liturgy. In this he refers to the joint Declaration signed by the Ecumenical Patriarch and himself, in which they announced the beginning of a theological dialogue between the Roman Catholic and the Orthodox Church, and the constitution of a mixed Catholic-Orthodox Commission to be responsible for this dialogue.

'With realism and wisdom, in conformity with the wish of the Apostolic See of Rome and also with the desire of the pan-Orthodox Conferences, it had been decided to re-establish relations and contacts between the Catholic Church and the Orthodox Churches which would make it possible to recognise each other and create the atmosphere necessary for a fruitful theological dialogue. It was necessary to create again the context before trying to rewrite the texts together.

'This period has rightly been called the dialogue of charity. This dialogue has made it possible to become aware again of the deep communion that already unites us, and enables us to consider each other and treat each other as sister-Churches. A great deal has already been done, but this effort must be continued.

'... This theological dialogue which is about to begin now will have the task of overcoming the misunderstandings and disagreements which still exist between us, if not at the level of faith, at least at the level of theological formulation. It should take place not only in the atmosphere of the dialogue of charity, which must be developed and intensified, but also in an atmosphere of worship and availability.

'It is only in worship, with a keen sense of the transcendence of the inexpressible mystery "which surpasses knowledge" (Eph. 3:19), that we will be able to size up our divergences and "to lay... no greater burden than these necessary things." (Acts 15:28) to re-establish communion. It seems to me, in fact, that the question we must ask ourselves is not so much whether we still have the right to remain separated. We must ask ourselves this question in the very name of our faithfulness to Christ's will for His Church, for which constant prayer must make us both more and more available in the course of the theological dialogue.

On Friday, November 30 Pope John Paul II celebrated Mass in Latin at an open air altar outside the House of Our Lady in Ephesus. The following is an extract from his address to the gathering, in which the Pope talked again of the need for unity between East and West within the Church.

There is one thing, in particular, that we wish to undertake today at the feet of her who is our common Mother: namely the commitment to push forward, with all our energy and in an attitude of entire availability to the inspirations of the Spirit, along the way that leads to the perfect unity of all Christians. Under her motherly gaze, we are ready to recognise our mutual faults, our selfishness and delays: she gave birth to one Son; we, unfortunately, present Him to her divided. That is a fact that causes uneasiness and suffering in us; an uneasiness and suffering to which my venerated predecessor Pope Paul VI referred at the beginning of the Brief which repealed the excommunication pronounced, very long ago, against the See of Constantinople: "Walk in love, as Christ loved us' (Eph. 5:2). These words of exhortation of the Apostle of the Gentiles concern us, we who are called Christians after the name of our Saviour, and they urge us on, especially in this time which commits us more strongly to expanding the field of love."

'A long way has been covered since that day; but other steps remain to be taken. We entrust to Mary our sincere resolution not to rest until the end of the way is reached. We seem to hear from her lips the Apostle's words: let there be no "quarrelling, jealousy, anger, selfishness, slander, gossip, conceit and disorder" among you (2 Cor. 12:20). Let us accept open-heartedly this motherly admonition and let us ask Mary to be close to us to guide us, with a gentle and firm hand, along the ways of complete and lasting brotherly understanding. In this way there will come true the supreme wish, expressed by her Son when He was about to shed His blood for our redemption: "That they may all be one; even as Thou, Father, art in me, and I in Thee, that they also may be in us, so that the world may believe that Thou has sent me" (John 17:21)'.

Africa

May 2 to 12, 1980

Zaire – May 2 to 5 and 6
The Congo – May 5
Kenya – May 6 to 8
Ghana – May 8 to 10
Upper Volta – May 10
Ivory Coast – May 10 to 12

On Saturday, May 10 Pope John Paul II celebrated Mass near the Cathedral in Oagadougou, the capital city of Upper Volta, for a congregation of many thousands. The following is an extract from the Pope's homily, in which he made an appeal for the drought-stricken people of the Sahel region of West Africa.

'Men are thirsty for love, for brotherly charity, but there are also whole peoples who are thirsty for the water necessary for their life, in special circumstances which are present in my mind, now that I am among you, in this land of Upper Volta, in this area of Sahel. If the problem of the progressive advance of the desert arises also in other regions of the globe, the sufferings of the people of Sahel which the world has witnessed, invite me to speak of it here.

'... a great deal remains to be done, to educate men to respect nature, preserve it and improve it, and also to reduce or prevent the consequences of what are called "natural" catastrophes.

'It is then that human solidarity must be manifested to come to the help of the victims and the countries which cannot cope at once with so many urgent needs, and the economy of which may be ruined. It is a question of international justice, especially with regard to countries that are too often overtaken by these disasters, whereas others are in geographical or climatic conditions which must, in comparison, be called privileged. It is also a question of charity for all those who consider that every man and woman is a brother and a sister whose sufferings must be borne and alleviated by everyone. Solidarity, in justice and charity, must know no frontiers or limits.

'... I cannot give an account of the history and the details of this tragedy: they are in all your memories anyhow. It would be necessary to recall at least the time taken to become aware of the drama brought on by a persistent drought, then the movement of solidarity which spread at all levels, local, national, regional and international. A great deal was done, by the citizens and Governments of the countries concerned as well as by the various international institutions. The Church also played an important part.

'... And yet, how many victims for whom help came too late! How many young people whose development has been stunted or compromised! Even now the danger has not been averted.

'... That is why, from this place, from this capital of Upper Volta, I launch a solemn appeal to the whole world. I, John Paul II, Bishop of Rome and Successor of Peter, raise my suppliant voice, because I cannot be silent when my brothers and sisters are threatened. I become here the voice of those who have no voice, the voice of the innocent, who died because they lacked water and bread; the voice of fathers and mothers who saw their children die without understanding, or who will always see in their children the after-effects of the hunger they suffered; the voice of the generations to come, who must no longer live with this terrible threat weighing upon their lives. I launch an appeal to everyone!

'Let us not wait until the drought returns, terrible and devastating! Let us not wait for the sand to bring death again! Let us not allow the future of these peoples to remain jeopardised for ever! The solidarity shown in the past has proved, through its extent and efficacy, that it is possible to listen only to the voice of justice and charity, and not that of selfishness, individual and collective.

'... You, international organisations, I beg you to continue the remarkable work already carried out; and to speed up the persevering implementation of the programmes of action already drawn up. You, heads of states, I beg you to contribute generous aid to the countries of Sahel, in order that a new effort, a large-scale and sustained one, may remedy even more effectively the drama of drought.

'... I also wish to address particularly your Catholic brothers in the world, those in the most privileged countries... I say to you: now, those who are hungry and thirsty in the world are at your door! Modern means make it possible to help them. You must not rely only on national and international political responsibilities. Beyond the universal duty of solidarity, it is your faith that must lead you to examine your real possibilities, to examine, personally and in the family, if what is too often called necessary is not actually superfluous. It is the Lord who invites us to do more.'

France

May 30 to June 2, 1980

In the evening of Saturday, May 31 the Holy Father concelebrated Mass in the Basilica of Saint-Denis in a working suburb of Paris. The basilica was full, and the Mass was relayed by loudspeaker to the hundreds of thousands of people gathered outside in the square. After the Gospel the Pope went outside the basilica and preached his homily to the crowds. The following is an extract from this address.

'I know that many workers, Frenchmen and foreigners, live and work here, often under precarious conditions as regards housing, wages and jobs.

'... this present day urban life makes human relations difficult, in the hectic rush, never ended, between the place of work, the family lodging and the shopping centres. The integration of the children, of the young, of the old, often raises acute problems.

'... I shall now tackle a difficult reflection on man's work and on justice. Let all those whose lives I have just evoked rest assured that I keep in mind their situation, their efforts, and that I wish to manifest all my affection to them as well as to their families.

'There exists a close connection, there exists a particular connection between man's work and the fundamental environment of human love which bears the name of the family.

'Man has been working from the beginning to subdue the earth and dominate it. We take this definition of work from the first chapters of the Book of Genesis. Man works to earn his living and that of his family. We take this definition of work from the Gospel, from the life of Jesus, Mary and Joseph, and also from everyday experience.

'... When man works to provide for his family's subsistence, that means that he puts all the daily toil of love into his work. For it is love that brings the family into being, it is love that is its constant expression, its stable environment. Man can also love work for work's sake, because it enables him to participate in the great work of dominating the earth, the work willed by the Creator.

'... In the course of my life, I had the... divine grace, to be able to discover fundamental truths about human work, thanks to my personal experience of manual work. I shall remember as long as I live the men with whom I was linked in the same work-yard, whether in the stone quarries or in the factory. I shall not forget the human kindness that my fellow workers showed towards me. I shall not forget the discussions we had, in free moments, on the fundamental problems of existence and of the life of workers. I know what value their home, the future of their children, the respect due to their wives, to their mothers, had for these men, who were at the same time fathers of families. From this experience of some years, I drew the conviction and the certainty that man expresses himself in work as a subject capable of loving, oriented towards fundamental human values, ready for solidarity with every man...

'In my experience of life, I learned what a worker is, and I bear that in my heart. I know that work is also a necessity, sometimes a dire necessity; and yet man wishes to transform it to measure up to his dignity and his love. His grandeur lies in that... It is false to say that the worker has no country. He is, in fact, in a special way, the representative of his people, he is the man of his own house. In human work are inscribed above all the law of love, the need of love, the order of love.

'... The world of human work must therefore be above all a world constructed on moral strength: it must be the world of love, and not the world of hatred. It is the world of construction and not that of destruction. The rights of man, of the family, of the nation, of mankind, are deeply inscribed in human work. The future of the world depends on respect for them.

'... the great society of workers, if they are constructed on moral power – and it should be so! – must consequently remain sensitive to all... dimensions of injustice which have developed in the modern world. They must be capable of struggling nobly for every form of justice: for the real good of man, for all the rights of the person, of the family, of the nation, of mankind.'

Brazil

June 30 to July 11, 1980

On Tuesday, July 1 Pope John Paul II celebrated an open air Mass at the Praca Israel Pinheiro, on the outskirts of Belo Horizonte, for a gathering of young people and students. The following is an extract from the Pope's homily on this occasion.

'The greatest wealth of this country, which is immensely rich, is you. The real future of this "Country of the future" is enclosed in the present of you young people. Therefore this country, and with it the Church, looks to you with expectation and hope.

'Open to the social dimensions of man, you do not conceal your determination to change radically the social structures that you consider unjust. You say, rightly, that it is impossible to be happy when you see a multitude of brothers who lack the minimum required for a life worthy of man. You also say that it is not right that some people should waste what is lacking on the table of others. You are resolved to construct a just, free and prosperous society, in which one and all will be able to enjoy the benefits of progress.

'In my youth I lived these same convictions.

'As a young student, I proclaimed them with the voice of literature and art.

'God willed that they should be tempered in the fire of a war whose atrocity did not spare my family. I saw these convictions trampled upon in many ways. I feared for them, seeing them exposed to the tempest. One day I decided to confront them with Jesus Christ: I realised that He was the only one who revealed to me their real content and value and that in this way I could protect them against the inevitable wear and tear of time, in its mysterious workings.

'All this, this tremendous and precious experience, taught me that social justice is true only if it is based on the rights of the individual. And that these rights will be really recognised only if we recognise the transcendent dimension of man, created in the image and likeness of God, called to be His son and the brother of other men, and destined to eternal life. To deny this transcendency is to reduce man to an instrument of domination, whose fate is subject to the selfishness and ambition of other men, or to the omnipotence of the totalitarian state, erected as the supreme value.

'... I learned that a young Christian ceases to be young, and has no longer been a Christian for a long time, when he lets himself be won over by doctrines or ideology that preach hatred and violence. But a just society cannot be constructed on injustice. It is not possible to construct a society that deserves to be called human without respecting, and, worse still, by destroying human freedom, denying individuals the most fundamental freedoms.

'Sharing as priest, bishop and cardinal the lives of innumerable young people at university, in youth groups, in excursions in the mountains, in clubs for reflection and prayer, I learned that a youth begins to grow old in a dangerous way when he lets himself be deceived by the facile and convenient principle that "the end justifies the means"; when he adopts the belief that the only hope of improving society is to promote struggle and hatred between social groups, that it is to be found in the Utopia of a classless society, which very soon reveals itself as the creator of more classes. I became convinced that only love draws closer things that are different, and brings about unity in diversity. Christ's words: "A new commandment I give to you, that you love one another; even as I have loved you" (John 13:34), then appeared to me, in addition to their incomparable theological depth, the seed and principle of the one revolution that does not betray man. Only true love contructs.

'If a young man such as I was, called to live his youth at a crucial moment of history, can say something to young people like you, I think he would say to them: do not let yourselves be used!'

Germany

November 15 to 19, 1980

The official meeting of the Holy Father with the authorities of the Federal Republic of Germany took place in the late evening of Saturday, November 15, at Brühl Castle in Bonn. The following is an extract from the address given by the Pope on this occasion, in reply to the greeting of President Karl Carstens.

'The history of your people and of the whole Christian West is rich in shining examples and valuable results of such a co-responsible and trustful collaboration between the State, society, and the Church. Eloquent testimonies of how the power of faith and the organization of the world are connected, are not only the splendid cathedrals, the venerable cloisters and universities with their vast libraries, and the many other cultural and social institutions, but also modern technical civilization and culture themselves, which cannot be understood without the decisive historical, spiritual, and moral contribution of Christianity since their origins. Even modern areligious and anti-religious ideologies still bear witness to the existence and high value of what they endeavour to deny and destroy with all means.

'Because of its significant spiritual-religious, cultural, and scientific contribution, special recognition is due to the German people in the history of the Church and in the spiritual history of Europe. In its past there are certainly lights and shadows, as in the life of every nation, examples of the highest human and Christian greatness, but also abysses, trials, deeply tragic events. There are times in which the life of this nation corresponded to true human and Christian virtue, but there are also times that were in contradiction with the latter in civil and international life. But your country has always been able to rise again even from ruin and humiliations – as for example those of the last World War – and acquire new strength. Political stability, technical and scientific progress, and the proverbial diligence of the citizens have enabled the Federal Republic of Germany in the last few decades to achieve prosperity and social peace within its own boundaries, and beyond them high prestige and influence in the international community of peoples. There has still remained for your people, however, the painful division which – as I hope – may finally also find its fitting peaceful solution in a united Europe.

'Allow me, ladies and gentlemen, to stress with particular joy in this place, among the efforts for peace with which your country too tries to contribute in an authoritative way to worldwide understanding among peoples, the growing readiness for agreement between your citizens and the Polish people. In this connection no slight credit goes, as is known, also to evangelical Christians as well as to the bishops and Catholics in both countries. In all painful relations between peoples the following principle holds good: not the reckoning of the grave wrongs and sorrows inflicted upon one another, but only the desire for reconciliation and the common search for new ways of peaceful coexistence can pave the way and guarantee a better future of peoples.'

On the morning of Monday, November 17 Pope John Paul II met with representatives of the Council of the German Evangelical Church in the Museum Halls of Mainz Cathedral, in the country in which the Reformation began. The following is an extract from the Pope's address on this occasion, again on the theme of reconciliation and unity.

'I recall that at this moment in 1510-1511 Martin Luther came to Rome as a pilgrim to the tombs of the Princes of the Apostles, but also as one seeking and questioning. Today I come to you, to the spiritual heirs of Martin Luther; I come as a pilgrim. I come to set, with this pilgrimage in a changed world, a sign of union in the central mystery of our faith.

'... You know that decades of my life have been marked by the experience of the challenging of Christianity by atheism and non-belief. It appears to me all the more clearly how important is our common profession of Jesus Christ, of His word and work in this world, and how we are driven by the urgency of the hour to overcome the differences that divide us, and bear witness to our growing union.

'Jesus Christ is the salvation of us all. He is the only mediator, "whom God put forward as an expiation by His blood, to be received by faith" (Rom. 3:25).

'... We must leave no stone unturned. We must do what unites. We owe it to God and to the world. "Let us therefore pursue what makes for peace and for mutual upbuilding" (Rom. 14:19).'

The Far East

February 16 to 26, 1981

Pakistan – February 16
The Phillipines – February 16 to 22
Guam – February 22 to 23
Japan – February 23 to 26

On Wednesday, February 25 Pope John Paul II visited the Peace Memorial in Hiroshima and delivered an address to those gathered there. Hiroshima was devastated by a nuclear bomb on August 6 1945, and the following is an extract from the Pope's strong appeal for peace on remembering this event.

'War is the work of man. War is destruction of human life. War is death.

'Nowhere do these truths impose themselves upon us more forcefully than in this city of Hiroshima, at this Peace Memorial. Two cities will forever have their names linked together, two Japanese cities, Hiroshima and Nagasaki, as the only cities in the world that have had the ill fortune to be a reminder that man is capable of destruction beyond belief.

'It is with deep emotion that I have come here today as a pilgrim of peace. I wanted to make this visit to the Hiroshima Peace Memorial out of a deep personal conviction that to remember the past is to commit oneself to the future.

'I bow my head as I recall the memory of thousands of men, women and children who lost their lives in that one terrible moment, or who for long years carried in their bodies and minds those seeds of death which inexorably pursued their process of destruction. The final balance of the human suffering that began here has not been fully drawn up, nor has the total human cost been tallied, especially when one sees what nuclear war has done – and could still do – to our ideas, our attitudes and our civilisation.

'To remember the past is to commit oneself to the future. I cannot but honour and applaud the wise decision of the authorities of this city that the memorial recalling the first nuclear bombing should be a monument to peace. By so doing, the city of Hiroshima and the whole people of Japan have forcefully expressed their hope for a peaceful world and their conviction that man who wages war can also successfully make peace. From this city, and from the event its name recalls, there has originated a new worldwide consciousness against war, and a fresh determination to work for peace.

'... To remember the past is to commit oneself to the future. To remember Hiroshima is to abhor nuclear war. To remember Hiroshima is to commit oneself to peace. To remember what the people of this city suffered is to renew our faith in man, in his capacity to do what is good, in his freedom to choose what is right, in his determination to turn disaster into a new beginning. In the face of the man-made calamity that every war is, one must affirm and reaffirm, again and again, that the waging of war is not inevitable or unchangeable. Humanity is not destined to self-destruction. Clashes of ideologies, aspirations and needs can and must be settled and resolved by means other than war and violence. Humanity owes it to itself to settle differences and conflicts by peaceful means. The great spectrum of problems facing the many peoples in varying stages of cultural, social, economic and political development gives rise to international tension and conflict. It is vital for humanity that these problems should be solved in accordance with ethical principles of equity and justice enshrined in meaningful agreements and institutions. The international community should thus give itself a system of law that will regulate international relations and maintain peace, just as the rule of law protects national order.

'... Those who cherish life on earth must encourage governments and decision-makers in the economic and social fields to act in harmony with the demands of peace rather than out of narrow self-interest. Peace must always be the aim: peace pursued and protected in all circumstances. Let us not repeat the past, a past of violence and destruction. Let us embark upon the steep and difficult path of peace, the only path that leads to the true fulfillment of the human destiny, the only path to a future in which equity, justice and solidarity are realities and not just distant dreams.

'... To every man and woman in this land and in the world, I say: let us assume responsibility for each other and for the future without being limited by frontiers and social distinctions; let us educate ourselves and educate others in the ways of peace...

'... to everyone I repeat the words of the Prophet: "They shall beat their swords into ploughshares and their spears into pruning hooks; nation shall not lift up sword against nation, neither shall they learn war any more" (Is. 2:4).

'... And to the Creator of nature and man, of truth and beauty I pray:

'hear my voice, for it is the voice of the victims of all wars and violence among individuals and nations.

'Hear my voice, for it is the voice of all children who suffer and will suffer when people put their faith in weapons and war.

'Hear my voice when I beg you to instill into the hearts of all human beings the wisdom of peace, the strength of justice and the joy of fellowship.

'Hear my voice, for I speak for the multitudes in every country and in every period of history who do not want war and are ready to walk the road of peace.

'Hear my voice and grant insight and strength so that we may always respond to hatred with love, to injustice with total dedication to justice, to need with the sharing of self, to war with peace.

'O God, hear my voice and grant unto the world Your everlasting peace.'

Africa

February 12 to 19, 1982

Nigeria – February 12 to 17
Benin – February 17
Gabon – February 17 to 18 and 19
Equatorial Guinea – February 18

In the evening of Friday, February 12 the Pope visited President Alhaji Shehu Shagari of Nigeria at the State House in Lagos. The following is an extract from the address he delivered on this occasion.

'It is... fitting for me to express to you, Mr President, and to the government leader, and indeed to all the people of this great country, my deep appreciation of what the Nigerian people have achieved, not always without suffering and sacrifice, since their independence over two decades ago. I experience a deep joy in seeing how Nigeria, together with numerous other African nations, has acceded to full national sovereignty and is able to take its future in its own hands, according to the richness of its own genius, in respect for its own culture, and in consonance with its own sense of God and of spiritual values. It is my conviction that all Africa, when allowed to take charge of its own affairs, without being subjected to interference and pressure from any outside powers or groups, will not only astound the rest of the world by its achievements, but will be able to share its wisdom, its sense of life, its reverence for God with other continents and nations, thus establishing that exchange and that partnership in mutual respect that is needed for the true progress of all humanity.

'I therefore desire to pay homage to the significant contribution which the Nigerian nation has made and is making, in the first place, to the African continent. You forcefully stand up for political freedom and for the right of all to a place on the African continent. You spare no efforts to help remove all discrimination against people because of their colour, race, language or social status. You have offered help to countries in greater need, and you champion brotherly relations and economic collaboration between African nations. Nigeria is looked to, to lead the way in promoting a magnanimous policy of receiving and assisting refugees and helping them to resettle through humane repatriation, or by programmes bettering their lot.

'... In consolidating national unity within you own nation, you are strengthening the unity of Africa.

'... Nigeria has been blessed by the Creator with a rich human potential and with natural wealth. Such gifts, received in humble gratefulness, are also a constant challenge, for the goods of this world are given by the Creator for the benefit of all. Public authorities are entrusted with the sacred assignment to channel these riches to the best interests of the people, that is, for the betterment of all and for the future of all.

'... Development projects must always have a human face. They cannot be reduced to a purely materialistic or economic endeavour. The human person must always be the ultimate measure of the feasibility and the success of an economic or social programme.

'... Thus are rejected such elements as corruption, bribery, embezzlement of public funds, domination over the weak, callousness towards the poor and handicapped.

'... Mr President, yours is a land of promise, a land of hope. In its efforts to develop, it is bound also to suffer the pressures that so often arise from conflicting demands and from the sheer magnitude of the task. Among the problems that invest the developing world is a disproportionate urbanization that can create slum conditions, place the disinherited and the less fortunate on the margin of society, and link want and poverty to crime and to the loss of moral values. Only the united efforts of all the citizens under enlightened leadership can overcome difficulties such as this. Only the harnessing of all the forces for the common good, in true respect of the supreme values of the spirit, will make a nation great and a happy dwelling place for its people.'

Portugal

May 12 to 15, 1982

On Thursday, May 13 Pope John Paul II met with those who care for and maintain the Shrine of Our Lady of Fatima at the Paul VI Pastoral Centre in Fatima. The following is an extract from the Pope's address on this occasion.

'There goes up from my heart a word of great understanding and appreciation for all of you, Little Handmaids of Our Lady of Fatima, and the others who provide services here for pilgrims; and also for you the workers who have given your commitment for the works of this impressive complex.

'... I know well, through direct experience, the value of your services and dedication to assist and help the pilgrims to feel at ease in this blessed place. But I know and appreciate even more what you more or less consciously do with generosity and self-sacrifice to offer the occasion for a loving encounter, through the heavenly Mother, with our Father in Heaven, and to strengthen in the heart of every pilgrim faith and the Christian meaning of life. Often there is born here a new encounter with oneself and a greater docility to the voice of Mary Most Holy, whose maternal appeals always converge in the words "do whatever He (Christ) tells you" (John 2:5). And now very many people, thanks to your help and interest, return ready to follow the paths, new to them or forgotten, of penitence, prayer, honesty, goodness, justice and grace.

'In your filial devotion to Our Lady, you are also the instruments of the merciful God, serving your brothers and sisters, especially the sick and the most needy. This is for your good, since you are obeying the Word of the Master, with a view to "eternal life": "Each time that you have done these things for one of the least of my brothers, you have done it for me" (Matt. 25:40). With your concrete acts of humanity and charity, you are performing the work of evangelization: and "the poor have the Good News preached to them" (Luke 7:22).

'I will explain it in another way: the Good News must be proclaimed, first of all, with the testimony of our capacity to understand and welcome; with the radiation, in an absolutely simple and spontaneous way, of our faith in values that are beyond current values and of hope in something which is not visible and surpasses imagination. By virtue of this demonstration of love, without speaking, there is bound to blossom in the heart of whoever sees your "good works" the question: why are they like that and why do they act this way? What is it – or who is it – that inspires and induces them to be full of goodness?

'Please God that you may continue to let yourselves be enlightened by this "reason for the hope which is in you" (1 Peter 3:15) and that this may give you courage to carry on, with serenity, joy and love, the tasks that you have generously accepted, as a way of living as Christians, and may you try to transform these into a filial homage to the Mother of God and our Mother.'

Great Britain

May 28 to June 2, 1982

In the afternoon of Tuesday, June 2 the Holy Father met with young people from England and Wales at Ninian Park in Cardiff. The following is an extract from his address on this occasion.

'I have come to this land as a pilgrim pastor, a servant of Jesus Christ. I have come to proclaim Christ's Gospel of peace and reconciliation; I have come to celebrate His saving action in the sacraments of the Church. I have come to call you to Christ.

'Before I go away, there is something very important that I wish to emphasise... It is prayer. Prayer is so important that Jesus Himself tells us: "pray constantly" (Luke 21:36).

'... My dear young people, it is through prayer that Jesus leads us to His Father. It is in prayer that the Holy Spirit transforms our lives. It is in prayer that we come to know God: to detect His presence in our souls, to hear His voice speaking through our consciences, and to treasure His gift to us of personal responsibility for our lives and for our world.

'It is through prayer that we can clearly focus our attention on the person of Jesus Christ and see the total relevance of His teaching for our lives. Jesus becomes the model for our actions, for our lives. We begin to see things His way.

'Prayer transforms our individual lives and the life of the world. Young men and women, when you meet Christ in prayer, when you get to know His Gospel and reflect on it in relation to your hopes and your plans for the future, then everything is new. Everything is different when you begin to examine in prayer the circumstances of every day, according to the set of values that Jesus taught. These values are so clearly stated in the Beatitudes: "Blessed are the merciful, for they shall obtain mercy. Blessed are the pure of heart, for they shall see God. Blessed are the peacemakers, for they shall be called children of God" (Matt. 5:7-9).

'In prayer, united with Jesus – your brother, your friend, your Saviour, your God – you begin to breathe a new atmosphere. You form new goals and new ideals. Yes, in Christ you begin to understand yourselves more fully. This is what the Second Vatican Council wanted to emphasise when it stated; "The truth is that only in the mystery of the Incarnate Word does the mystery of man take on light". In other words, Christ not only reveals God to man, but He reveals man to himself. In Christ we grasp the secret of our own humanity.

'But there is more. Through prayer you come to experience the truth that Jesus taught: "The words that I have spoken to you are spirit and life" (John 6:63). In Jesus, whom you get to know in prayer, your dreams for justice and your dreams for peace become more definite and look for practical applications. When you are in contact with the Prince of Peace, you understand how totally opposed to His message are violence and terrorism, hatred and war. In Him you experience the full meaning of an interpersonal relationship that is based on generous love. Christ offers you a friendship that does not disappoint, a fidelity beyond compare.

'... In all the circumstances of your lives, you will find that Jesus is with you – He is close to you in prayer. It is prayer that will bring joy into your lives and help you to overcome the obstacles to Christian living. Remember the words of Saint James: "Is any one among you suffering? Let him pray" (James 5:13).

'My dear young people, it is easy to see why Christ told us to pray all the time, and why Saint Paul insisted on this so much. (Luke 21:36, Romans 12:12, 1 Thess. 5:7). It is in prayer that God finally brings us into union with himself, through our Lord Jesus Christ, His Son, who lives and reigns with Him and the Holy Spirit for ever and ever.

'... It is my hope today, as I return to Rome, that you will remember why I came among you. And, as long as the memory of this visit lasts, may it be recorded that I, John Paul II, came to Britain to call you to Christ, to invite you to pray!

'Dear young people, this explains why, in the Church of today, you are the hope of tomorrow. And so I urge you, in the words of Saint Paul: "Pray at all times in the Spirit... and also for me, that utterance may be given me in opening my mouth boldly to proclaim the mystery of the Gospel... that I may declare it boldly, as I ought to speak... Grace be with all who love our Lord Jesus Christ with unfailing love" (Eph. 6:18-20, 24). Amen.'

Argentina

June 11 to 12, 1982

Pope John Paul II arrived in Buenos Aires on Friday, June 11. He was met at the airport by Cardinal Aramburu, Primate of Argentina and Archbishop of Buenos Aires, and by President Galtieri. The following is an extract from the address given by the Pope during the welcoming ceremony.

'Praised be Jesus Christ!

'He repeats to us again: "My peace I give to you; not as the world gives do I give it to you" (John 14:27).

'Blessed be the Lord who allowed me to come to this dear land of Argentina.

'I wanted to come here in order to tell you with my own lips the feelings which I expressed to you in my personal letter which, at the end of last month, I addressed to you, beloved sons and daughters of the Argentine nation, on the eve of my pastoral journey to the Churches in England, Scotland and Wales.

'If, during that apostolic visit – which was meant to be, and in fact was, a continuous prayer for peace, as much as a service rendered to the cause of ecumenism and to the Gospel – my thoughts and my affection were also with you, my presence today is intended to be visible proof of such love in an historical moment as sorrowful for you as this one is.

'... my visit is meant to be marked by the same pastoral and ecclesial character which places it beyond any political intention. It is simply a meeting of the father in the faith with his children who are suffering: of the brother in Christ who points Him out once more as the way of peace, of reconciliation and of hope.

'... In this spirit, permit me from this very moment to invoke Christ's peace on all the victims, on both sides, of this armed conflict between Argentina and Great Britain; to show my affectionate closeness with all families who mourn the loss of some loved one; to ask the governments and the international community to take measures to avoid greater damage, to heal the wounds of war and to facilitate the restoration of areas for a just and enduring peace and progressive serenity of hearts.

'... at this moment mankind must once more ask itself about the absurd phenomenon of war, in whose scenario of death and pain only the negotiating table, which could and should have prevented it, remains valid.

'With these wishes made a prayer, which I invite all of you to join, I invoke divine protection and comfort on each person and family of the beloved Argentine nation, first of all upon the orphans, the victims of the war, upon all those who are suffering from infirmity or uncertainty concerning the fate of a loved one. May the Apostolic Blessing, which with great affection I impart to everyone, be a pledge of my universal favour and the reconciliation of hearts.

On the morning of Saturday, June 12 Pope John Paul II met the bishops of Argentina, representatives of CELAM, and the presidents of the Episcopal Conferences of the Latin American countries, in the Buenos Aires Metropolitan Curia. The following is an extract from the Pope's address on this occasion, in which he continued his appeal for an end to the Falklands conflict.

'I well knew that in directing my steps toward Great Britain – in carrying out a strictly pastoral mission which was not only the Pope's but the entire Church's – that someone could perhaps have interpreted such a mission in political terms, deflecting it from its purely evangelical significance. In any case, I maintained that fidelity to my own ministry required that I not halt in the face of possible inexact interpretations, but carry out the mandate to proclaim with gentleness and firmness the *verbum reconciliationis*.

'... I come to join my voice and entreaty to yours. As I did in Great Britain, I come to pray for those killed in the conflict, to bring comfort and consolation to so many families anguished by the deaths of their loved ones. But I come above all to pray with you and with your faithful that the present conflict may find a peaceful and stable solution with respect for justice and for the dignity of the respective peoples.'

Switzerland

June 15, 1982

On Tuesday, June 15 Pope John Paul II travelled to Switzerland, where he addressed a number of international organisations in Geneva. The following is an extract from his address to the International Labour Organisation.

'My thinking aims at reflecting, in a coherent way, one fundamental idea and one basic preoccupation: the cause of man, his dignity and the inalienable rights flowing therefrom. Already in my first Encyclical *Redemptor Hominis*, I stressed the fact that "man is the first road which the Church must travel in fulfilling its missions; it is the first road and the fundamental road of the Church, mapped out by Christ himself". That is also the reason why... I felt I should devote a major document of my papacy to human labour, to man at work – *homo laborem exercens*. For not only does work bear the imprint of man, but it reveals to man the true meaning of his existence – work considered as a human activity regardless of its concrete content and circumstances. Work is endowed with "this basic dimension of human existence" through which "man's life is built up every day". From work "it derives its specific dignity, but at the same time contains the unceasing measure of human toil and suffering and also of the harm and injustice which penetrate deeply into social life within individual nations and on the international level".

'The problems of work – problems that have repercussions in so many spheres of life and at all levels, whether individual, family, national or international – share one characteristic, which is at one and the same time a condition and a programme, and which I would like to stress before you today: solidarity. I feel impelled to place these considerations before you partly because solidarity is inherent in one way or another in the very nature of human work, and also because of the objectives of your Organisation and above all the spirit which imbues it.

'... The problem of work has a very profound link with that of the meaning of human life... this... observation indeed enables us to set human work, in whatever way it is performed by man, within man himself, in other words, in his innermost being, in the essence of his nature, in what makes him a man and therefore destined to work. The conviction that there is an essential link between the work of every man and the overall meaning of human existence is the whole foundation of the Christian doctrine of work... and it permeates the teaching and activities of the Church, in one way or another, at each stage of its mission throughout history. "Never again will work be against the worker; but always work will be... in the service of man" – it is worth repeating today the words spoken... by Pope Paul VI. If work must always serve the welfare of man, if the programme of progress can only be carried out through work, then there is a fundamental right to judge progress in accordance with the following criterion: does the work really serve man? Is it compatible with his dignity? Through it, does human life achieve fulfilment in all its richness and diversity?

'We have the right to conceive of human work in this way; and we also have a duty to do so. We have the right and the duty to consider man not according to whether or not he is useful in his work, but to consider work in its relation to man, to each man, to consider work according to whether or not it is useful to man.

'... All the major problems of man in society are now world problems! They must be approached on a worldwide scale, in a realistic spirit, of course, but in an innovative, critical spirit as well.

'... a new world conscience must be created; each of us, without denying his origins and his membership of his family, his people and his nation, or the obligations arising therefrom, must regard himself as a member of this great family, the world community.

'... we must also seek a fresh significance in human work seen in a world context and therefore set ourselves fresh tasks. This also means that the worldwide common good requires a new solidarity without frontiers.

'... A society of solidarity is built up day by day, first by creating and then by preserving the conditions on which the free participation of all in the common effort effectively depends... The right to associate freely is a fundamental one for all those who are connected with the world of work and who constitute the work community. It means that no working man need be either alone or isolated; it expresses the solidarity of all in the defence of the rights which are rightfully theirs and flow from the requirements of their work; it affords a normal channel for participating actively in the performance of work and everything related to it, while being guided at the same time by a concern for the common good. This right presupposes that the social partners are truly free to form or join an associatin of their own choosing and to run it. Although the right to freedom of association seems beyond a doubt to be one of the basic rights most generally recognized, as attsted by International Labour Convention No. 87, yet it is severely threatened, often flouted either in its principle or – more often – in one of the substantive aspects, with the result that freedom of association is disfigured. It seems essential to point out that cohesion among the forces of society, always desirable in itself, must be the outcome of free decisions by those concerned, taken in full independence from the political athorities and arrivedat in full freedom as regards the determination of the internal organisation of trade unions, their operating methods and their activities. The working man must assume responsibility for defending the truth, the true dignity of his work. He must not be prevented from exercising that responsibility, though also bearing in mind the good of the community.'

Spain

October 31 to November 9, 1982

On Wednesday, November 2 more than a million people gathered in the Plaza de Lima of Madrid, where Pope John Paul II celebrated a special Mass for families. The following is an extract from the Pope's homily on this occasion.

'Allow me, in keeping with the word of God proclaimed in the liturgy today, to remind you of the moment in which, through the sacrament of the Church, you became spouses before God and before men. In that important moment the Church in a special way called upon and solemnly invoked the Holy Spirit to be with you in accordance with the promise which the apostles received from Christ: "The Comforter, the Holy Spirit which the Father will send in my name, will teach you all things and will remind you of all that I have said to you" (John 14:26).

'... today, more than ever, this interior impulse of the Spirit is... necessary so that with Him you, Christian spouses, although living in environments where the norms of Christian life are not held in due respect, or where they are not duly honoured in social life or in the communications media most accessible to the home, may be able to fulfil the Christian plan of family life, while resisting and overcoming with the strength of your faith whatever contrary pressures may present themselves.

'... Jesus Our Lord, speaking of marriage made reference to "the beginning" (Matt. 19:8) that is, to the original plan of God, to the truth about marriage.

'According to this plan, marriage is a communion of indissoluble love. "This intimate union, as a mutual giving of two persons, and the good of the children demands total fidelity from the spouses and requires its indissoluble unity". Therefore whatever attacks conjugal indissolubility, inasmuch as it is contrary to God's original plan, is also contrary to the dignity and the truth of conjugal love.

'... you, Christian spouses, are called to bear witness to these words of the Lord: "What God has joined together, let no man put asunder" (Matt. 19:6).

'... according to God's plan, marriage is a community of indissoluble love ordered to life as a continuation and complement of the spouses. There is an unbreakable relationship between conjugal love and the transmission of life, in virtue of which, as Paul VI taught: "Every conjugal act must remain open to the transmission of life". On the contrary, as I wrote in the Apostolic Exhortatio *Familiaris Consortio*: "The innate language that expresses the total reciprocal self-giving of husband and wife is overlaid, through contraception, by an objectively different language, namely, that of not giving oneself totally to the other. This leads not only to a positive refusal to be open to life, but also to a falsification of the inner truth of conjugal love".

'But there is another aspect, still more serious and fundamental, which refers to conjugal love as a source of life. I am speaking of the absolute respect for human life which no person or institution, private of public, can ignore. Therefore, whoever denies protection to the most innocent and weakest human person, to the human person already conceived, even though not yet born, would commit a most serious violation of the moral order. The killing of an innocent child is never legitimate. Such would undermine the very foundation of society.

'What sense would there be in speaking of the dignity of man, of his fundamental rights, if an innocent human being is not protected, or even if the point is reached of providing means and services, private or public, for the destruction of defenceless human lives? Dear spouses! Christ has given you His Spirit so that you do not forget His words. In this respect His words are very serious: "Woe to him who despises one of these little ones... their angels in heaven always contemplate the face of the Father" (Matt. 18:10). He wished to be recognised for the first time by a child still in his mother's womb, a child who rejoiced and leapt for joy in His presence.

'... Dear brothers and sisters! Beloved spouses and parents! I have recalled some essential points of God's plan for marriage, for the purpose of helping you hear in your hearts the words directed to you by Christ and which the Spirit continually recalls to you.

'"The law of the Lord is perfect, refreshing the soul... giving wisdom to the simple. The precepts of the Lord are right" (Psalm 19:7-8). The law of the Lord which ought to govern your conjugal and family life is the only way of life and of peace'

Central America

March 2 to 9, 1983

Costa Rica – March 2 to 4 and 6
Nicaragua – March 4 to 5
Panama – March 5
El Salvador – March 6
Guatemala – March 6 to 8 and 9
Honduras – March 8
Belize – March 9
Haiti – March 9

In the late evening of Monday, March 7 Pope John Paul II met the rectors of Guatemala's five universities, together with representatives of the students, in the Apostolic Nunciature in Guatemala City. The following is an extract from the address which the Pope delivered on this occasion.

'I express my profound esteem for your work, which I have shared as a teacher for some years of my life. In this work I have been able to observe the importance of your mission, which in the group of these peoples is called to exercise a decisive influence, not only in the sphere of persons, but also of nations. In fact, it is well known that culture shapes societies. Thus, when it is desired to build more elevated and just forms of society, it is necessary to pay attention to the cultural world, since this is a question not only of seeking new and more just ways of distributing wealth, but a better distribution of culture and of the consequent social influence.

'The indispensable element will have to be the reference to the spiritual and moral values of man, which in your case have been made concrete in the Christian vision which enlivens you and which has been a characteristic of the centres which you represent.'

On the same occasion the Holy Father consigned a written message to the representatives of the Guatemalan university world with whom he met. The following is an extract from this message.

'... As you well know, the university was born in Europe, in the very bosom of the Church, as an almost natural extension of the roles carried out by the Church in the field of teaching, education, research and cultural service. Beginning with modest schools, originating in the cathedrals and monasteries, faculties and centres of higher learning gradually developed, at first supported and then instituted and confirmed by the Church in their academic prerogatives and autonomies.

'... my intention is... to emphasize the role which the Church has tried to fulfil in this age-old experience through the universities. From the very beginning it has aspired to cultivate the sacred and profane sciences in order to investigate the works of God and to serve society.

'... The Church often recalled that the role of the university was to defend man, his rights and his freedom.

'Suffice it to recall here the prophetic voice of the great Bishop Francisco de Maroquin who, one hundred years before the creation of the prestigious University of St Charles in Guatemala, proclaimed the university's Christian and human mission.

'For him, the university ought to be consecrated to the progress of divine and human sciences, and to the defence of man's rights. This spirit, constantly recalled by the Church, contributed to the flourishing of a new culture, open to the service of the Latin American man and to the advancement of his identity. From these universities have come in great measure the men and women who have formed the Latin American nations and who have determined their autonomy and cultural vocation, always sustaining the community spirit of the peoples of this continent.

'... In fact, the university and the Church are devoted, each in its own way, to the search for truth, to the progress of the spirit, to universal values, to comprehension and to the integral development of man, to the exploration of the mysteries of the universe. In a word, the university and the Church want to serve man unselfishly, trying to respond to his highest moral and intellectual aspirations.

'... the Church addresses itself in a very particular way to the present university students to tell them: let us together try to defend man, whose dignity and whose honour are seriously threatened. The university, which by vocation is an unselfish and free institution, appears to be one of the few institutions of modern society which, along with the Church, is capable of defending man in himself; without deceit, without other pretext and for the sole reason that man possesses a unique dignity and deserves to be esteemed for himself.

This is the superior humanism taught by the Church. This is the humanism which I propose to you for your noble and urgent works, university students and educators. Allow, me therefore, to exhort you to use all the legitimate means at your disposal: teaching, research, information, dialogue, in order to bring to term your humanistic mission converting yourselves into builders of this civilization of love, the only one capable of sparing man from being man's enemy.'

Poland

June 16 to 23, 1983

On Wednesday, June 22 Pope John Paul II visited the Jagellonian University in Krakow. This was founded on May 12, 1364 by King Casimir the Great, and is the oldest university in Poland. The professors, and representatives from amongst the students, welcomed the Holy Father in the Aula Magna with the singing of "Gaude, Mater Polonia". The Rector delivered an opening address and conferred an honorary doctorate on the Pope. The following is an extract from the discourse which the Pope then delivered.

'I cannot conceal that it is with particular emotion that I cross the threshold of the "Jagellonian Alma Mater". For many years, as a resident of Krakow, I regularly came across this complex of buildings that conceal the University inside – and yet for all this it has lost nothing of its greatness. It did not become commonplace. It remained great with that fundamental greatness which it possesses in the history of our country and in the cultural history of Poland, Europe and the world. This is how one of its students, Father Peter Skarga, saw it when he called the Academy of Krakow "a happy gift of the Polish Kings and the ornament of this Crown". In my daily contact with it, throughout the forty years I lived here, never for an instant did I lose my awareness of being associated with something great. It is one of those things that determines the place of my country in the cultural history of man and the universe.

'I first entered the walls of the "Collegium Maius" as a ten-year-old elementary school pupil, to attend the degree ceremony of my elder brother, who graduated in the Faculty of Medicine of the Jagellonian University. I can still visualise that ceremony in the Great Hall of the University.

'... The... years of my studies in Krakow coincide with the period of the Second World War and the Nazi Occupation. I began my studies in the autumn of 1938 in the then Philosophy Faculty, being inscribed in the Faculty of Letters. That one year of study before the war is deeply impressed on my memory; the whole university environment, the names of the great professors under whom I had the privilege of studying, the faces of my friends, men and women from most of whom I was separated by the events of the years 1939-1945. With all the greater joy I see some of them present here today. I wish to place in their hands my gratitude for all that I owe to the Faculty of Letters of the Jagellonian University. Still today I reap the benefits of those studies that, in fact, were very brief and fragmentary.

'In the period of hiding during the Occupation, while at the same time working in a factory at Borek Falecki, I began studies in the clandestine Faculty of Theology of the Jagellonian University. It was the autumn of 1942. Amid the terrible trials of the war, I gradually discovered within myself a vocation to the priesthood – and I entered on a new road.

'As I return within its walls today... I feel – as I always have in the past – the historic greatness of the Jagellonian University, with which Providence allowed me to link my earlier years, even though in a somewhat fragmentary way. Through the prism of that unforgettable and irreplaceable experience, I embrace the more than six centuries of the University's existence at the heart of my country's existence.

'"For entire centuries, the University has served truth and the Republic", writes the Reverend Konstanty Michalski, "sharing its good and bad fortune, its successes and disasters, so that the whole Republic has been able to say with Jagiello to the Polish Academy: My daughter, bone of my bone and blood of my blood".

'The University is like a big family. All united by mutual love of the truth – that truth which is the very foundation of man's development in his own humanity. It is also the foundation of the development of society in its most profound identity.

'During my visit to UNESCO on 2 June, 1980 I said: "I am the son of a nation which has lived the greatest experiences of history, which its neighbours have condemned to death several times, but which has survived and remained itself. It has kept its identity, and it has kept, in spite of partitions and foreign occupations, its national sovereignty, not by relying on the resources of physical power, but solely by relying on its culture. This culture turned out in the circumstances to be more powerful than all other forces... There exists a fundamental sovereignty of society which is manifested in the culture of the nation".

'And we all know what part the Jagellonian University played in the creation and the spreading of this culture which forms the spiritual sovereignty.'

France

August 14 to 15, 1983

For the first time in history a Pope celebrated Mass at the Grotto of the Apparitions in Lourdes, on Monday, August 15, the feast of the Solemnity of the Assumption of the Virgin Mary. Pope John Paul II concelebrated Mass with the cardinals and bishops of France. The following is an extract from his homily on this occasion.

'"A great sign appeared in the sky, a woman clothed with the sun" (Rev. 12:1).

'We have come on pilgrimage today towards this Sign.

'It is the solemnity of the Assumption into heaven: now the Sign attains its fullness. A woman is clothed with the sun of the inscrutable Divinity, the sun of the impenetrable Trinity. "Full of grace": she is filled with the Father, the Son and the Holy Spirit who give themselves to her as one God – the God of creation and of revelation, the God of the covenant and of the Redemption, the God of the beginning and of the end. The Alpha and the Omega. The God-Truth. The God-Love. The God-Grace. The God-Holiness.

'A woman clothed with the sun.

'Today we are making a pilgrimage to this Sign. It is the Sign of the Assumption into Heaven, which occurs above the earth and, at the same time, rises from the earth, from this earth in which the mystery of the Immaculate Conception was implanted. Today these two mysteries come together: the Assumption into Heaven and the Immaculate Conception. And today, they are shown to be complementary.

'Today, for the feast of the Assumption into Heaven, we come in pilgrimage to Lourdes where Mary told Bernadette: "I am the Immaculate Conception".

'We have come here because of the extraordinary Jubilee marking the year of the Redemption. We want to fulfil this jubilee close to Mary.

'Lourdes is the best place for such proximity.

'Here, once, "the Beautiful Lady" spoke to a simple young girl of Lourdes, Bernadette Soubirous, reciting the Rosary with her and entrusting various messages to her. In making this pilgrimage to Lourdes, we want to experience once again this extraordinary nearness which has never ceased here, but has rather grown stronger.

'This proximity to Mary is like the soul of this sanctuary.

'We come on pilgrimage to Lourdes to be close to Mary.

'We come on pilgrimage to Lourdes to get closer to the mystery of the Redemption.

'No one is more deeply involved in the mystery of the Redemption than Mary. And no one is in a better position to bring this mystery home to us. She is at the very heart of the mystery. We pray that the very heart of this mystery will beat more strongly in all of us during this extraordinary Jubilee Year.

'We find ourselves in Lourdes on the solemnity of the Assumption of Mary into Heaven, when the Church proclaims the glory of her definitive birth in heaven.

'... The liturgy... shows us the Assumption of Mary into heaven under three aspects. The first aspect is the Visitation, in the house of Zachariah.

'Elizabeth said: "Blest are you among women and blest is the fruit of your womb... Blest is she who trusted that the Lord's words to her would be fulfilled" (Luke 1:42,45).

'Mary believed the words spoken to her on behalf of the Lord. And Mary received the Word who took flesh in her and who is the fruit of her womb.

'The redemption of the world is based on the faith of Mary. It was linked to her "Fiat" at the moment of the Annunciation.

'... The Assumption of the Mother of Christ into Heaven is part of the victory over death, that victory which originates in the Resurrection of Christ...

'... In Christ all will come to life again, but each one in proper order: Christ the first fruits and then... all those who belong to Him" (1 Cor. 15:22-23).

'And who belongs to Christ more than His Mother? Who was redeemed by Him more than she was? Who co-operated in the Redemption more closely than she did by her "Fiat" at the Annunciation and by her "Fiat" at the foot of the Cross?

'Thus, it is at the very heart of the Redemption achieved through the Cross on Calvary, it is in the very power of the Redemption revealed by the Resurrection, that the victory over death which the Mother of the Redeemer experienced, that is, her Assumption into Heaven, finds its origin.

'... Her birth in Heaven is the definitive beginning of the glory which the sons and daughters of this earth must attain in God himself in virtue of Christ's Redemption.

'Mary is the first of those who are redeemed. In her also has begun the transformation of the history of the universe into the Kingdom of God.'

Austria

September 10 to 13, 1983

On Sunday, September 11 the Holy Father concelebrated Mass in Donaupark in Vienna, at the close of 'Katholikentag', the great meeting of Austrian Catholics. The theme of the 'Katholikentag' was hope. The following is an extract from the Pope's homily on this occasion, delivered to more than two hundred thousand of the faithful.

'The parable of the Gospel we have just heard tells of a young man who, proudly and self-confidently, left his father's house for a distant country where he expected more freedom and happiness. But when he had squandered his fortune and suffered the indignities of bondage such as he had never experienced before, his hope sank. Finally admitting his guilt to himself, he remembered his father and set off for his father's house, hoping against hope.

'It is at this very point in the Gospel that we read: "I will set off and go to my father". This profound parable, in fact, epitomises the eternal drama of man: the drama of freedom, the drama of ill-used freedom.

'The Creator has given man the gift of freedom. Thanks to this freedom he can shape and organise the world, create the wonderful products of the human mind with which this country and the world abound: science and the arts, business and technology, our entire civilisation. Freedom makes man capable of that unique form of human love which is not merely a consequence of natural attraction, but of a free decision of the heart. Freedom makes him capable of the most sublime expression of human dignity: the love and worship of God

'But freedom has its price. All those who are free ought to ask themselves: have we preserved our dignity in freedom? Freedom does not mean licence. Man must not do all he can do or that he wishes to do. There is no freedom without bounds. Man is responsible for himself, for his fellow human beings, for the world. He is responsible to God. Any society that plays down responsibility, law and conscience will undermine the very foundations of human life. Devoid of a sense of responsibility, man will squander himself in reckless living and, like the prodigal son, suffer the indignities of bondage and lose his home, and his freedom. Unrestrained selfishness will make him misuse his fellow men, or insatiably strive for material wealth. Where the ultimate values are no longer respected, marriages and families will break up and there will be no respect for the life of others, especially of the unborn, the old and the sick. The worship of God will give way to the worship of money, prestige or power.

'Is not all of the history of mankind also a history of the misuse of freedom? Are not many of us following in the steps of the prodigal son? In the end, their lives will be wasted, their love betrayed, their misery self-inflicted, and they will face fear and despair. "For all alike have sinned and are deprived of the divine splendour" (Romans 3:23). And they will ask themselves: "Where have I got to? Is there a way out?"

'... Christ's parable, however, does not leave us in outer darkness, in the misery of the sinner in all his abasement. The words "I will set off and go to my father" make us aware of the longing for the good that still persists in the heart of the prodigal son, and of the light of unfailing hope. In these words the perspectives of hope open before him. And such a perspective will always be open to us, since each individual and, indeed, all mankind, may set off to go to the Father. This is the essential truth, the central message of the Gospel.

'The words "I will set off and go to my father" are evidence of a change of heart. For the prodigal son continues, "I will say to him, 'Father I have sinned against God and against you'" (Luke 15:18). At the very centre of the Good News we find the truth of *metanoia*, of penance, of a change of heart.

'Why? Because the parable reveals what lies in the heart of hearts of all men, actively present and permanently active in spite of sin and even through sin: the insatiable longing for truth and love, undeniable evidence of how the heart and mind reach out far beyond the creation towards God. For man, this is the point of departure towards a change of heart.

'At the same time it is the point of departure for God. In the parable, God's point of departure is presented with utmost simplicity, yet in deeply moving and convincing words. The father is waiting. He is waiting for the return of the prodigal son, as though he was sure that his son would return. The father goes out into the streets which his son might take to come home, for he wants to meet him.

'... The son in his unbridled quest for freedom is, it seems to me, the image of man in the society of the highly developed nations. Rapid technological and economic progress and rapidly rising standards of living have brought about fundamental changes in that society. Many were overcome by the euphoric feeling that man at long last had become able to take control of the world and to mould its future. Proud self-confidence made many of them turn away from their ingrained belief that God is the cause and object of all being. God, it seemed to them, had become expendable.

'But this self-confident exodus, this rejection of God, was soon followed by great disillusionment coupled with fear: fear of the future, fear of the capabilities man has acquired. Indeed, fear of man himself. Austria, at the centre of Europe, has not been spared such developments. And now you are looking for new ways, for answers to the problems of our times.

'Remember again your spiritual home! Turn round, return to God and organise your lives and society in accordance with His laws.'

The Far East

May 3 to 11, 1984

Korea – May 3 to 7
Papua New Guinea – May 7 to 9 and 10
The Solomon Islands – May 9
Thailand – May 10 to 11

In the evening of Friday, May 11 Pope John Paul II met members of the Government and the Diplomatic Corps at the Government Palace in Bangkok. The following is an extract from the Pope's address on this occasion.

Through the courtesy of the Thai Government, I had the opportunity this morning to visit the Refugee Camp at Phanat Nikhom, a processing and transit centre for over seventeen thousand men, women and children who have been exiled from their own countries and have sought asylum here in Thailand. It was a particularly moving experience for me, because, as I looked into the faces of so many suffering human beings, at the same time I realised that there were thousands more in a similar situation, living in the various other camps in this country.

The sad lot of these courageous and unfortunate people cannot be ignored by the international community.

'... The poverty of these victims of political unrest and civil strife is so extreme on virtually all levels of human existence, that it is difficult for the outsider to fathom it. Not only have they lost their material possessions and the work which once enabled them to earn a living for their families and prepare a secure future for their children, but their families themselves have been uprooted and scattered: husbands and wives separated, children separated from their parents.

'... Many of the refugees have endured great dangers in their flight by sea or land. All too many were given up for lost or died en route, often the victims of shameless exploitation. Arriving here completely destitute, they have found themselves in a state of total dependence on others to feed them, clothe them, shelter them and make every decision for their future.

'... The desperate appeals of these suffering men, women and children have been heard by many compassionate people, both in Thailand and round the world, who offer a ray of hope.

'... I wish to express my gratitude to the Government and people of Thailand. They are to be thanked, especially for having agreed to be, for many years now, the country of first asylum for thousands and thousands of refugees from other parts of south-east Asia. The international community knows the difficulties which they have encountered. These difficulties are not only of a material nature. The internal and external political order of the nation has been affected by the steady influx of refugees. The departure of these same people to resettlement countries has not proceeded at nearly the same rate.

History will record the sense of hospitality, the respect for life and the deeply rooted generosity shown by the people of Thailand. These national traits have enabled the Thai authorities to overcome many obstacles and thus provide a measure of hope for so many people living on the verge of despair. To His Majesty the King and to the Government and people of Thailand I renew my deep appreciation.

'... However, the many efforts being made towards relieving the sufferings of the refugees should not be a convenient excuse for the international community to stop being concerned for the ultimate future of these people. The fact remains that it is something repugnant and abnormal for hundreds of thousands of human beings to have to leave their own countries because of their race, ethnic origin, political convictions, or religion, or because they are in danger of violence or even death from civil strife or political turmoil. Exile seriously violates the human conscience and the norms of life in society; it is clearly contrary to the Universal Declaration of Human Rights and to international law itself.

'Consequently, the governments of the world and the international community at large must focus their attention on long-range political solutions to the complex problem.

'Resettlement alone can never be the final answer to these people's plight. They have a right to go back to their roots, to return to their native land with its national sovereignty and its right to independence and self-determination; they have a right to all the cultural and spiritual relationships which nourish and sustain them as human beings.

'In the final analysis, then, the problem cannot be solved unless the conditions are created whereby genuine reconciliation may take place: reconciliation between nations, between various sectors of a given national community, within each ethnic group and between ethnic groups themselves. In a word, there is an urgent need to forgive and forget the past and to work together to build a better future.'

Switzerland

June 12 to 17, 1984

The Holy Father arrived at the Kloten Airport near Zurich in the early morning of Tuesday, June 12, when he was welcomed by ecclesiastical and civil dignitaries. The President of the Swiss Confederation, Leon Schlumpf, delivered a welcoming address. The following is an extract from the Pope's response.

'Even before historical events united in one State the free cities and cantons of this region of the Alps, it was the Christian religion which united the men and populations of these majestic mountains and valleys, despite their various origins and languages, in the one Church of Jesus Christ. From the earliest times Christianity has been deeply rooted in the souls and the traditions of the Swiss people. It is my hope that the various meetings of the coming days serve to help us reflect anew on this common Christian vocation, and as the People of God of the New Covenant, together with Christ, to praise and thank God, the Creator and Father of all people for His "marvellous deeds" (1 Peter 1:9-10).

'The challenge which the modern age represents for mankind and for Christianity grieves us Christians all the more for the unhappy divisions and polarizations which divide us today as in the past. The longed-for common witness of all Christians, to Christ and to mankind redeemed by Him, in an increasingly secularised world, commits us to ever greater efforts to overcome gradually, in full truth and in the love of Christ, all the obstacles which divide, from within and from without, "that the world may believe" (John 17:21). For this reason I am happy in particular for the meetings which I will have during my visit with our separated brothers and sisters in the faith. May God grant that these meetings deepen our mutual understanding and strenthen and further develop our commmon witness to the Faith.

'With this visit I wish to express esteem to all the beloved people of Switzerland, which enjoys great respect in the community of nations, not only for its flourishing economic well-being, but also for its excellent hospitality and firm international cooperation. Its traditional neutrality has guaranteed it long periods of peace and social progress and at the same time has created the conditions for an extraordinary humanitarian commitment, especially in times of severe international conflicts. I would like to recall here in particular as representative of all the other humanitarian organisations, especially for the needy peoples in developing countries, the institution and humanitarian activity of the International Red Cross.

On Wednesday, June 13 Pope John Paul II met with young people in the Ice Stadium at Fribourg. The following is an extract from his address on this occasion.

The future of the world seems rather gloomy to you. Unemployment, famine, violence, the threat to humanity from the stockpiling of armaments capable of terrible destruction, the economic disparity between north and south, the spiritual poverty which comes with the consumer society in many countries, are many causes of anxiety and worry.

'To you, young people, I say: do not allow yourselves to be disheartened by defeatism and discouragement! You are tomorrow's world. The future depends primarily on you. From us, the elders, you inherit a world which can deceive you; but it has its riches and its miseries, its values and its counter-values. The extraordinary progress of science and technology is ambivalent. It can be used for good and for evil. It can save human lives or destroy them. It can allow a better and more equitable distribution of the world's goods, or on the contrary, permit a growth of their accumulation by small groups while increasing the misery of the masses. It can favour peace or, on the contrary, threaten humanity with frightful destruction.

'Everything depends on the use that is made of the progress in science and technology. Ultimately, everything depends on the hearts of men. It is the hearts of men which must be changed. Various systems which foster injustice and suffering must certainly be modified, but the hearts of men must be transformed at the same time.'

Canada

September 9 to 20, 1984

On the morning of Monday, September 10 Pope John Paul II visited the handicapped in the Francois-Charon Centre in Quebec. The following is an extract from the Pope's address on this occasion.

'I have very much wanted to meet personally with you, you who suffer in your bodies from illness or accident. I would like to greet each and every one of you, as well as all those who surround you with affection and assistance, and who help you to love life and to make it blossom in you like a gift from God.

'... A word of encouragement must... be given to the concern this centre has for integrating the spiritual dimension into its work of human rehabilitation.

'... The human person constitutes a whole – body and soul – and every personal event – trial, effort or healing – has a spiritual dimension.

'... I see in... this a sign of the value that your people attach to the dignity of the disabled, in spite of the fascination the modern world feels for productivity, profit, efficiency, speed, and records of physical strength.

'... I would like to say... clearly and forcefully: the handicapped person is a human subject in the full sense with all the innate, sacred and inviolable rights that that entails. This is true whether the person be handicapped by physical disability, whether due to birth defect, chronic disease or accident, or by mental or sensory deficiency. It is true, too, no matter how great the person's affliction might be. We must facilitate his or her participation in all facets of social life and at all possible levels: in the family, at school, at work, in the community, in politics and religion. In practice, this presupposes the absolute respect of the human life of the handicapped person from his or her conception through every stage of development.

'... Up to this point... I have spoken of the nobility of this tenacious fight against physical evil and of all the technical competency, courage, solidarity and hope that it involves. This is indeed the will of God.

'But the mystery of your suffering is deeper still, and I would like to descend into its depths with you, as I did... on the occasion of the Feast of Our Lady of Lourdes: "At the heart of all human suffering appears the inevitable question: Why? It is a question about the cause, the reason; it is also a question about purpose, and, finally, meaning. Almost every person enters suffering protesting, quite humanly: 'Why?'...". The person suffering addresses this question to God as Job did, and also to Christ. Even though one identifies the secondary cause of the handicap, even though one hopes to overcome it and manages to do so through will and rehabilitation, the subjective problem remains: Why this suffering? Why this restriction at this time in my life?... Christ gives an answer from His cross, from the depth of His own suffering. It is not an abstract answer, it is a call which requires time for us to hear.

'Christ gave universal redemptive value to His own suffering which appeared to be imposed on Him from without. He accepted it out of obedience towards His Father and out of love for humanity in order to free it from its sin, the ultimate cause of suffering and death. And if we agree to do so, we also can participate in this redemption. This agreement is neither fatality nor resignation to suffering, which remains an evil against which we must continue to struggle. But God shows us how to draw good from evil by offering up our suffering with the Cross of Christ. I'm sure that many of you are having or have had this experience in faith. The pain remains. But the heart is serene and peaceful. It overcomes the feeling of the uselessness of suffering. It opens itself to love and helps those around to go out of themselves, to give themselves. Such a heart bears witness to faith and hope. It believes that in the mystery of the Communion of Saints it has something to offer for the salvation of its brothers and sisters throughout the world. It enters into the redemptive mission of Christ.

'... with Christ you must love life: "I have come so that they may have life and have it to the full" (John 10:11). Natural life in your body, in your rehabilitated functions, in your senses; the life of the intellectual faculties and of your ability to love. But also, the more mysterious, supernatural life which God gives believers at baptism, His divine life, a sharing in the life of the Trinity. This life is invisible to the eye, but it gives people their inner beauty and their hidden strength; it lasts and grows beyond this earthly life.'

Spain and Central America

October 10 to 13, 1984

Spain – October 10 to 11
Dominican Republic – October 11 to 12
Puerto Rico – October 12 to 13

The highlight of the Holy Father's pilgrimage to Latin America was the inauguration of the 'Novena' in preparation for the fifth centenary of the discovery and the evangelisation of America, to be commemorated in 1992-93. The solemn ceremony, a Liturgy of the Word, took place on Friday, October 12, in the Olympic Stadium in Santo Domingo, the capital of the Dominican Republic. The following is an extract from the Pope's address on this occasion.

'The Letter of Pope Leo XIII, at the conclusion of the fourth centenary of Columbus's accomplishment, speaks of the designs of Divine Providence that guided the "event that was *per se* the greatest and most marvellous among human deeds", and which by the preaching of the faith made an immense multitude come "to the hope of eternal life".

'In its human aspect, the arival of the discoverers at Guanahani meant a fantastic widening of mankind's frontiers, the mutual discovery of two worlds, the appearance of the entire inhabited world before the eyes of man, the beginning of universal history in its process of interaction, with all its benefits and contradictions, its lights and shadows.

'... It was the vigorous breaking forth of that universality willed by Christ for His message, as we read in St Matthew.

'... The Church... does not wish to ignore the interdependence that existed between the cross and the sword in the phases of the first missionary penetration. But neither does She wish to forget that the spread of Iberian Christianity brought to the new peoples the gift inherent in the origins and development of Europe – the Christian Faith – with its charge of humanity and its capacity for salvation, dignity and fraternity, justice and love, for the New World.